SUBHASH CHANDRA BOSE

The Springing Tiger

Hugh Toye

JAICO PUBLISHING HOUSE

Ahmedabad Bangalore Chennai
Delhi Hyderabad Kolkata Mumbai

Published by Jaico Publishing House
A-2 Jash Chambers, 7-A Sir Phirozshah Mehta Road
Fort, Mumbai - 400 001
jaicopub@jaicobooks.com
www.jaicobooks.com

SUBHASH CHANDRA BOSE:
THE SPRINGING TIGER
ISBN 81-7224-401-0

To be sold only in India, Bangladesh, Bhutan,
Pakistan, Nepal, Sri Lanka and the Maldives.

First Jaico Impression: 1991
16th Jaico Impression (Enlarged Edition): 2010
34th Jaico Impression: 2025

Printed by
Pashupati Printers, Delhi

To My Father and Mother

CONTENTS

FOREWORD

On February 15th, 1942, at Singapore, some eighty-five thousand men, the remainder of the British forces in Malaya, surrendered to the Japanese. About twenty thousand more had already been killed or had previously been captured. The final surrender was the culmination of a disaster as complete and dramatic as any that has befallen British arms anywhere in the world; in the East, there had been nothing like it since the annihilation of a British army in the gorges of the Kabul River just a hundred years before. Of the troops who fell into Japanese hands, more than half, nearly sixty thousand altogether, were Indians; in the course of their captivity, rather less than half of them, about twenty-five thousand, threw off their allegiance and joined what was called the Indian National Army; this was the army of 'Free India', a 'provisional government' that claimed to be a national state under the Presidency of Subhash Chandra Bose – the subject of this book – and to be allied with the Japanese. In military law, they thus committed the offences of mutiny, desertion and waging war against the King.

Yet more than half the Indians, some thirty-five thousand, stood firm to their allegiance, facing continuous privation and hardship, sometimes torture and death, rather than be false to the salt they had eaten and the oaths they had taken when they enlisted; meanwhile, their comrades, men of sister battalions of the same regiments, drawn from the same stock, with the same traditions, won glory for their colours and the admiration of their fellow soldiers – British, American, Germans alike – in North Africa, Italy and Burma. Why did these other troops go over to the enemy? Was their act, as most British soldiers thought, a simple betrayal of faith? Or was it, as many Indians came passionately to believe, an outburst of nationalist fervour?

That is one question of interest to anyone concerned with the motives for human behaviour. A second is how these men were treated at the end of the war. The decisions taken have been criticised with bitterness and from varied quarters; it is the kind of criticism which is easy after the event, but in the circumstances of the time, I do not believe any other general line of policy could have been taken. And though I recall several long statements setting out the grave – and very real – dangers involved in every possible course of action, I know of no constructive alternative ever put forward and rejected.

In the whole story, the personality of Subhash Chandra Bose plays an important part, with which Mr. Toye has dealt in his book; here, as an introduction to his book, are the barest outlines, sketched from another angle. Among the twenty-five thousand technically guilty of mutiny there were, in proportions about which one can hardly be precise, men whose motives fall into four classes. Some – and I would judge few – joined the I.N.A. with the intentions of rejoining the British forces when they saw a chance; some – and I would judge the majority – were puzzled, misinformed, misled, and on the whole believed the course they took was the most honourable open to them. Others were frankly opportunist, some really were fervent nationalists: in both these classes, I would suppose there were nothing like so many as in the second. And of course these categories were not clear-cut; there were men whose motives were thoroughly mixed and some mixture in almost all.

The Indian Army consisted of volunteers – even in the war when it grew to two million and a half – and men came to the colours partly because the pay, food and clothing were by Indian standards very good, partly because in India the soldier's profession has always been held in honour. There had been for a century and a half Indian officers, promoted from the rank, who might command a platoon, or in emergency a company, and who held a subordinate form of commission signed by the Viceroy, the higher officers who held a King's Commission were until 1919 British. Of the officers with the King's Commission, regular or emergency, I should suppose that, by the time of Singapore, approaching one-fifth were Indians.

The men were taken away from their higher officers when they were captured. They often had no source of news that was not Japanese and they were told that Britain was defeated and the war was over. I knew the men and lower-grade-officers of one of these battalions well: in particular, I remember their Subadar-Major, whose position was something between those of Adjutant and Regimental Sergeant-Major, a straightforward little man from the remoter hills. They were Himalayan peasants, very credulous and curiously humble in their attitude to the world beyond their hills, magnificent soldiers when firmly led, but when deprived of firm leadership too conscious of their own lack of knowledge and experience to offer much resistance to propaganda. To this battalion was sent an Indian officer who had held a King's Commission and had for a short time served with them before the surrender. He told them that the war was over and that they had the choice between digging latrines for the Japanese and once more becoming soldiers – but this time in the service of an Independent India. They chose to be soldiers.

The behaviour of this battalion was, I believe, typical of many. It did contain an element of nationalism: the men had long been aware of India's progress towards independence and felt for it a natural sympathy of an undefined, uncritical nature which was normally not strong enough to compete with the hold of the Army; of this hold the strands were discipline, regimental pride, loyalty to individual officers, good food and fair treatment. But now they were actively misled and to men of this category – I believe the great majority of the twenty-five thousand – it came as a surprise to find themselves fighting against their former comrades. Such men were quick to desert or surrender from the I.N.A., the 'Indian National Army'.

Among the King's Commissioned Officers, educated men, the conflict between two sets of values was much more continually present. They were used to hearing their Indian friends describe as patriotism what their British fellow-officers called disloyalty. Yet they had held the King's Commission and enjoyed its benefits, knowing that some Indians – and no doubt occasionally their own hearts – charged them with treachery. One must respect such a man as Subhash Chandra Bose, who resigned from the Indian Civil Service because he sincerely believed it his duty to India; that respect can hardly be extended to all who changed sides in adversity and who a second time chose the more comfortable path. But it would be wrong to imply that opportunism was the sole motive. The story of Mohan Singh, told in this book, provides one example of an officer who made his choice from a genuine conviction and was prepared to suffer for his beliefs. And the personality of Bose must have been an overriding factor with many.

The Japanese overreached themselves and were defeated in the long stubborn battle for Imphal, General Slim's victorious army poured southward through Burma, and the I.N.A. – disillusioned, defeated, starving and in rags –

crawled in to surrender, by twos and threes, by platoons, by battalions. By international and military law, they could have been tried by court-martial for mutiny and desertion and shot on the spot. But clearly the problem was a big one with political implications; it was not faced at the time – there was too much to do – and they were sent back to India as though they had been prisoners of war. The Indian public at this stage did not know of their existence. But when the war with Japan suddenly ended, the problem could be postponed no longer; the police had to be told about the I.N.A. and the Government had to decide what was to be done with them.

All were guilty of an offence legally punishable by death, but of course there could be no question of executing twenty-five thousand men. It would have been cruel, impolitical and unjust. On the other hand, the offences of mutiny and desertion could not be condoned – and this in the interest not so much of abstract justice as of the future of the Indian Army. To the new India, that Army would be valuable possession if it preserved its discipline; without it, a serious danger. It was decided that in the first place those who had joined the I.N.A. with the intention of deserting from it should be classed as White and restored to their former privileges, while the Greys – those who had been misled – should be summarily tried, dismissed and released. The Blacks would remain; they were those who had been well aware of what they were doing and among them the Blackest were those who had previously been in positions of trust and responsibility and those who had tortured, flogged or killed their comrades, either to make them join the I.N.A. or after they joined to punish them for attempted desertion. For a few of the Blackest, the law should take its course; for the other Blacks, the death penalty would be commuted for imprisonment of varying lengths, in most cases short.

That was the decision taken within a few weeks of the armistice with Japan; it is difficult to believe that any body of humane and responsible men in that position at that time would have decided on a different course of action. I defended it in the Assembly in Delhi in 1946 and I would defend it again today. But events moved with extreme rapidity and in a way no one foresaw – and I concede at once that if the way things would go had been foreseen it would have been far wiser to adopt a different handling in regard to the public. It would have been better to pick out some of the Blackest at once and try them very quickly, delaying for a few weeks the announcement that the I.N.A. had existed, keeping the secret till the trials were over, and then announcing a policy of clemency for the rest. It would not have been easy; lawyers need time to prepare a case and there was a vast mass of evidence to pick through, some of it three years old; some of the Blacks would have escaped through lack of time to consider their cases. And it would not have been an easy secret to keep. Still, it might have been done – if anyone had thought of it. But no one did.

The policy was right; the public handling – as it turned out – was seriously wrong. The public handling proceeded on two assumptions: first, that Indian public opinion would recognise the justice, and indeed clemency, of the policy proposed; and secondly, that it would not swing round to an opposite view within a few weeks. The first assumption was correct; the policy was announced to the Press – I drafted the communique myself – and it met at first with gratified approval, even from the Congress leaders. Few Indians had felt that the War was their war and few had been much concerned that we should win it; there was, however, relief that there was no more danger of Japanese bombs, a deluded hope that prices would now fall, a quickened pulse at the thought of constitutional advance and some distaste at the news that there had been Indians who had tortured Indians to fight against Indians.

But within a few weeks all this was changed. In a wave of nationalist emotion the I.N.A. were acclaimed heroes who had fought for the freedom of India; no political leader who valued his future could stand aloof – all must offer to defend the martyrs. There was an I.N.A. Defence Fund, I.N.A. Flag Days. No evidence against the I.N.A. could be believed for a moment; it was treachery to regard the least action of one of them with less than reverent loyalty. And in the face of this storm of public feeling – at which Congress leaders were secretly as much perturbed as the British – the original policy was changed; India was very near independence and it was surely incongruous to punish men for casting off an allegiance which the state was in any case on the point of relinquishing. To do so would certainly cause a fury of indignation that might jeopardise the whole settlement between Britain and India.

A second decision was taken that, though all should be tried and found guilty, dismissal would be the punishment for waging war against the King. The I.N.A.'s claim to have been fighting for patriotic motives would be taken at its face value and its members would be treated as though prisoners of war; only those who had committed acts of brutality would be liable on conviction to death or imprisonment. This decision was felt by many Englishmen to be a betrayal, not only of the thirty-five thousand prisoners who had stood firm but also of the victorious Indian Army. And in a sense it was a betrayal. It shook the Indian Army; it disturbed the villages to which I.N.A. men went back; it played a part in the naval mutinies of February 1946. All the same, I believe that in the extraordinary circumstances of the time it was the right choice between two bitter alternatives. To have persisted on the old line would have led to a betrayal of Britain's true purpose in India.

A postcript must be added to this highly compressed – and highly controversial – outline. It concerns an error of judgement and a blunder. The first prisoner to have been tried in the original plan was a King's Commissioned Officer who – so the prosecution evidence alleged – had ordered two would-be deserters to the British to be hung up by their extended arms and flogged by a whole battalion; one of them was dead when taken down. It had originally been proposed to hold the trials in the remote spot where they would not attract much attention; so sure was Field-Marshal Auchinleck that this case would horrify Indian opinion that he gave orders that the trial should be public and held in an accessible place. The Red Fort at Delhi was chosen because it was near the capital and because the Press and a controlled number of the public could get there without inconvenience. But in the slogans of the I.N.A. the Red Fort had been the spot where the tricolor of the new India was to be planted. The choice of scene was taken as a deliberate taunt, an insolent and provocative act of triumph over the vanquished. It heightened the fury of partisanship and helped to make the trials a symbol of India's national pride.

That was the error of judgement. Then at the last moment a technical legal difficulty arose in the flogging case and it was postponed; in its place as put the trial of three other accused, who, it was said, were charged with behaviour no less brutal. But this was not so. Each of these men had proceeded on lines that – once it was conceded that the I.N.A. was a combatant army – were in accordance with the normal conduct of war. One of them, for instance, had caught men deserting, had ordered them to be tried by a court martial and had confirmed the sentence of death the court passed, a sentence which was carried out in accordance with international convention. That is not the same as flogging a man to death or torturing him. The men were released, rightly in view of the previous decision, and I believe that both Britain and India owe Field-Marshal Auchinleck a debt for a hard decision. But the accused ought not to have come to trial at that stage and in that way. Perhaps the substitution of this trial for the first made little difference to Indian public opinion; in the hysterical atmosphere of the time, the flogging evidence would have been disbelieved. But it was a blunder and I do not propose to say where I think the blame lay beyond saying that it did not adhere to the Commander-in-Chief.

I have outlined, briefly and dogmatically, two aspects of the I.N.A. affair. In the behaviour of the men who went over to the enemy as much as in the sudden surge of Indian opinion in their favour, one factor on which I have deliberately not dwelt was the personality of Subhash Chandra Bose. In this 'study of a revolutionary' Mr Toye has made the first attempt from the British side to assess this man's character and recount the events of his life. It is a story with an interest of its own. There are elements in Bose's character which are repellent to an English reader – his arrogance and refusal to compromise, the assurance with which a man who could not bear to see suffering proposed that India should pay a 'blood sacrifice' to get liberation the way he chose; there is the unbelievable lack of realism which could dismiss as unimportant the invasion of Italy and the landings in Normandy. Yet these very certainties were an essential part of his leadership.

Power corrupted him; he grew more arrogant, more intolerant, more certain. But no one can doubt the stature of the man, his intellectual scope and the passion with which he held his convictions. The writer began this study after long months spent as an Intelligence Officer carefully sifting evidence; it is perhaps not too fanciful to suppose that he first acquired that kind of intellectual involvement with his prey that Sleeman, more than a hundred years before, had felt with the Thugs. But from that intellectual involvement has grown a deep if critical admiration for Bose and a sympathetic understanding of the Indian revolutionary movement; I find myself agreeing again and again with the analysis in his last chapter, though I am not sure that the I.N.A. trials were really to the advantage of the Congress or that they made much difference in the end to the date or form of independence. His book is a contribution to the history of India and essential to anyone who holds views – which are almost certain to be passionate, one way or the other – on the I.N.A. and the way the I.N.A. were treated.

PHILIP MASON

AUTHOR'S NOTE

In 1949 I started to write an exhaustive factual account of the Indian Independence Movement which flourished under German and Japanese patronage during the Second World War. The work took five years, got me the reputation of a troglodyte, and was quite unreadable. Here I have tried to tell the same story through a study of Mr. Subhash Chandra Bose, the Indian revolutionary nationalist who dominated the whole affair.

It is a story little known in the Western world, and even in India it has received only piecemeal and fragmentary treatment. It may be said to have started with the escape of Mr. Bose from police surveillance in Calcutta during January 1941, and his appearance in Berlin two months later. Quickly coming to terms with the Nazis, Bose formed from prisoners of war captured in the West an 'Indian Legion', which he saw one day marching into India with the German Army. Stalingrad and El Alamein in 1942 put an end to this dream, but by now the Japanese, who had started in Malaya an Indian Independence League and an 'Indian National Army', needed Bose's help to control the large Indian communities of South-East Asia.

In 1943, therefore, Bose journeyed to the Far East. He took charge of the Independence League, formed a 'Provisional Government of free India,' campaigned vigorously and with the success to raise money and recruits, prepared to enter India at the head of an Indian National Army division with the Japanese in 1944. The division was virtually wiped out during the Imphal campaign, but a second division was already arriving in Burma and a third, recruited from the civilian Indian population of Malaya, was under training in Johore. The second division disintegrated after the British-Indian Fourteenth Army crossed the Irrawaddy early in 1945. The third remained to defend Malaya, to which, in June 1945, Bose returned to continue at least his propaganda war. He was already thinking of ultimate refuge in Russia with some of his Cabinet Ministers, and this was still in his mind, when two months later, he was fatally injured in air accident in Formosa.

Published sources of material on the subject are now numerous. By far the most important is the record of the Court Martial at Delhi, November 1945, of three prominent Indian National Army Commanders. With the many appendices and exhibits, the account of this trial constitutes the fullest collated record of the Movement in South-East Asia from 1943 onwards. I refer to it frequently, sometimes simply as 'I.N.A.CM.'

For permission to quote freely from the published works of Mr. Subhash Chandra Bose, my thanks are due to his nephew, Mr Sisir K Bose of the Netaji Research Bureau, Calcutta. I should like to thank Mr. D.K. Roy for the extensive quotation I have made from his book *The Subhash I Knew*, and Mr. K.P.K. Menon for much first-hand material. I am indebted to Mr. Alfred Tyrnauer for the facsimile on page 61, the original of which is in his possession; to Mr. Nirad Chaudhuri and Mr. Shah Nawaz for permission to quote from their works; and to Messrs. Lawrence & Wishart for my quotations from *The Indian Struggle*. Extracts from *The Goebbels Diaries* edited by Mr. Louis P. Lochner and from *Ciano's Diary* and *Ciano's Diplomatic Papers*, both edited by Mr Malcolm Muggeridge, and reproduced by kind permission of Messrs. Hamish Hamilton and Messrs. William Heinemann respectively. Other indispensable sources are acknowledged in notes to the text.

Indian readers will, I hope, forgive the liberty I have taken with the spelling of the name 'Bose'. Two Boses figure dominantly in the story. Rash Behari Bose and Subhash Chandra Bose. To avoid confusing Western readers I have referred to the former as Rash Behari Basu, using a widely accepted alternative spelling.

I have been fortunate in the many friends who have helped and encouraged me in the preparation of this work. In particular thanks are due to Mr. David Anderson, himself an authority on the subject, who most generously urged me to write about it; to Mr. Christopher Blond who made me start again: to Professor Rushbrook Williams whose generous advice shaped the present form of the book; to my wartime colleagues Mr. Carl Ivens and Professor E.W. Herd who each contributed specialist knowledge; and to Miss Hazel Palmer who has typed two successive versions with unwarranted patience and incredible speed.

- HUGH TOYE

Cyprus, December 4th, 1957.

NATIONAL ANTHEM OF AZAD HIND

May Good Fortune, Happiness and ease rain down upon India;
On Punjab, Sindh, Gujarat, Maratha on Orissa and Bengal,
On the Indian Ocean, on the Vindhya Mountains,
On the Himalayas, the blue Jamuna and the Ganges.
May thy ways be priased, from Thee our life from thy body our hope.
May the rising sun shine down upon the world and exalt the name of India
In every heart may thy love grow and thy sweetness take shape.
So that every dweller in every province.
Every faith united, every secret and mystery put aside.
May come into thy embrace, in plaited garlands of love.
May the rising sun shine down upon the world and exalt the name of India.
May the early morning with the wings of a bird praise Her.
And with all the power and fullness of the winds bringing freshness into life.
Let us join together and shout: 'Long Live India', our beloved country.
The rising sun shines upon the earth, exalting the name of India.
Victory! May India's name be praised.

Translated by C.H. IVENS

I

THE EXILES

Towards dusk on a soaking December day in 1941, a group of Indian soldiers waited at the verge of the jungle near a village in North Malaya. They were drenched, half-starved, ragged, stinking with swamp mud, and utterly exhausted by three days of blundering through the jungle in torrential, tropical rain. Now one of their officers, a young Sikh, Captain Mohan Singh, had gone to explore the village and discover what treatment they might expect there. For they were fugitives, survivors of the 1/14 Punjab Regiment, which had been surprised and scattered by Japanese tanks on December 11th near the Siamese Border. They had travelled far through the thick, swampy country; now perhaps they had reached friendly territory, where they might recover from shock and suffering before they faced the nightmare battle again.

It was not to be. The captain returned to tell them that the enemy had advanced far beyond them into Malaya. They were still hopelessly isolated, cut off from their comrades by fifty miles of perilous forest. Utter despondency overtook them. Famished, wretched, desperate as they were, even Japanese captivity seemed better than their present misery. Sadly their British colonel and two Indian officers led them to the village police station, and sent a message of surrender to Alor Star, twelve miles away. The Japanese replied that they would collect them next day.

Instead of a Japanese guard there rode into the village on the morning of December 15th a Sikh gentleman of friendly appearance, in a car flying the flag of the Indian National Congress. Yes, he said, it was the Indian soldiers he had come to see: he would take charge of them and be responsible for their good treatment. A little later a Japanese officer arrived to confirm his words and to conduct the party to Alor Star. The British colonel was taken away separately, but the two Indian officers travelled with the Sikh: he said he was Giani Pritam Singh of Bangkok, a holy man working for Indian independence. He had a treaty with the Japanese and intended to raise an independent Indian Army. The Japanese officer they had seen, Major Fujihara, had instructions to treat them not as prisoners of war, but as honoured friends of Japan. Japan meant to achieve the liberation of India from British rule: she asked her friends to help her as her victorious armies marched on.

At Alor Star they found that Pritam Singh had already set up an office of what he called the 'Independence League of India'. The local Indians had welcomed him and now did their best for the forlorn and destitute soldiers. Late that night Major Fujihara sent for the two officers and began to talk to them. Had Pritam Singh made everything clear, he asked. Did they now understand that Japan took no pleasure in making prisoners of fellow-Asiatics, fellow-sufferers from the oppressive arrogance of the West? Japan was marching to victory over the white-skinned foreigner: she had already proclaimed a Co-Prosperity Sphere in which the countries of the East could be independent partners. With the defeat of Great Britain other liberated countries, could join it: Malaya, Burma, India who had suffered so much. Fujihara was a great talker, enthusiastic, charming, friendly, indefatigable, persuasive even through an interpreter. Furthermore he believed in what he was saying, and something of his sincerity gradually communicated itself to Captain Mohan Singh and drew him into the argument.

For already the Indians were wondering why such a meagre personality as Pritam Singh had been chosen to lead so great an enterprise. The Sikh missionary was politically incompetent – how could he ever deal with the complications of diplomacy? There was a leader already outside India, a leader who would be acceptable to all Indians, a man of the highest political repute. They thought he was now working in Germany: his name – Subhash Chandra Bose.

Pritam Singh too had spoken of Bose. Fujihara did not comment, but brought the conversation back to the Co-

Prosperity Sphere, Greater East Asia, 'Asia for the Asiatics', India's 'shackles of slavery' Mohan Singh asked what all these phrases meant, but in vain. The talk flowed on about the Indian National Congress and its repudiation of the war, about the high ideal of Freedom and at last reached the point of the argument. Freedom said Fujihara, was not to be achieved by sitting in an armchair, still less on the earthern floor of an ascetic's cell. Gandhi was only a religious leader and could not bring about any political change. To change a world there must be an army and soldiers fighting. It was soldiers who made history. Then he turned to Mohan Singh and asked him in effect: 'And what are you going to do about it? You are a soldier, it is for you to choose. Your old master is dead. If you really want freedom for your country you must aspire to do something active. You must raise an Indian National Army.'

Two influences weighed on Mohan Singh when he heard this proposal: the whole subconscious drag of the Indian nationalist mind, and the sudden shattering calamity which had sealed the fate of the British not only in Malaya, but it seemed in all the Far East. He wrote afterwards of his political feelings:

> I could not convince my conscience that it was right for Indians to shed their blood for an end which was not applicable to them. Britain, faced with the imminent danger of invasion, had declared that she was fighting for freedom, democracy and other high-

> sounding principles. She besought others to come to her help. Even at the most critical period of her national history, and when she was using India to fight for her own freedom, she refused to consider the question of India's freedom. Instead, she ordered the arrest of Indian leaders because they were considered guilty of asking freedom for India. Why should we Indians fight for a thing for others, the mere mention of which for ourselves was considered sufficient crime for the greatest of us to be put behind bars?
>
> Then why were we Indians fighting? The only answer I could find was that we were fighting merely as deluded, befooled, mercenary heroes at the expense of poor India for the sole benefit of Britain, thus helping Britain to keep India in subjection with Indian men, money and materials.

This was the nationalist argument with a vengeance. Before war came Mohan Singh had not been more perturbed by the demands of Indian nationalism than most Indian officers. Now the British were gone – there was no doubt in his mind about that – what was his duty, where lay his interest now? He was a nationalist: he was ready to act if India would benefit. But were not the Japanese simply a new race of oppressors? Already they were trying to use Indian prisoners as fifth columnists: this surely was the proof. His protests were vigorous and outspoken. 'Such petty exploitation here,' he said, 'will do you no good: by defeating the British in Malaya you may shake them, but you can only overthrow them in India. If you go there now, the whole populace will join with them to resist you. We are the only people who can defeat the British in India, and we will only take up the cudgels if we are sure that you will not exploit us in your turn.'

Here was the half-promise for which Fujihara had been hoping. On December 17th he took Mohan Singh to see the Japanese Commander-in-Chief and placed all Indian prisoners under his control. Now, as he followed the Japanese advance down into Malaya, the Indian was won by the real friendship he thought he found in Fujihara, and by the useful service he himself was enabled to perform as he took over more and more Indian soldiers. The prisoners for their part were glad to accept the protection from the Japanese which he seemed to provide, and cheered the propaganda speeches he began to make in fulfillment of his side of the bargain.

By the end of December 1941, Mohan Singh had made his choice. With the consent of a committee of prisoners, he had agreed to organise an Indian National Army which would work with the Independence League of Pritam Singh and eventually fight the British.[1] For political decisions beyond that he looked to the leadership of Subhash Chandra Bose, upon whose name all doubts, all uncertainties were cast. Bose was the Man of Destiny: for

---

[1] See Appendix I, No.1

him they would shed their blood: let the Japanese secure his support and leadership. So much Fujihara promised to do, and Mohan Singh pledged his own trust in return. He would start 'patriotic education' of the soldiers. He would prepare to raise an army. While he was doing this he would see more of the Japanese and consult the many civilian Indians in Malaya whose support would be required. The Army was to be raised from Indians, directed by Indians, used for the purposes of India: he would do nothing irrevocable until he was sure of that. Fujihara let him so think and looked to his other instructions.

It is indeed time to consider exactly what those instructions were, and what was the origin of this strange alliance between Sikh missionary and Japanese invader. The roots lay deep in history, for this remarkable intrigue was in the line of the many revolutionary attempts which Indians had made against British rule. The Japanese were using one of the leaders whom the Germans had employed to disturb India during the First World War, and some of the same ideas.

In 1912 a group of Indian revolutionaries, having been prevented from agitation in India, found a safe field of activity among the Indian settlers on the West Coast of the USA. In San Francisco they founded a newspaper, The Ghadr (Revolution), which was distributed in the large Indian communities of the Pacific ports and regularly smuggled into India. In 1914 the 'Ghadrities', as they came to be called, were able to induce several thousand

Sikhs to sail for home, bent on trouble. Despite Government precautions, many reached the Punjab. As they did so, war broke out in Europe and original conspirators, now openly pro-German, moved to Berlin. There the Indian Revolutionary Society flourished, using the German diplomatic posts in Shanghai, Batavia and the USA to assist its agents in India. Chief of these agents was Rash Behari Basu, a terrorist who had been concerned in the attempt to assassinate the Viceroy, Lord Hardinge, in 1912 and in other outrages. The major rebellion he now plotted in the Punjab was forestalled by the police, but Basu escaped to Shanghai where he helped the Germans in two other schemes for Indian revolution in 1915. In 1916 he fled to Japan and came under the protection of Toyama, head of the Black Dragon Society, a political bandit of immense power who defied Japanese government attempts to arrest the fugitive for extradition to India. In the course of time Basu married Toyama's daughter, became a Japanese citizen and founded a Japanese branch of the Congress 'Indian Independence League', which was still alive in 1941.

In 1915, too, the Ghadr conspirators had set up in Kabul with German assistance what was called the 'Provisional Government of India', which tried in vain to seduce some of the Indian Princes from their Imperial allegiance. In India, as conspiracies failed, hundreds of revolutionaries were interned, imprisoned or transported. Many more escaped to sanctuaries in the Far East as Rash Behari had done: many returned there when released after the war. The

Ghadr Society of San Francisco, neutralised when the USA became combatant, was revived in Russia's interest when war was over and wove new intrigues among its old comrades in the cities of the Far East. Then in the early 'thirties there were more exiles seeking refuge from the unhappy political struggle in India, and Bangkok, in particular, became a centre of Indian discontent which British influence there could not allay. Thus in 1941 there was abundant material for Japan to use if she wished to try her hand at Indian revolutions.

At first she had no thought of doing so. The outspoken hostility of the Indian National Congress to her aggression in China seemed to rule out the possibility of using Indian nationalism. But in June 1941, when her plot to employ Burmese revolutionaries in the invasion of Burma was developing, Giani Pritam Singh approached the Japanese Embassy in Bangkok with an offer of Indian nationalist help. Imperial Headquarters in Tokyo became interested. An Intelligence Officer, Major Fujihara, was briefed to use Pritam Singh in the invasion of Malaya; he might perhaps obtain cooperation for the Japanese Army from the eight hundred thousand Indians in the country, he might even win over some Indian troops. Fujihara gathered in Bangkok a handful of interpreters and Intelligence Officers to work with the nine Indians recruited by Pritam Singh. From this group sprang the 'Independent League of India' which was being carried through Malaya, and the winning of Mohan Singh with its unhoped-for consequences.

When Singapore fell the Japanese handed over to Captain Mohan Singh all the forty-five thousand Indian prisoners captured there. His organisation catered for their immediate needs. He himself, and the acute, nationalist Indian lawyers and intellectuals of Malaya and Siam, considered the political issues. Their discussions were pursued at Tokyo in March 1942, under the chairmanship of Rash Behari Basu: the Indian Independence League was provisionally established throughout Japanese Asia, and an agenda prepared for a fully representative conference of Indians to be held at Bangkok in June.

The Japanese, meanwhile, at the instance of Fujihara, sought a tripartite Axis declaration on Indian Independence, and invited Subhash Chandra Bose to leave Germany for the wider opportunities of leadership which they could offer him in the Far East. Bose was momentarily more interested in a tripartite declaration for which he campaigned vigorously. Mussolini was willing, Hitler reluctant; after the Fuhrer's final refusal on May 29th, Bose turned his eyes to the East.

There could be no doubt that a welcome awaited him there. The Indians assembled on June 15th 1942, at Bangkok heard with enthusiasm the message he sent them from Germany, and unanimously invited him to assume the leadership as soon as he could. His words seemed to answer their doubts and to add to their deliberations the moral sanction for which they had been seeking. There was a new militance and a self-confidence which had been lacking in the earlier discussions. The same leaders led them – the Malayan contingent which had formulated all policy so far, and which controlled a majority of the votes – but in the two months that had gone by many Japanese less liberal than Fujihara had been encountered, and many more stupid. Suspicion of Japanese intentions was now hardly disguised and the demand for specific assurances from Japan as to freedom from interference was almost peremptory. The assembled Indians intended, moreover, to be guided by Indian National Congress principles; beyond that point they would go only under the leadership of S.C. Bose. In a radio-telephone conversation with Rash Behari, Bose accepted their invitation, but a year was to pass before he reached South-East Asia.

The Thirty-five Resolutions of the Bangkok Conference[2] implied Japanese agreement in so many particulars, that official ratification by Japan was clearly necessary before the 'Council of Action' of the Indian Independence League – the Executive Committee of five with Rash Behari as President – could proceed with confidence on its programme. Japanese assent to the foundation of the League and Indian National Army[3] could be assumed, but specific acceptance of at least five points seemed indispensable:

1. Control by the League and I.N.A. of all Indian prisoners.

---

[2] See Appendix I, The Bangkok Resolutions.

[3] Hereafter referred to frequently as the I.N.A.

2. The status of the I.N.A. as an army freely allied with Japan.
3. Unfettered League control of the I.N.A.
4. The absolute independence of India after liberation.
5. League control of the property in East Asia of Indians who had left as refugees.

Japanese acceptance of these terms, and their agreement to the liberal democratic constitution of the League, would have looked a little like recognition of a provisional government of India. It was the Council's intention to take nothing less. The Japanese, with the connivance of Rash Behari, temporised, and it was six months before an open breach occurred.

The Conference had taken place against a background of unrest and agitation in India which culminated in the disturbances of August 1942. The Council of Action as it waited for recognition by the Japanese, followed Indian developments with eager attention. The words 'Quit India' were being muttered, Rash Behari added his broadcast portion of incitement and defiance, open rebellion loomed near. There could be no greater stimulus to an independence movement. All action possible in advance of Japanese ratification was taken. The main League Secretariat was set up in Bangkok and territorial branch headquarters throughout the Japanese East: members of the Council of Action took charge of their departments: broadcast propaganda was intensified under central direction, and agents were recruited for espionage and subversion in India.

In this same atmosphere Mohan Singh had slowly led on his officers and men to the formation of the Indian National Army. He had listed some twenty-five thousand volunteers before the Bangkok Conference. When he returned to Singapore after it as General Mohan Singh, with impressive badges of rank and with at last sufficient public sanction to quieten lingering doubts, recruiting began in earnest. By the end of August 1942 forty thousand prisoners of war had signed a pledge 'to join the Indian National Army under Mohan Singh'. There were several reasons for this success. First, the pledge to Mohan Singh by name: all thought that this would enable their leader to release them if things went wrong. Secondly, the I.N.A. offered personal liberty, comparative comfort and freedom from the labour gangs of the Pacific Islands, where several thousand Indians prisoners had already gone. The third factor was the ambition of the Indian camp commanders, some of whom sought to improve their personal standing with Mohan Singh by presenting long lists of volunteers. Harsh methods of persuasion were used, including several corporal punishment, and the Bidadari 'Concentration Camp', hitherto the normal military detention centre, became a place of terror the mere threat of which could often induce a man to 'volunteer'.

Mohan Singh was largely ignorant of this coercive

recruitment. Not that there was any softness about his regime. He ruled with high-handed arrogance, and was always prepared to act sternly towards those who made propaganda against his Army. He would warn officers that they must not influence their men. If they did not comply he would remove them to a special 'Officers' Separation Camp', where ridicule, propaganda and discomfort were used to bring them round. About one hundred and twenty officers and Viceroy's Commissioned Officers were 'separated' in August and September 1942, and there were times when they were treated altogether as outlaws.

The Japanese agreed in August to the raising of a combat division of the Indian National Army. This was ready, an armed force of sixteen thousand three hundred officers and men, on September 10th. Mohan Singh was soon asking for a second division to be formed from his twenty-four thousand surplus volunteers and for facilities to train civilian recruits. His ultimate aim, he told Colonel Iwaguro, head of the Japanese liaison organisation, was an army of two hundred and fifty thousand men: this would not be difficult, for his recruiting officers in Malaya had been overwhelmed with civilian offers of service. But the expansion of the Indian National Army was governed by factors which Iwaguro's diplomacies could not affect – the running-down of the Japanese forces in Malaya and the labour requirements of their vast new airfield programme. The I.N.A. at its present strength was quite enough for the depleted Japanese garrison in Malaya to handle in an emergency; it could not therefore be allowed to expand until part of it had moved to Burma. Furthermore, Iwaguro knew that so far from handing over all Indian prisoners to Mohan Singh, the Japanese must eventually take back for labour overseas even the surplus volunteers. This had to be concealed as long as possible. The recruitment of civilians had to be delayed and the movement of the 1st Division to Burma hastened.

Mohan Singh's patience was soon exhausted. There were other issues. Although its 1st Division had been warned for Burma, the I.N.A. had still not even been publicly recognised; if the Japanese accepted the Bangkok Resolutions, he thought, there should be some acknowledgment of the I.N.A. as a new allied army, some declaration of its status. There had also been Japanese interference with Indian broadcasting in Singapore and Mr. K.P.K Menon, the Council of Action member responsible, had protested in vain. Then, early in November, Mohan Singh received a report on the handling of Indian property in Rangoon. This was the last straw.

The Bangkok Resolutions had asked that the property of absent Indians be entrusted, as a source of revenue, to the League. In Burma there were many deserted Indian houses left in the great Indian exodus of 1942, but the Japanese did not at first hand them over. Eventually, to ease their own administrative difficulties, they proposed that the League should manage such property on their behalf. In the ensuing discussions they declared that the Bangkok Resolutions had never been accepted, and that the Council of Action had no status: all was at the discretion of the local Japanese commanders. Furthermore, said the Japanese:

> Absentee property according to international law is enemy property. What property do you have here? You are all paupers. You must acknowledge the generosity of the Japanese in entrusting you with the management of absentee property at all.... As for Indian prestige, that is secondary to the execution of the Commander-in-Chief's orders.
>
> ....Puppets? What is the harm in being puppets? You should be proud to be puppets of the Japanese.

Then in Japanese, which one of the Indians understood:

> You cannot argue with these people because the Indian way of arguing amounts to indulging in useless feats of hair-splitting. In my view they should just be toid that the Commander-in-Chief has every right to direct, guide and control the League.

Nothing could be clearer than this. Mohan Singh resolved to prevent any major I.N.A. movement to Burma until japan had given satisfactory assurances. If she refused, he would disband the I.N.A.

The Council of Action steadily supported its chief military member. It demanded an official reply to the Bangkok Resolutions, recognition of itself as the supreme executive of the Indian Movement, a guarantee of Indian sovereignty after liberation, public recognition of the I.N.A., and facilities for its expansion. On December 1st Iwaguro gave the Japanese reply: Japan recognised no obligation regarding the Bangkok Resolutions; there would be no further Government statement on India at present; all Indian soldiers would revert forthwith to Japanese control except for the Indian National Army Division. I.N.A. expansion, he said, was a matter for the Japanese and they would not be hurried. After this meeting Mohan Singh was told that a draft of soldiers was required for Burma on December 5th. He refused point blank to provide it.

For a few days individual Japanese tried to save the situation. Even Fujihara was called down from his new staff appointment in Saigon to intercede with his old friends. Throughout, Mohan Singh's boldness was remarkable. He told the Japanese that if they tried to replace the British in India, India would fight them; she did not want the sort of bogus independence given to Manchuria. As for Malaya 'the way you are crushing the Malayans here and completely Japanising them has created suspicions. No basis of cooperation was left. Only Rash Behari Basu wavered, and for him his colleagues had nothing but contempt. On December 8th 1942, all the members of the Council of Action except Basu, resigned.

Some Indians in Malaya, fearful of the consequences of antagonising the Japanese, now urged that at least the League be saved as a community organisation. Basu promised to continue the work himself, reach a definite understanding with the Japanese, and report to his countrymen within a reasonable time. But first he tried to strengthen his own position by wresting control of the I.N.A. from Mohan Singh. On December 29th, when this had proved impossible, Mohan Singh was summoned to Iwaguro's office, dismissed from his command, and arrested. The I.N.A. was not unprepared. Mohan Singh's order of dissolution came into effect as soon as his arrest was known. He disappeared quietly into internment, first in a remote part of Singapore Island, then on a small island in the Johore Strait and finally in Sumatra until the war ended.

For the next six weeks Rash Behari Basu was occupied in the salvage of the I.N.A. This was easier than might have been expected. The Japanese refused to recognise the dissolution and denied that I.N.A. soldiers could return at will to prisoner-of-war status. Colonel Iwaguro addressed the officers and undertook to obtain another Japanese Government statement of policy. Then a small issue, promoted by the few who had disagreed with Mohan Singh throughout the crisis, came completely to obscure the greater one. Within a few days the question was not whether Mohan Singh had been justified in dissolving the I.N.A., but whether his position had entitled him to do so. To return to the prison camps was no small matter – had the personal pledge rightly been given to Mohan Singh? Had Rash Behari acted legally in dismissing him? Could the Japanese properly refuse to recognise the dissolution and where, in that case, did I.N.A. members stand? Thus the issues of principle were clouded and Iwaguro was given his chance. Soon the talk was not of whether the I.N.A. should, continue, but on what terms. At the beginning of February leading officers were told that Subhash Chandra Bose was on his way from Germany. This was decisive; every doubt was now deferred. After February 13th 1943, the I.N.A. was progressively reorganised and revived.

From the manner of its revival a number of reflections must be drawn. There was patriotism in the origin of the I.N.A. – Mohan Singh was without doubt sincere in his desire to do only what would benefit India and his appeal to his fellow prisoners had been genuinely patriotic – but during the months in which the I.N.A. was established other factors – comfort, amenities, security – had emerged which in January 1943 were powerful enough to outweigh all others.

Mohan Singh's freedom of action, his safeguard against Japanese insincerity, the power he thought he had in the last resort of dissolving the I.N.A., had thus departed long ago. He might formally abolish his creation, but he could not uproot his ideas from the other hearts in which he had planted them. So there was a certain reluctance about the dissolution. Officers and men took off their badges and insignia but did not burn them in accordance with others; most were readily available for resumption six weeks later. Logically, pay should have been renounced as soon as the I.N.A. was dissolved, for although I.N.A. pay was no more at this time than the rate to which prisoners of war were entitled under the Geneva Convention, it was far more than the genuine prisoners were receiving. Yet officers continued to draw money because Rash Behari said that the cash they were receiving came from his personal account, and those few who refused did so with an air of nobly exceeding their duty. Then Rash Behari and the Japanese were able to throw in uncertainty of status, legal issues and appeals to jealousy and ambition, so that when reconstruction of the I.N.A. was proposed, with twice as many staff appointments as before, the question was, to the majority, one merely of face – the more credit, be it said, to the thirty officers and four thousand men who preferred joining their ten thousand comrades already in the cruel camps of the South-West Pacific, to continuance in the I.N.A. on Japanese terms.

While Rash Behari was occupied with military affairs the League in Malaya had waited with mounting impatience for him to report as promised on an understanding with the Japanese. At length, on February 21st, the Malayan League leaders called on him to put forward his solution of the deadlock and to suspend League activity until he had done so. But the Japanese would tolerate no further argument; under clear threats of violence, resistance from the League collapsed. Rash Behari's confidence had now recovered; he moved his headquarters permanently from Bangkok to Singapore and, on April 3rd, assumed dictatorial powers in the Indian Independence Movement, on grounds of its entry upon 'active service'. To confirm this he summoned a new representative conference to Singapore at the end of April and confronted it with a new constitution. There would be no more 'unnecessary arguments': the Bangkok Resolutions were scrapped; objections could be answered by Subhash Chandra Bose.

It was indeed clear that S.C. Bose would have a free hand. His friend Colonel Yamamoto, lately Military Attache in Berlin, had been appointed to succeed Iwaguro; the League had been transformed into a simple dictatorship, and the subordination of the Indian National Army to it clearly established. Rash Behari left Singapore at the beginning of May 1943 to await Bose in Tokyo. None knew yet how he would arrive, where or when, for the Japanese Admiralty had kept their secret well. But the Indian communities of all Japanese Asia awaited him with impatience. The first promise of his coming had been made more than a year ago; surely now he would rescue them from their difficulties and from their fears of the Japanese.

2

SUBHASH BABU

Subhash Chandra Bose was born to Bengali parents on January 23rd, 1897, at Cuttack in Orissa, where he lived for the first sixteen years of his life. They were years of violence. In them the frustrated nationalism of Bengal, tinged with religious revivalism, spread from the few to the many, till the whole province was in the grip of terrorism. The partition of Bengal in 1905 had precipitated the mischief. This measure, proposed for cogent administrative reasons, was carried out in the teeth of Hindu opinion and sentiment. Bengali nationalism, rooted in a language and literature of its own, and older than any all-India feeling, saw it as a wanton outrage and a challenge to patriotism. Had Bengalis no religion, no self-respect? Were they less able than the newly victorious Japanese to stand up to the Western interloper? Agitation became hysterical. Racial hatred began to take root. Terrorism became the ultimate act, all that enslaved and frustrated man could do against hopeless injustice. The revolutionaries collected arms, manufactured bombs and, in schools and colleges throughout Bengal, organised recruitment for the terrorist clubs. Year by year violence increased; magistrates, police officers, witnesses were attacked; funds were stolen to support the organisation. Counter-measures, any attempt to restore public security, was deemed oppression. The hysteria grew. There seemed to the nationalist no hope of a peaceful liberation: 'Only military power, actual or potential, could drive out the British.'[1]

The repeal of partition in 1911 brought relief but no reconciliation. The target was now simply foreign rule. By 1917 there had been 161 incidents classed as outrages in which fifty-six persons had been murdered, eighty-four wounded and 800,000 rupees stolen. Of all these only thirty-three cases had been solved by the police, and although many men were sent to goal, only four were convicted on capital charges. The foreigner was thus not merely oppressive but to a degree powerless to punish; good terrorist organisations and prompt vengeance on informers reduced the risk and aided recruiting.

So Bengal dreamed dreams of revolt, and her poets sang great songs of freedom. These were the songs of Bose's boyhood. He must have heard them, for half the revolutionaries belonged to the rich and educated Kayastha caste from which he was sprung. His own family background was stable. His father, Janakinath Bose, was an able, public-spirited lawyer of broad social interests and orthodox nationalism: from 1905 he was Public

[1] N.C. Chaudhuri, Biography of an Unknown Indian, p. 245.

Prosecutor in Cuttack and from 1912 a member of the Bengal Legislative Council. He was a man of moderate means and of great ambition for his eight sons and six daughters. His wife, a strong, sensible woman, ruled her large family firmly. The sixth son Subhash, stood in awe of his father and mother, and looked with envy on children whose contact with their parents seemed closer. But it was a healthy, disciplined home and he learnt to respect industry and good behaviour.

Before he was five, Subhash was sent to the Baptist Missionary School which his brothers attended. Here for seven years he underwent a normal English education, showing great promise as a scholar, and suffering the unhappiness which often comes from failure at sport. But Bengali had now become a compulsory subject for the Calcutta matriculation: when he was twelve Subhash went to an Indian school, the Ravenshaw Collegiate School, in order to prepare for it. Here uneasiness at games troubled him less and he found more sympathy with his love of gardening and nature study. He was a reserved, serious boy; an avid reader, introspective, his mind turning in upon itself in a precocious concern for religious truth, self-control and psychic harmony. The *sadhus* and pilgrims at Puri, near his home, fascinated him; he was attracted by Yoga and mysticism. There was active compassion which would drive him to seek opportunities of social service, a slow political awakening and some contact with the secret societies of Calcutta. The conflict between mystic and man of action thus came early to him. It was made clearer when, at the age of fifteen, he came by chance on the writings of Swami Vivekananda who taught salvation through service, service to humanity and particularly to Mother India. He read all he could of Vivekananda and Vivekananda's master, the saintly and ascetic Ramakrishna Paramahansa. Selfless service became his ideal. He began to read philosophy at the Presidency College, Calcutta, in 1913.

Formal philosophic study served only to intensify the inner struggle. How was the ideal to be attained? In 1914, unknown to his parents, he went with a friend on a search through Northern India, looking for a spiritual master to show him his way. But the holy places of Hinduism held no leader for him, and he returned to his sorrowing family convinced only that he had some mission to fulfill. We find him soon afterwards arguing philosophy with his father and writing of it to a friend:

> He asked me whether the statement about the reality of God as against the unreality of the world might not amount to a mere theory. I said, 'It might but only as long as one simply mouthed it, for the moment it is realised it becomes a living truth of experience and, what is more, it can be realised. For those who said so had realised it; therefore we too can follow in their footsteps.'
>
> 'But whoever realised it?' he challenged, 'and where is the proof?'

> 'The sages realised it,' I returned, 'and the proof is their testimony, namely the Upanishads:– "I do know the Great Being whose colour is the dazzle of the sun and who is stationed beyond the gloom".[2]

Nevertheless, in the disillusion that followed his vain pilgrimage, political activism began to assert its hold on Subhash. He was already a leader among the students, playing a full part in college life. He had started a debating club – because 'the country will need great debaters, parliamentarians – when we are free, that is'.[3] He wanted to promote quick thinking and self-reliance, for 'we Indians are too dependent on others – for action, views, initiative, everything'.[4] Among his fellows he was not talkative, but in discussion, whether in the debating club or in argument with his friends, his speech was warm and urgent. Self-contained, holding aloof from secret societies, almost passionate in his desire for social service, with a certain loftiness of character, but never unsociable or puffed up, he still seemed to some to be destined for the life of contemplation.

Then there occurred the incident which Bose afterwards called the turning point of his career: he was expelled from his college for his leading part in an assault on one of the English lecturers. The lecturer had been indiscreet and impatient, the students too ready to take offence.

---

[2] Letter to Hemanta Kumar Sarkar.

[3] Dilip Kumar Roy, The Subhash I Knew, p. 22

[4] Ibid. p. 23

Hostility had grown. There had been angry protests against remarks he had made, and Bose had led them. The students were excited, militant, determined to dramatise, to see the affair as a test of the manhood of Indian Youth, and hence of India's own future. 'India has entered on a new life...,' he wrote at this time. 'Blessed are we that we are living in this auspicious hour... Cast off despair and look yonder to the new light before us, and follow it.'[5] Such a mood in a pupil was more than difficult. Tension increased. At length an exasperated lecturer reacted perhaps too roughly, against a group of noisy students on a verandah outside his classroom. That afternoon a party of them assaulted one of his colleagues. Bose had been present and his leadership was taken for granted; he would neither deny it nor apologise and was expelled in February 1916.

Whether this was a harsh punishment is open to argument: the affair received so much publicity that magnanimity may have been difficult. But of its effect upon the proud young undergraduate there can be no doubt. All was high tragedy. In his own eyes he was a victim of racial prejudice, struck down for protesting against an insult to his Motherland. He appeared to bear his sentence with equanimity, retired to Cuttack, devoting himself to strenuous nursing, social work and the process of mental discipline he called self-analysis. The injury was not forgotten: he brooded over it with all the vehemence of

[5] Letter to Hemanta Kumar Sarkar, February 1st, 1916.

his nineteen years, added other examples of racial prejudice – and these were not hard to find in the Calcutta of 1916 – racial hatred ate into his soul. He came to glory in the strictures with which he had been dismissed. He had been 'the most disturbing element in the college,' had he; he would create other disturbances for them to remember. To show himself superior to the white-faced foreigner now became his one-pointed aim. India also must show herself superior. To help her accomplish this was, he felt, in some way his mission.

Academic studies meanwhile made little progress. Bose's father, who had not been unsympathetic, had nevertheless refused to let him continue them elsewhere, insisting that his course in Calcutta be first completed. He was readmitted to the University in July 1917. There was no further setback. He joined the University Training Corps, spending many happy days in it during 1918, became a member of the Students' Consultative Committee and in 1919 took first-class honours in philosophy. It was apparent that academically nothing could stand in his way. To his father it was also clear that the nationalist turbulence of Bengal at this time would tempt him sorely: let him therefore go to England and sit for the Indian Civil Service: let power and dignity cure him. The father's decision was sudden and the son's dilemma acute. Does not power corrupt? If he succeeded, what of his nationalism? Yet he had already refused to join the terrorists. He knew the people – of course he did, so many of them were of his own caste and kind – but he felt that the time was not ripe for violent revolution.

With many misgivings he agreed to go. This was no change of heart: to enter the Indian Civil Service was still consistent with Indian Nationalism, and the examination would serve him as a final test of his superiority over the European. His over-sensitivity easily found for him further examples of racial prejudice in England. He could still write from Cambridge in November 1919: 'What gives me the greatest joy is to watch the whiteskins serving me and cleaning my shoes.'[6] This racial complex lost its edge with time, it was on occasion overcome, but its continuing, influence was the root cause of the arrogance which he was always apt to display towards the British.

At Cambridge Bose began to make English friends, to enjoy the freedom and the give and take of the Union. In spite of himself he was impressed: 'People here have a sense of time. Many are their defects, but one must bow one's head to their merits.'[7] He admired their energy, love of discipline and *esprit de corps*. Deliberately, and with the single-minded concentration that was now the most obvious characteristic of this strange young man, he set out to make himself personally acceptable to them so that he could study them better. The manners of his fellow Indians made him blush: 'Let your one ambition,' he

---

[6] The Subhash I Knew, p.53, footnote.

[7] The Subhash I Knew, p.50, footnote.

would tell them 'be to leave behind an impression here of flawless spruceness.'[8] And to his friend, Dilip Kumar Roy, in outraged protest: 'Don't for God's sake fling your arms about like lassos!'[8] The freedom of gesture natural to an Indian was, he saw, one cause of the English assertion he resented most of all – that Indians were not fit, not civilised enough, for self-rule. Always shy with women, he affected to regard feminine society as a danger to be shunned; he thought he had mastered sex, and he solemnly disapproved of the behaviour of the less restrained. But censoriousness won him no friends; his countrymen called him a humourless prig, and he retaliated by ignoring the Indian student community. He became more concentrated than ever: his methodical work, his abstinence and scrupulous personal discipline made him the envy of his compatriots.

There was not, of course, a sense of humour: yet it was possible for him occasionally to laugh and relax. Years later he told how Mr. Roy had imparted to him some appreciation of music, and nourished his sense of laughter and beauty. But Roy had to drag him from his books: because of the atmosphere of high seriousness in which he had been brought up 'he needed laughter more than the likes of us'.[9] He was also able, exceptionally, to forget his shyness of women: he sometimes stayed in England with Dr. Dharamvir, whose wife was English; she was perhaps in

[8] Ibid, p. 75, 76

[9] Ibid, p. 130

a better position than most to realise and cope with his racial difficulties, and they became good friends.

The harsher qualities were those of success. Bose passed the Civil Service open competitive examination brilliantly in 1920, attaining fourth place, a considerable achievement for one who had been in England barely eight months. But the direction of Indian nationalism was now changing. When Bose set out for England, Mr. Gandhi had not thrown himself into unqualified opposition to British rule. The tragic massacre of Amritsar had only just taken place, and its full horror was still obscured by the seriousness of the disturbances which had occasioned it. In 1920, when, despite official action against General Dyer and the repudiation of his methods by the House of Commons, the English people as a whole appeared to support what he had done,[10] Mr. Gandhi turned away. The Indian National Congress adopted his programme of non-cooperation and his call to Indians to renounce their British titles and appointments.

---

[10] April, 13th, 1919, Riots in Amritsar had got out of hand, and four Britons had been murdered by the mob when the military Commander, Brig-Gen. Dyer, was called in to restore order. Finding a large-meeting in Jallianwala Bagh, a confined space in the city, assembled in defiance of his proclamation, he ordered the party of Gurkhas with him to open fire; 379 people were killed and 1,200 left wounded on the ground. At a subsequent inquiry Gen. Dyer implied that he had intended by his action to check the spread of rebellion. This statement lead to deprivation of his command, in the House of Commons. There was, however, much sympathy for him in Britain, and this added fuel to public agitation in India.

Subhash debated the matter with his family, particularly with his brother Sarat; even Sarat urged him not to resign – life in the service would be tolerable, there was honourable work to be done, the British temper was changing. But to Subhash they seemed to miss the point: 'I must either chuck this rotten service and dedicate myself whole-heartedly to the country's cause, or I must bid adieu to all my ideals and aspirations'.[11] No Indian had yet resigned from the Indian Civil Service. If he failed here he would never respect himself again: nothing else was worth considering – he did not intend to marry and he had 'at heart no worldly ambitions'.[12] His mind was made up in January 1921: he would offer himself for work at the Congress National College in Calcutta, and on the new nationalist paper *Swaraj*. He resigned from the Indian Civil Service in April.

The Under-Secretary of State for India sent for him. 'I told him,' said Bose later, 'that I did not think one could be loyal to the British Raj and yet serve India honestly, heart and soul.'[13] His father was grieved, but the son had faced the father's distress and would not be diverted: 'If we build our ideals thinking first and last of our family happiness, won't the ideals be wonderful!

He returned to India in July 1921, to throw himself at the feet of Mr. Gandhi. Gandhi had just made his promise of

[11] Letter to his brother (An Indian Pilgrim, p. 128).
[12] Letter to his brother (An indian Pilgrim, p. 128).
[13] The Subhash I Knew, pp. 71, 72

independence for India within a year, and Bose had put his own interpretation upon it. A few months earlier he had talked with Mr. Roy about the possibilities of revolution in India. Indian Revolution, he had said, was full-grown when the Russians were learning the trade: even now things were being hatched, ... only this time the birds will not be let out until they are full-fledged. And then there will be such music at that new dawn'[14] His face flushed with excitement, 'but for this to be conceivable those stalwarts of the Swadeshi[15] days just had to be. And you call them failures? Can't you imagine the beauty of it all, the appalling beauty of that courage – of an infant organisation of a tiny handful – which dared to throw down the gauntlet to the mighty British'. Bose was impatient for battle and thought that this was what Gandhi offered.

His return, then, was as a would-be revolutionary, eager to be called upon for some deed of daring that would justify, to himself and to his family, his spectacular sacrifice of orthodox brilliance. He found Gandhi in Bombay, and the fascination he experienced can be seen in his own account of that first interview:

> I remember vividly the scene of that afternoon.....I was ushered into a room covered with Indian carpets. Almost in the centre, facing the door, sat the

[14] Ibid., p. 292.

[15] 'Swadeshi' - 'home-made-'; the 'Swadeshi Movement' was the boycott of British goods from 1905 onwards.

> Mahatma, surrounded by some of his closest followers. All were clad in home-made khadi. As I entered the room I felt somewhat out of place in my foreign costume and could not help apologising for it. The Mahatma received me with his charactreristic hearty smile and soon put me at ease, and the conversation started at once. I desired to obtain a clear understanding of the details – the successive stages – of his plan, leading on step by step to the ultimate seizure of power from the foreign bureaucracy. To that end I began to heap question upon question and the Mahatma replied with his habitual patience.[16]

But instead of action, he found non-violence, instead of a revolutionary plan, the pious hope that the British would be 'converted' by Gandhi's methods. Bose left him in disappointment, convinced that he had no 'clear idea of the successive stages of the campaign which would bring India to her cherished goal of freedom.' He went home to Calcutta to work under C. R. Das, the Bengali patriot who had given up his lucrative legal practice for poverty and nationalist agitation. With Das he was to learn many lessons.

S.C. BOSE IN POLITICS

The immediate cause of Mr. Gandhi's turn against the

[16] The Indian Struggle, pp. 66-67.

British in 1920 was the Amritsar Massacre. Let us pause here to consider what were the deeper reasons, the origins of the rising uneasiness of India under British rule, why it was that a brilliant young man could resign, from the highest service to which he could have aspired. For after this critical year in Indo-British relations neither side saw clearly any more: the dismal cycle of unrest, propaganda and repression built up a massive racial hatred which bedevilled Indian politics for twenty-seven years, and the eventual disappearance of the British, even as partners in the Government of India, certain. Bose was one estimable youth lost to the forces of moderation: there were many others, men whose fathers had worked sincerely for India with the British but who for themselves found only the way of revolt.

Indian independence had been the stated aim of British rule for a hundred years. By a series of liberal reforms Indians had been brought into the Government, first into local, then into provincial administrations, until in 1909 responsible parliamentary government was coming into view. There was a curious contradiction about this constitutional progress; although the reformers denied again and again that parliamentary democracy was suitable or intended for India, the steps they took moved them steadily in this direction. To the question 'If not parliamentary democracy, then what sort of government?' there was no answer: there would be leisure, it was assumed, for that issue when India was ready to rule herself: in the meantime there were urgent practical problems to be solved now. It was as if the British were walking down a corridor which had only one door, they had always said that they would leave the corridor and every step brought them nearer the door, yet with every step they said that they had no intention of passing through it. Thus it was very easy for Indians to believe that while there might be steps, the door would never open and the British would never go. Meanwhile the institutions, the steps, were bringing to Indians the desire, and increasingly the fitness, to do without the British. That was the political grievance.

There were others. Not only did the British deny that they would leave India in the foreseeable future, their conduct gave no hint of withdrawal They planned the great new capital city, New Delhi: measures to equalise the positions of Indians and Europeans before the law were rejected: Governments could still carry out vast projects of wide effect on the lives of the governed arbitrarily, and in the teeth of Indian opinion: the Indian Civil Service was still overwhelmingly British, although provision for Indian entry had been made by Parliament in 1870. Finally, with the participation of Indians in government, social contact between Indians and Europeans had decreased and there had grown up a discreet but effective colour bar.

When the First World War broke out in 1914, the mood of Indian nationalism was becoming one of despair. Some thought revolution inevitable, others continued to hope.

Then in August 1917 the British Government stated its intention of taking substantial steps towards responsible government in India as soon as possible. The British had now said for the first time, not only that they would leave the corridor but that they would pass through the door. When Mr. Edwin Montagu, the Secretary of State for India, went to India in November 1917, to work out with the Viceroy what the next steps were to be, he saw immediately that this was Britain's last chance to save her position there:

> If the results of our deliberations are either something which India will not accept, or a niggling, miserly, grudging safeguard, fiddling with the existing order of things, we shall have defrauded and defrauded irreparably – for they will never believe us again – a vast continent whose history is our glory, and whose hopes and aspirations, fears and tribulations it is pathetic to see.[17]

Mr. Montagu and the Viceroy certainly did their best to draft reforms which India, as well as the British Parliament, would accept. But beyond the grievances which political reforms could remedy, they saw the social grievances, 'the feeling in the minds of many an educated Indian that neither birth nor brains, enlightenment nor loyalty are regarded by the Englishmen in India as making him quite one of themselves'. 'If there are Indians,' they

---

[17] E.S. Montagu, *An Indian Diary*, pp. 10-11

said, 'who really desire to see India leave the empire, to get rid of English officers and English commerce, we believe that among the springs of action will be found the bitterness of feeling that has been nurtured out of some manifestation that the Englishman does not think the Indian an equal.'[18] This was not a matter which could be remedied by Parliament. The complete change of heart in the British community in India which could have removed it might have been possible over a long period of peace and security. Unhappily these conditions were not granted.

In 1919 when the new reforms were still in the making, the introduction of the Rowlatt Bill,[19] against the strongest public opinion India had ever manifested, started a fatal chain of events. The issue became not the necessity for the bill – which was arguable[20] but the willingness of those who governed to consider Indian opinion when it went against their own, and their capability of undergoing that social transformation without which the coming reforms would fail. The reforms were opposed by many Europeans, particularly by those who thought that Indian nationalism should be treated with a firm hand. The passage of the Rowlatt Bill seemed to be an expression of this view, and it undermined the confidence which Mr. Montagu had built up in 1918. The unrest which followed in the Punjab gave the exponents of the firm hand their

---

[18] Preamble to the *Montagu-Chelmsford Report*.

[19] To permit the Government to retain in peacetime some of the emergency powers it had taken to quell rebellion during the war.

[20] It was never used.

opportunity. The tragedy of Amritsar followed and, in the sordid haggling over responsibility in 1920, not all the integrity which had been lavished on India, nor all the outpouring of liberalism at home could avail. It seemed that India had been defrauded after all. Certainly she never believed the British again.

This was the atmosphere of Subhash Chandra Bose's entry into Indian politics in 1921. For the next two years he served a hard political apprenticeship under the eye of Mr. C. R. Das – in the Congress National College of which he was Principal, on the nationalist newspaper *Swaraj* and as member in charge of publicity on the executive of the Bengal Provincial Congress Committee. Mr. Das was a more aggressive nationalist than Mr. Gandhi, even as Bengal Congress opinion was more turbulent than that of the Congress as a whole. Bose quickly won his confidence and was soon at the heart of Congress affairs in Calcutta. He attended Gandhi's secret conference in September 1921, taking down the Mahatma's answers and listening to his instructions for the new non-cooperation programme. In the next two months he was prominent in the agitation against the Prince of Wales's visit, and undertook the leadership of the Congress Volunteers in Calcutta. The Volunteers were soon declared illegal. 'I feel the handcuffs on my wrists,' said C. R. Das, 'and the weight of iron on my body. It is the agony of bondage.' Civil disobedience in Bengal was commenced on December 1st.

To Bose's disappointment he was not at once arrested. Das teased him for his long face and called him 'Our crying Captain', as he waited for the blow to fall. It came on December 10th: Bose received his first gaol sentence for parading illegally: it was not long enough for him: 'Only six months,' he said to the magistrate: 'have I then stolen a chicken?' But it was a good start for a political cadet. Mr. Das was sentenced at the same time and much of their imprisonment was spent together. Bose served his leader humbly, cooking his food and learning with him the sharp lessons of discomfort. Das's demeanour impressed him deeply: he was thoughtful always for others and treated all with an equality of kindliness. For Bose he came to stand in the place of the guru he had sought so long.

They talked continually of the political struggle and of what they would do when released. They were overwhelmed with indignation when Gandhi withdrew civil disobedience in 1922. Bose shared his leader's dissatisfaction with general Congress policy. It seemed to them that the Congress boycott of the reformed provincial councils set up in 1919-1920 was altogether too simple a solution. It would be more effective to contest the elections, enter the councils and wreck them from within. As soon as he emerged Das started to urge the Congress to take this course. We find Bose in September 1922 making one of his first political speeches – 'about sincere work and patient suffering', social service and the removal of social evils. There followed for him six strenuous weeks in charge of Congress relief work in the flooded regions of Northern Bengal. His passionate energy in the presence of suffering and his capacity for organisation won lasting gratitude and increased his political stature in the province.

At the Congress Assembly of December 1922, C. R. Das as President, sought backing for his new idea: Bose was his secretary and active partisan. But although Gandhi was in gaol, his influence against the policy of 'council entry', as it was called, was too strong, and a month later Das resigned to form his own 'Swarajya Party'[21] and contest the 1923 elections. The Swarajya Party was still part of the Congress, and the prestige if not the official support of the Congress was partly responsible for its unhoped-for success in elections. It emerged at the beginning of 1924 as a strong minority group in the Central Legislature in Delhi and with sufficient strength in the Central Provinces and Bengal to force the respective Governors eventually to resume full control.

Meanwhile in April 1924 the Swarajists won control of the Calcutta Corporation. This could not be wrecked with impunity: Das became Mayor of Calcutta and S.C. Bose was elected Chief Executive Officer. Under its new constitution, the Corporation of Calcutta was largely independent and Bose found himself a privileged official with wide powers and a salary of about $ 3,000. At the age of twenty-seven he was thus in a far more responsible

---

[21] Self-government Party.

position than any which he could have occupied in the Indian Civil Service for many years. The new civic administrators wore Congress home-spun, reduced their own salaries, renamed streets and public places after nationalist heroes, improved the education, social welfare and public health services. It says much for the influence of Mr. Das that Bose was able to carry off the situation at all. He did so with less arrogance than might have been expected, but its irony did not escape him, and he was not above reminding senior British officials of the Corporation that they were now his subordinates. The severely constructive hard work of municipal affairs appealed to him, he became thoroughly absorbed in the detail, took his files home like any bureaucrat, and found himself for a time lost to the Congress as a political worker.

His downfall was nevertheless being prepared. There had been in 1923 a recrudescence of violence in Bengal: the Swarajists were believed to be actively involved in terrorism. In 1924 the situation grew worse and the police could do little. 'Intimidation by anonymous threats became the order of the day... Everyone went about his business in fear of the secret societies.'[22] The old days of terror returned. In March 1924 Gopinath Saha was executed for terrorist murder. There was no doubt about his guilt, but his proud bearing made a deep impression. Taking leave of his mother he begged her to 'pray God that mothers in India should give birth to sons like him, and

---

[22] Lord Lytton, *Pundits and Elephants.*

every home be sanctified by a mother like his'. Then, for himself: 'May every drop of my blood sow the seeds of freedom in every home in India.'

Although he sponsored an official Swarajist condemnation of terrorism, Bose could not fail to be stirred by words like these. In his office he was accessible to all. He knew many of the revolutionaries, he would receive all kinds of visitors even late at night. Inevitably official suspicion turned against him: to the British he was that most sinister of objects, an enigma. He could not in fact have been an active conspirator, but when in October 1924 the suspected terrorist leaders were rounded up under an emergency ordinance, he was arrested as one of the most dangerous. No charge was ever brought, and such was the clamour against his arbitrary detention that, had a conviction been possible, the authorities could hardly have refrained from trying him. For two months he performed his municipal duties in Alipore Jail, then in January 1925 he was removed with seven others to the great fort of Mandalay in Burma.

The two years in Mandalay were to be among the most important in his life. He went there a fledgling, looking to his *guru* for guidance, and with a mass of student notions in his head, only recently seasoned with the experience and discussions of adult political life. When he left prison in 1927, he had a clear political conception of his own, Mr. Das was dead and he himself was widely regarded as the natural leader of Bengal. From the first he had realised that his imprisonment would not be all loss:

> The enforced solitude in which a *detenu* passes his day gives him an opportunity to think down into the ultimate problems of life. In any event I can claim this for myself that many of the most tangled questions which whirl like eddies in our individual and collective life are edging gradually to the estuary of a solution. The things I could only puzzle out feebly or the views I could only utter tentatively in days gone by are crystallising out more and more presentably every day. It is for this reason if for no other that I feel I will be spiritually a gainer through my imprisonment.[23]

But it was a hard school. At first inner rebellion against circumstance gave him no peace and he began to feel his health threatened. Then, he said, he returned to self-analysis, the 'throwing of a powerful searchlight' on his own mind, studying objectively his motives, and actions:

> The change in me was this, that I decided to be honest. I resolved that I must, as I watched my own movements, pass judgment on them as I would on those of any outsider. And I can tell you that the practice taught me not a little tolerance till it really came to this – though I don't know that I'll be able to achieve it in practice – that even in the thick of the fight (since fight one must) I felt one was

[23] Letter to Mr. Roy, May 2nd, 1925.

> obligated not only to be lenient to one's antagonists but to love them.[24]

Not that he claimed the lesson was final: to love one's enemies is always difficult because: 'self-love is too exacting to suffer the neighbour for long within its orbit.' But the realisation was there and with it a new moral strength.

In June 1925 he mourned the sudden death of Mr. C. R. Das:

> I gave him my heart's deep adhesion and reverent love not so much because I happened to be his follower in the arena of politics, as because I happened to know him....in his private life. He had no family, properly speaking, outside that of his colleagues and adherents. Once we lived together in jail for eight months: for two months in the same cell, for six months in adjacent ones. I took refuge under his feet because I came to know him thus....[25]

This was a 'cataclysmic loss' for the youth of Bengal. It was cataclysmic for Bose too: as never before he was on his own. The mental activity went on. He thought about his past – his old argument with D.K. Roy about the contemplative life and the life of action kept coming to the surface. This question too was crystallised: too much

---

[24] The Subhash I Knew, p. 178.
[25] Ibid.. p. 324.

seclusion might atrophy the active side of a man, 'the majority ought to take to action and service as the main plank of their contribution'. India needed activists, he concluded, to rescue her from her chronic inertia. The precious fruits of contemplation should come from the select few whose proper milieu it was. The artists and musicians also had their places: 'Flood our whole countryside, my friend,with songs, and recapture for life the spontaneous joy we have forfeited.' He could not be an artist himself, he lacked the capacity; but he acknowledged the artist's importance and had cultivated appreciation.

His political conclusions can be studied in the speeches he made after his release. Independence was to be won by the development of the Congress organisation into a parallel government. Each department and instrument of administration should be duplicated by the Congress. Labour should be organised, political education provided for the masses, all preparations should be made for the Socialism in which he wholeheartedly believed. How the Congress could capture power was also now clear to him: the nationalist movement would culminate in a general strike and civil disobedience which would together make the administration of the country impossible. The jails would be full and the Government demoralised because it could no longer count on the loyalty of its servants. The bureaucracy would then be 'forced to yield to the demands of people's representatives'.

The future constitution would be republican. Bose rejected

Dominion Status because he feared that it would perpetuate British capitalist interests in India. There must be no 'repressive ordinances'; barriers of wealth, class and caste must go; women must have equality of status with men, and there must be no distinction between Hindu and Muslim at election times. He regarded communal representation in the legislatures as a device for dividing India and supporting foreign rule. He was sure that if the communal question was ignored it would vanish, and this view he held to the close of his life.

At the end of 1926 he was nominated as a candidate for the Bengal Legislative Assembly: his friends hoped that his election would force the Government to release him. The manoeuvre failed. In spite of eloquent and skillful arguments that his enforced absence was a breach of privilege invalidating the proceedings of the Assembly he remained in prison. The great red-brick fort of Mandalay, with its fairy-tale royal palace which he could see from the verandah of his cell, with its relics of the atrocious King Thibaw whom the British deposed in 1885, and its memories of other Indian nationalists imprisoned there was to hold Bose for a few months more. Already his health had begun to give way. In 1927 it broke down and the Government of Bengal offered release on condition that he go to Switzerland without setting foot in India. This he contemptuously refused:

> Ideas will work out their own destiny and we, who are but clods of clay encasing sparks of the divine

fire, have only to consecrate ourselves to these ideas. A life so consecrated is bound to fulfill itself, regardless of the vicissitudes of our material and bodily existence. My faith in the ultimate triumph of the idea for which I stand is unflinching, and I am therefore not troubled by thoughts about my health and future prospects.

... I am not a shopkeeper and I do not bargain. The slippery path of diplomacy I abhor as unsuited to my constitution. I have taken my stand on a principle and there the matter rests. I do not attach such importance to my bodily life that I should strive to save it by a process of haggling. My conception of values is somewhat different from that of the market place and I do not think that success or failure in life should be determined by physical or material criteria. Our fight is not a physical one and it is not for a material object.... 'We wrestle not against flesh and blood but against principalities, against powers, against the rulers of the darkness of this world, against spiritual wickedness in high places.'

Our cause is the cause of freedom and truth: as sure as day follows night, that cause will ultimately prevail. Our bodies may fail and perish but, with faith undiminished and will unconquerable, triumph will be ours. It is however for Providence to ordain who of us should live to witness the consummation of all our efforts and labours, and as for myself, I am content to live my life and leave the rest to Destiny.[26]

He was in any case too ill to go to Switzerland without prolonged convalescence, and it was this that decided his unconditional release on May 16th. In November, fit enough to be drawn back into full political activity, he was elected Chairman of the Bengal Provincial Congress Committee. In the same month a British Parliamentary Commission was appointed to consider the next step in India's constitutional development. But Indian nationalism had long been thinking in terms of early Domination Status: a mere routine commission established under the 1919 Constitution, although appointed well in advance of the prescribed date, provided simply a new focus of attack. Hindu and Muslim alike were soon in full cry. This was once again the atmosphere of 1921, the air in which Bose's personality thrived. He loved the roaring, chanting nationalist audiences; their acclamation had for him the sound of popular sanction, and it gave him strength, eloquence and confidence. Gone was the philosophic humility and mysticism of his days in jail; instead of the recurrent refrain 'at times I feel as if I am groping in the dark', there was a loud cocksureness,[27] a complete, even overweening confidence, supported and intensified by the adoration of the crowds. 'A subject race has nothing but politics,'[28] he shouted; 'There is no power on earth which can keep India in bondage any longer,'[28] 'Consecrate your

[26] Letter to his brother from Insein Gaol, May 8th, 1927.

[27] The Subhash I knew, p. 105.

[28] October 29th, 1929.

lives at the altar of freedom;[29] 'India shall be free the only question is when.'[30]

The importance to Bose of the mass audience is strangely revealed in a speech of advice to young politicians which he made at about this time:

> ... You will have to handle large crowds in order to preserve your control over them. You may have to play to the gallery on certain occasions. You may also have to bring yourselves down to the level of the masses in order to keep your communion with them.

On the other hand, he continued, it may be necessary to swim against the tide:

> If you wish to solve the fundamental problems of our national life you will have to look miles ahead of your contemporaries. The mass mind is often unable to cut itself off from present-day moorings and visualise the future. If you propose remedies to anticipate and counteract favourite evils, it is not improbable that the mass mind will refuse to accept your prescription. On such an occasion you must summon up courage to stand out alone.... One who desires to swim with the tide of popular approbation on all occasions may become the hero of the hour – but he cannot live in history.[31]

---

[29] December 18th, 1929.

[30] November 29th, 1929.

[31] Nagpur, November 29th, 1929.

Of Bose it may be said that although he did not hesitate, on occasion, to oppose the majority, he never doubted the crowd's authority if its voice agreed with him. In this lay great danger, for his driving vehemence was such that he could carry a crowd with him and then himself be carried away by the enthusiasm he had generated.

1928 had given Bose new opportunities for distinction in Congress affairs, a rising distinction which held him in the long-drawn-out process of establishing his political succession to C. R Das in Bengal. With Jawaharlal Nehru, he had become a General Secretary of the Congress in December 1927. He was a member of the All Parties Committee which worked out in the summer of 1928 an Indian answer to the challenge of the Parliamentary Commission. When this answer recommended acceptance of Dominion Status, he shared with Mr. Nehru in the formation of the 'Indian Independence League' to campaign against any qualification of independence. Everywhere he painted his own picture of the way to freedom and addressed urgent words to Indian youth. His eloquence became more practiced, his rhetoric more skilful, his stature as a leader greater and more widely accepted: he commanded the parade of 'Congress Volunteers' at the 1928 Congress Assembly: his 'Volunteers. Fall in', and the smartness and precision he had inculcated, impressed the pacifist Congressmen in spite of themselves; he intervened in a steelworkers' strike at Jamshedpur and brought it to a favourable settlement: he led the funeral procession through Jatin Das of

Calcutta, one of his Congress Volunteers who had starved himself to death in Lahore prison in September 1929. He was still unconcerned, it was noted, with women – except to enrol them in the political struggle – and it was beginning to be said that he had forsworn marriage until India was free. This, and his abstention from alcohol, became a definite part of his public reputation.

The next crisis in the Indian struggle was now drawing near. In October 1929 the Viceroy, Lord Irwin, after some months of consultations in England with the new Labour Government, stated clearly on its behalf that Dominion Status was 'the natural issue' of India's constitutional progress, and that a Round Table Conference would be held after the publication of the report of the Parliamentary Commission. For a few weeks it seemed that this gesture would win the cooperation of the nationalist leaders. But the phase passed and 1930 saw the commencement of a full-scale civil disobedience campaign. Bose was arrested on his birthday, January 23rd, for leading an 'Independence' procession, and sentenced to a year's imprisonment. In jail he was once more serene: hardly a month ago, in the Congress Assembly, he had trumpeted: 'I am an extremist and my principle is – all or none'; now he mixed quietly with his Congress friends, reading, meditating, writing, praying in a secluded corner of the prison room which he had partitioned off with a sheet. There were incidents even in prison; he was injured in April when he intervened between the jail staff and some prisoners he thought were being roughly handled; in July he staged a hunger strike against prison treatment. But apart from such exuberances, he took the rest which, after two strenuous years, he needed.

When he emerged from prison on September 25th he was Mayor of Calcutta, because the elected Mayor – also a prisoner – had failed to take the oath within six months. He was to be elected Chairman of the All India Trade Union Congress in the following year – and the welfare of civil disobedience prisoners occupied him for the next three months. Then, early in January 1931 he insisted on visiting a disturbed area of Bengal which had been forbidden to him and was imprisoned for seven days. Hardly had he been released when he was injured and arrested while leading a demonstration on 'Independence Day', January 26th. He had been warned privately by a senior police officer not to take part: 'Tell your boss,' he replied to the messenger, 'that I will break the law.' In court, as a Congressman, he could make no defence but he spoke vigorously as Mayor about conditions in the lock up in which he had spent the night. Six weeks later he was released with other political prisoners under the agreement between Mr. Gandhi and the Viceroy, known as the Gandhi-Irwin Pact. There followed ten months of liberty before the new crisis, on Gandhi's return to India from the Second Round Table Conference in December 1931, led to a new trial of strength.

While Gandhi had been negotiating. Bose had abstained from embarrassing him, although he saw no hope of a successful issue. But as the unrest of 1931 began to grow he became a thorough nuisance to the authorities in Bengal, criticising, inciting, prying into any situation of political delicacy, displaying a haughty detachment to British officials who impeded him, disregarding orders, injunctions, prohibitions, smelling out, he might have claimed, injustice, cruelty and oppression. He was naturally included in the general arrests of leading Congressmen on January 2nd, 1932. Two days earlier he had written for a friend.[32]

> Do you want the fragrance of the full-blown rose? If so, you must accept the thorns. Do you want the splendour of the smiling dawn? If so, you must live through the dark hours of the night. Do you want the joy of liberty and the solace of freedom? If so, you must pay the price. And the price of liberty is suffering and sacrifice.
>
> *Subhash Chandra Bose*
>
> Bombay,
>
> 21.12.31

None was readier than Subhash Chandra Bose to pay that price. He had never spared himself, and the years since his illness in Mandalay had taken the most that he could give. By the end of 1932 he was again gravely ill; on February 22nd, 1933, he was released, on condition that he went to Europe for the medical treatment recommended by his

[32] D.K. Roy, The Subhash I Knew.

doctors. This time the condition was welcomed. He entered Dr. Furth's sanatorium in Vienna on March 11th.

The doctors regarded his condition as serious and prescribed a long course of treatment, but the phase of complete prostration soon passed. Bose met Mr. Vithalbhai Patel, a great Congressman and patriot who was also now an invalid in Vienna. The two men watched events in India closely. In April Mr. Gandhi's correspondence with the Viceroy showed a softer mood: then, after a fast undertaken to force certain of his views on his countrymen Gandhi was released for reasons of health. On May 8th he suspended the civil disobedience campaign for which he had gone to prison in 1932.

To Bose and Patel in Vienna this was abject surrender. They discussed a joint statement they had drafted. Said Patel to the journalist,[33] who interviewed them: 'My young friend believes that an attack must be sharp like a dagger, whereas I hold one should not be careless in one's own house.' Bose intervened: 'Gandhi is an old, useless piece of furniture. He had done good service in his time but is an obstacle now.' – 'Maybe he is,' replied the older man, 'as an active politician. But his name is of great and permanent value.' The Round Table Conference, Bose held, had been a waste of time, for 'no real change in history has ever been achieved by discussions'. – 'But the only alternative is war!'

[33] Mr. Alfred Tyrnauer writing in the *Sunday Evening Post*, March 11th, 1944.

– 'What of it? India can well afford to bring a blood sacrifice for her liberation. 350 million miserable lives are waiting for deliverance.'

'There speaks the mind of young India,' said Patel, 'it may be a brilliant mind and it may be a foolish one. It maybe creative and it may be suicidal. But it is here and if the gods are thirsty what can we do but offer our blood?' The joint statement condemned Mr. Gandhi as a failure: it was time for a new deal in the Congress and a new leader. If the Congress as a whole could not change, there would have to be a new radical party within it.

For the moment this was an idle threat. Neither Bose nor Patel hoped for much immediate progress in India. Both thought that the best chance lay in arousing sympathy for India abroad, that world opinion would force the British to relax their grip. Bose was inclined to go further than this, and was sorely tempted to accept a Russian invitation. It was not that he was a Communist – he had often proclaimed that Communism was not the solution for India – but he was willing to learn all that Russia could teach him of revolutionary technique and to accept any help she could offer against the British. Patel dissuaded him, for he saw clearly that such a link would hamper Bose's service to India.

There were other powers who could be courted as allies. In May, Bose obtained permission to go to Germany. A series of visits followed, to Berlin, Rome, Prague, Warsaw,

Istanbul, Belgrade, Bucharest: some of them he repeated several times in the next two years. Meanwhile, in October 1933, Mr. Vithalbhai Patel had died and had made Bose the trustee, not only of some of his ideas, but of a considerable fund for the propagation abroad of knowledge about India. Bose was greatly moved by the confidence of his dead friend, and encouraged in his foreign contacts, he insisted even more on the importance of world opinion, was more urgent than ever for action. He called impatiently on his friend, Dilip Kumar Roy, to leave his yogic cell and help in the work of interpreting India abroad. Gone was the calmness of mind and humility of his own seclusion. His was the way – he was sure of it – nothing else mattered, nobody else could know.

He wrote ceaselessly, upholding India's rights, exhorting his friends in India, championiong individuals against injustice. He could not bear to see suffering, nobody called to him in vain. He took great interest in the Indian communities in Europe, urging the students especially never to forget that they were India's ambassadors. He sponsored the formation of a Students' Association which was to help Indians all over the Continent. Those in Berlin, who had suffered particularly from Nazi arrogance, never forgot his help and inspiration.

Wherever he could, Bose made political contacts and constitutional studies. He met Dr. Benes several times, in 1936 he saw Mr. de Valera, he visited and was much encouraged by M. Romain Rolland, he was received by

Adolf Hitler, Ribbentrop and other members of the Nazi hierarchy. Of these latter he plainly asked when they were going to strike at Britain, 'so that we might also take up arms simultaneously against the British'. The Germans said they had no thought of this and that they hoped for a compromise. In the end Bose told them: 'Britain is our traditional enemy. We will fight her, whether you support us or not.'[34] He had no doubt that war in Europe would come and carried away the overwhelming impression of its imminence when he went home in 1936.

Meanwhile Gandhi had turned from active politics to village welfare. Some of the Congress leaders followed him, some remained in jail, some thought once more to work for freedom by constitutional means. This led to a measure of reconciliation with the Government. As the 1935 Constitution became law, the Congress was inclined to take part in the elections for which it provided, and to proceed constitutionally.

The more radical nationalists, the men who would have followed S.C. Bose had he been in India, formed the Congress Socialist Party in 1934. Bose sympathised, but no reform, no new party within the Congress would now serve. Gandhi could not see beyond the grasping of power and democratic elections: Bose was fast leaving such ideas behind:

---

[34] On to Delhi, pp. 67-68.

> In India we want a party that will not only strive for India's freedom but also produce a national constitution, and after winning freedom will put into operation the whole programme of national reconstruction. There can be no question of a Constituent Assembly... Likewise there can be no question of giving up power....[35]

In November 1934 Bose published his own account of Indian nationalism, *The Indian Struggle*. In it he rejected both cooperation with the constitution and the compromises of a wavering, declining Gandhi, and pointed to a new way for India, a middle way. This lay not between democracy and dictatorship but between Communism and Fascism, two different, forms of dictatorship. Bose had been stirred by what he had seen in Rome and Istanbul – a strong party organisation in the one, Mustapha Kemal's swift modernisation of a backward oriental state in the other. India was in need of material and social reconstruction on the same scale and must be governed by a dictator. There must be 'a strong Central Government with dictatorial powers for some years to come... Government by a strong party bound together by military discipline'.[36] Only by these means could India be held together while she was achieving statehood.

At the end of 1934 Bose flew to India because of the

---

[35] Article written after visit to Rome in 1934.

[36] The Indian Sruggle pp. 344-345.

illness of his father, but reached home too late to see him alive. Rai Bahadur Janakinath Bose[37] had long been reconciled to his brilliant son, and had learnt to be proud of the distinguished rebel he had become. After the obsequies Subhash would have liked to remain: howbeit there could be no question of release, and he sailed again for Europe on January 10th, 1935. During this year his health was abundantly restored and by its end the urge to re-enter the struggle in India was irresistible. He made up his mind at the beginning of 1936. The Congress Assembly was soon to discuss whether to take part in the new elections. Mr. J. L. Nehru who was to be President, urged him to come. The discussions would be critical, and he must throw his weight against any compromise with the British. In March 1936 he announced that he was returning to India and received formal warning that he would be arrested when he did so. This he openly scorned. What did it matter, he thought, his arrest now would simply bind the Congress to support him, whatever Gandhi might think of his behaviour in Europe and of the opinions in his book. He reached Bombay on April 8th and was arrested on landing, shouting to the crowds who awaited him: 'Keep the flag of India's freedom flying.' Protests in England and a vote of censure in the Indian Parliament were in vain. In India authority said that he was plotting to introduce 'Irish methods of warfare' into India, while at home the Government refused to intervene, for,

[37] He had given up his title 'Rai Bahadur' in 1930 as a gesture of protest against alleged maltreatment of nationalist prisoners.

'unhappily Mr. Bose is a man who, while of great ability, has always directed his ability to destructive... purposes.'[38]

Detention was not this time physically oppressive: he spent much of it interned in his brother's house near Darjeeling. Mr. Roy met him again soon after his release on March 17th, 1937. He found him much improved, mellowed, more self critical and less intolerant. There was also a new common touch: he had learnt to talk to simple people and to value them.

The Congress had just emerged victorious from the first elections under the Act of 1935, and during the summer it decided to form Congress Ministries in seven provinces. Bose took little part in this decision, and returned to the hills after his release to stay until October with his old friends Dr. and Mrs. Dharamvir. He then conferred with Mr. Gandhi in Calcutta, agreeing to accept nomination as Congress President in 1938. There followed six weeks at Badgastein and, in January 1938, a brief visit to England. On London, Mr. Attlee, Mr. Ernest Bevin and Sir Stafford Cripps welcomed him; there was a reception at the Dorchester: 'English people who met him for the first time were impressed alike by his pleasant, quiet manner and the decisiveness with which he discussed Indian affairs.'[39] He was back in Karachi on January 23: 'Matrimony?' he said to a questioner, 'I have no time to

---

[38] Lord Zetland, Secretary of State for Inda, reported in The Times, December 2nd, 1936.

[39] Manchester Guardian, January 11th, 1938.

think of that.'

Bose was now a man of more than national stature. Abroad he ranked after Gandhi and Jawaharlal Nehru as an Indian politician. Within India his personality had proved to many the most attractive of the three. In some places his reputation rivalled that of Gandhi himself, and his nomination as President of the Congress at the early age of forty-one was without doubt an attempt by the Mahatma to consolidate with the orthodox Congress those considerable left-wing elements, in Bengal and elsewhere, which actually preferred Bose's leadership. Inevitably, therefore, Bose saw it as more than the formal compliment which it had been for some years: he was going to be nobody's man of straw, and while he realised the necessity for Congress unity, he meant to mould its policy if he could. An eventual rupture with Gandhi could thus hardly be avoided. When it came it was Bose's second turning point.

3

THE REBEL PRESIDENT

Hitherto we have seen Bose as a rebel against the British Raj. Through the events of the last chapter ran also the thread of his growing dissent from the doctrines of Mr. Gandhi. In this one the progress of that dissent must be traced more particularly, for it was as a rebel, not merely against the British, but against what we saw as the dead hand of the Congress Dictator, that his full political manhood was attained.

In *The Indian Struggle,* written in 1934, Bose himself gives the early history of the disagreement. It began with that first meeting in 1921. Fresh from Cambridge, elated by the conscious sacrifice of his career, Bose had asked the Mahatma for orders. There were no orders. Gandhi seemed to think that if the Congress could sit long enough in reproachful silence upon Britain's door-step, the scandal of India's treatment would somehow smite the British conscience. Not all his followers thought that Gandhi's quietism would work and some hoped that once civil disobedience was started, they could convert it into something more active. Bose found his place among these and in December 1921 enthusiastically went to prison, only to discover that at the first serious incident of violence Gandhi took fright and withdrew. To sound the order of retreat, said Bose, 'just when public enthusiasm was reaching boiling point, was nothing short of a national calamity.'[1]

Gandhi's imprisonment in 1922 removed him from immediate direction of the Congress and Bose joined C.R. Das in promoting the Swarajist plan of obstruction in the legislatures, of which they had talked in prison. The Mahatma's influence was strong enough to prevent this being adopted as official Congress policy at the end of 1922, and the Swarajya Party was formed in consequence. The leading Swarajists went to prison in 1924 and this particular dispute faded out. Bose brooded meanwhile in Mandalay, perhaps thinking, as so many did, that Gandhi's political career was at an end. The Mahatma would not go far enough for him, non-violence plagued him: the British would never awaken to the realities of the Indian situation until confronted with force. He had not yet personally opposed Mr. Gandhi – he had been politically far too young – but he came to believe that a new and more vital leadership, prepared if necessary to resort to violence, was indispensable.

In 1928, both men were back in politics. Bose, now

[1] The Indian Struggle, p. 90.

reaching political maturity, went to see Gandhi and for the first time urged his own plan of action. He saw in the feeling aroused by the Congress against the Parliamentary Commission an opportunity for the revolution he desired and begged Gandhi to give a decisive lead. The British, he thought, should be easy to overthrow: 'Only our cooperation enables a handful of Englishmen to rule our country."[2] But Gandhi's mind was elsewhere:

> The reply... was that he did not see any light, though before his very eyes the peasantry of Bardoli were demonstrating through a no – tax campaign that they were ready for a struggle.[3] While the country was ready, the leaders were not.[4]

Not only this, but Gandhi was prepared to accept the recommendation of the All Parties Committee about Dominion Status. The formation of the Independence League to fight this idea, which Bose shared with Jawaharlal Nehru, was his first open challenge to Gandhi. By the end of the year he was speaking more directly, deploring the passivism of Gandhi's school of thought:

> ....a feeling and impression that modernism is bad, large scale production an evil, wants should not be increased and the standard of living should not be raised... and that the soul is so important that

---

[2] May 30th, 1929.

[3] The Indian Struggle. p. 170.

[4] Ibid. p. 181.

> physical culture and military training can be ignored.[5]

Mystics would always hold an honoured place in India, he said, 'but it is not their lead we shall have to follow if we are to create a new India, at once free, happy and great.... We have to live in the present.'

In the Congress Assembly of 1928 Bose spoke of a fundamental cleavage in the Congress on the Dominion Status issue. "What we feel most acutely,' he said, 'is that at a most critical juncture in our history our older leaders have failed to rise to the occasion.'[6] His opposition was still respectful and he moved his counter-resolution almost with an air of apology. With its defeat he accepted a year's postponement of the full-scale independence struggle. But during 1929 he developed his own ideas of what that struggle was to be. While the Congress as a whole thought of it as a gesture of resistance, Bose looked forward to it as the planned attempt to seize power. He condemned the Viceregal pronouncement on Dominion Status in October 1929 and refused to sign the All Parties manifesto issued in reply. In this he lost his chief ally; Jawaharlal Nehru, who was to preside over the Congress assembly in December, was persuaded by Mr. Gandhi to sign the manifesto.

When the assembly met, Gandhi proclaimed complete

---

[5] All-India Youth Conference, Calcutta, December 25th, 1928.

[6] Statement in Subjects' Committee of Congress, December 1928.

independence as the Congress goal, and the Indian Independence League was soon forgotten.[7] 'But', said Bose, 'the programme laid down by his resolution is not such as to carry us towards the goal of complete independence.'[8] He moved a counter-resolution embodying his whole personal faith. Let the Congress turn itself into a parallel government by expanding its structure, organise the people in support, and then commence such a massive civil disobedience that normal administration would be impossible. The Congress Party would be the only body capable of dealing with the situation, and control of the country would simply fall into its hands.

Mr. Gandhi's final rejection of Dominion Status had brought to his side many who would otherwise have supported Bose. The counter-resolution was decisively rejected. There was another issue here. Having failed to influence the Congress as a whole, Bose sought representation in the Congress Working Committee for the opinion he expressed, so that after the assembly dispersed the extreme view would continue to be heard in Congress counsels. The executive, he thought, should represent all shades of party opinion and not simply that of the majority. Mr. Gandhi was now strong again: he could afford to ignore the vehemence of young Mr. Bose and calmly watched him lead his sixty-two supporters in protest out of the assembly: only sixty-two, barely worth

---

[7] But not in Japan, see p. 6.

[8] Speech at Lahore Congress, December 1929.

half a seat in the Working Committee. But he sensed the depth of feeling behind the demonstration: he wrote to C.F. Andrews at this time of the violent reaction of young India and confessed he saw no other way of holding it within bounds than for himself to lead a non-violent campaign – a safe outlet, he believed, for youthful passion. The civil disobedience campaign of 1930 was thus a partial concession to Bose's view and Bose drew encouragement from it.

Then, in March 1931, came the Gandhi-Irwin Pact. As soon as he was out of jail, Bose, who felt that the Congress resolve for complete independence might weaken in the Second Round Table Conference at which it was to be represented, went to convey his misgivings to Gandhi in Bombay. The Mahatma reassured him and when the Congress assembly met at the end of March Bose merely recorded his dissatisfaction. For he could not but acknowledge Gandhi's immense popular appeal at this time. 'I travelled with him,' he says, 'for some days, and was able to observe the unprecedented crowds that greeted him everywhere. I wonder if such a spontaneous ovation was ever given to a leader anywhere else. He stood out before the people not merely as a Mahatma but as the hero of a political fight.[9] It was indeed pointless for the angry young man to oppose him. Gandhi held to his course, and the presence of his scantily clad figure in London at the negotiations in the autumn of 1931 brought the British

[9] The Indian Struggle, p. 241.

people, perhaps for the first time, face to face with their responsibility for solving India's problem. But Bose was convinced that the conference would be abortive. 'I cannot persuade myself.[10] he said, '....that anything substantial will come out of the conference in the present temper and mentality of the British Government... When the result... is announced, it will be time for the people to take such action as they think fit.'

In fact the crisis of January 1932 had little to do with the failure of the Round Table Conference. There had been considerable unrest in India during 1931 and the Government had taken stern measures to control it. On his return to India on December 28th Mr. Gandhi complained of these as breaches of his pact with Lord Irwin. But Lord Irwin had gone and the Conservatives were back in office; the new Viceroy refused absolutely to discuss Gandhi's complaints and the Working Committee called for a resumption of civil disobedience. Bose went to prison with the rest, and for fifteen months his voice was silent.

There followed in April 1933 the attack on Gandhi by Bose and Vithalbhai Patel in Vienna. This was the strongest criticism of Gandhi that any Congressman had dared to utter. In his book Bose was even more vigorous. The Congress old guard was of a low intellectual level; few, he said, of its leaders had the capacity to think for

---

[10] Speech at Calcutta, July 4th, 1931.

themselves. 'The entire intellect of the Congress has been mortgaged to one man.'[11] Gandhi had again retired and Bose discussed his place in world history as if his career was over. It was no longer simply a matter of the way to freedom; Bose wanted to see a plan for Free india. To Gandhi it was enough to win freedom: the disturbance of India's economic structure and the writing of the constitution could wait. In fact Gandhi did not mind if that were done by some other leader or party afterwards. To Bose the three were inseparable. He was a Socialist and could not leave the reconstruction of India to capitalism, nor could he trust the making of a constitution to the processes of democracy. The hand that won freedom must not lose its grip. Otherwise, he argued, the vested interests, parasites and toadies now waiting on the British would rob the people of the prize for which they had fought. No, after freedom let the constitution and the Socialist State be established; let the strong hand that made them retain control, until they were firm enough to stand against the corrupting influences democracy would liberate.

Bose believed that Gandhi had failed for five reasons. He had failed because he had not understood his opponents; because he had not made a plan; because he had not sought international help; because he tended to trust the British, and because he hovered between his two roles, political leader and world teacher. The future of India, said

---

[11] The Indian Struggle, p. 86.

Bose, lay with 'those radical and militant forces that will be able to undergo the sacrifice and suffering necessary for winning freedom"[12] for 'the strength of a leader depends not on the largeness but on the character of one's following.'[13] Equally he believed that his appreciation of the opposition and of his own following was correct, and that he would consequently succeed.

There were indeed some grounds for thinking that Gandhi would never again control the Congress as in the past. For four years after his release in 1933 his leadership has withdrawn. It was still exerted in a sense through Jawaharlal Nehru who was, in one aspect of his personality, the Plato to Gandhi's Socrates. But the non-violent doctrines, well as they sounded on the lips of the Mahatma, came less fluently from Nehru who had as lately as 1929 rivalled Bose in his opposition to them. Nehru's personal popularity increased, but he failed to supply the Congress with that quality of leadership which had, since 1919, given it the dominant voice in India.

Consequently Bose's influence at home suffered less from his exile in Europe than it might have done. The Congress Socialist Party formed in 1934 was not the new, disciplined party of *The Indian Struggle*, which Bose saw eventually ousting the Congress from the heart of India. But it was a sign that left-wing opinion had not weakened.

---

[12] The Indian Struggle, p. 330.

[13] Ibid, p. 329.

When, therefore, Bose's book, with its open admiration of totalitarinianism, reached India in 1935 – and the Gestapo itself could not have kept it out[14] – its doctrines had an audience hardly less favourable than if Bose in person had been preaching them. For the evil of Fascism was much less obvious in India than elsewhere. Even the rape of Abyssinia seemed, to eyes clouded with hatred of exclusively British Imperialism, to have its justification, and British condemnation of it to be rooted in mere self-interest. Thus Bose's regard for Mussolini weighed little against him, and the onset of his ideas encountered a Congress for a time too unsure of itself to answer.

But what it lacked in this respect, the Congress began to make up in organisation. Under the strong guidance of Sardar Patel it began to permeate the social and administrative life of the country – even as Bose had long ago urged that it should – until, when the first elections of provincial autonomy were held in 1936, it gained majorities or emerged as the strongest party in seven out of the eleven provinces. Gandhi returned to active politics in March 1937, and after months of hard bargaining allowed the formation of seven Congress Ministers.

In 1933, 1934 and even 1935 Bose might, if he had been free in India, have formed his new party at Gandhi's expense. But when he was released in 1937 he found the Mahatma not only restored to nationalist leadership, but

[14] It was banned in India.

about to assume effective power through his mastery of seven Provincial Governments. Nevertheless Gandhi knew that in Bose there had arisen the only national figure capable of splitting the Congress and that this was still possible. Young Mr. Bose could no longer be ignored. When he had regained his political bearings after release, he met Gandhi for long and earnest discussions in Calcutta: the theme was 'unity'.

Unity could scarcely have had a stronger case. Gandhi had satisfied himself that in practice the Provincial Governors would not use their overriding powers against the Congress Ministries. Thus, for the first time, the Congress had a chance of legislating its way to freedom, or at least of turning some of its pet ideas into law. Bose had not favoured the acceptance of any part of the new constitution, and he had been against the formation of Congress Ministries. It was not so much a matter of principle, but that he believed that the Ministries, and with them the Congress, would-be in danger of corruption by the scant power they had been given. The detail of government would preoccupy them and obscure the long-sought goal. He himself, when set in high municipal office in 1924 had, he knew, for that time been lost to the Congress and to the Independence fight because he was overwhelmed with work. The Congress Ministries would certainly run into the same difficulty. It was a mistake to accept office until the fight was won.

But this issue had been decided. Now, with Gandhi's

proposal that he should be President of the Congress in 1938, Bose accepted the *fait accompli*. He saw the need for Congress unity both because of the growing likelihood of war in Europe, and to make effective the fight against the federal provisions of the 1935 Act. He entirely agreed with Gandhi that the proposed Federation of India would leave the British in real control and that it must be rejected, and he now admitted that the framing of the constitution must be left to an Indian Constituent Assembly after the British had left.

The Fifty-first Congress at Haripura in 1938 was Bose's political coronation. Proudly, in a Presidential car drawn by fifty-one bullocks through fifty-one gates of honour, he acknowledged nationalist India's fervent acclaim: not simply cheers for the new President, the new symbolic leader of the national struggle, but the fullness of hearts proud for his youth, his burning enthusiasm, his humanity, his new harmony with Gandhi. The moment meant much to him; he did justice to it in an immense speech ranging over the whole field of Congress policy from the national and the international points of view. In it he toned down somewhat the urgency of his Socialism. He said nothing about a new party, or about reform of the old one; Gandhi was once more the revered Mahatma and essential architect of independence. On the other hand Bose insisted that the Congress Party should look forward to retaining power when freedom was won. India could not escape an industrial revolution: this would not be a gradual process as in Great Britain, but must be a forced march as in Russia. For it the utmost strength of government would be required. 'The party will have to take over power, assume responsibility for administration, and put through its programme of reconstruction'. Otherwise, he deduced from the revolutions of Europe, there would be chaos. 'Only those who have won power can handle it properly'; this would not be Fascism, he said: opposition parties would not be banned and the structure of the Congress would remain democratic.

It was also necessary that the Congress should prepare this reconstruction programme in detail, so that there would be no delay or uncertainty when power was transferred. With the support of Nehru, though with no enthusiasm from Gandhi, Bose urged on the work of an 'All-India National Planning Committee' formed by Congress to produce it.

In his attitude to Britain, Bose was now almost of Gandhi's view:

> We have no enmity towards the British people. We are fighting Great Britain and we want the fullest liberty to determine our future relations with her. But once we have real self-determination, there is no reason why we should not enter into the most cordial relations with the British people.[15]

The alliance between Bose and Gandhi nevertheless remained precarious, and as 1938 wore on the strain upon

[15] Presidential Speech, 1938.

it increased. When the year began Bose had thought that the danger of war had receded. The Munich Pact showed him how mistaken he had been, and revived all he had ever thought of the use Indian nationalism might make of Britain's preoccupation nearer home. Nor had he always liked what he had seen of the Congress in action, whether in the Provinces or in the 'High Command' of which he was for the time official leader. There were moments of desperate loneliness. Once he begged his friend Dilip Kumar Roy not to go back to his yogic cell in Pondicherry because he needed someone he could trust: 'I have to hobnob day and night with scoundrels mostly. If you remained in Calcutta I would at least know that in the last resort there is one man I can go and confide in...'[16] At another time Roy proposed that Bose join him in seclusion. But no: Bose could not turn to Yoga with the brand 'Defeated by Life' upon him; he could not go even for a time, because he might lose the 'fire of fight', his fighting spirit. The choice had been made, the moods of humility were rare; yet the question could still be discussed. Mr. Roy maintains that the call to the life of contemplation never left his friend and was never finally refused, that he would ultimately have responded to the mystic within him. An autograph of this time reads:

> There is nothing that lures me more than a life of adventure away from the beaten track and in search of the Unknown. In this life there may be suffering,

---

[16] The Subhash I Knew, p. 36.

> but there is joy as well; there may be hours of darkness but there are also hours of dawn. To this path I call my countrymen.[17]

Surely here was a rare spirit, and a source of sustaining strength known to few.

In 1939 he was to need all that strength. He saw clearly that it was to be a critical year: war in Europe, 'England's difficulty', the supreme opportunity for the Congress, was at hand. Nobody – least of all Mr. Gandhi – could be trusted to make use of this opportunity. The Congress Ministries had enjoyed the taste of power, and the High Command, lording it over them, had become complacent: there was even a feeling that perhaps the federal provisions of the 1935 Act might also be more palatable than they looked. Against all sound advice, against his Working Committee, overmastered by the wish to force the issue with the British at once, Bose sought re-election as Congress President for 1939. Mr. Gandhi was unprepared for this: the divergence in their views could no longer be ignored and was beginning to be an embarrassment. But Bose, arousing at the election the sort of popular support he always could command, defeated Gandhi's candidate by a small margin and entered his second year of office.

If his health had not been on the verge of another breakdown. Bose might have survived what followed.

[17] Ibid, pp. 78-79.

Gandhi announced that he regarded the election as a personal defeat and hinted that he might retire. Bose denied that he opposed the Mahatma and tried to come to terms, but the Working Committee found the first excuse for resigning, and by the end of February Congress business was beginning to suffer. When the Congress assembly met on March 10th Gandhi was absent and Bose was lying on a stretcher: his photograph did duty for him in the Presidential procession. His address, short and without vigour, was read for him: some of the most important sessions he could not attend at all. The bold resolution he nevertheless proposed, demanding self-determination for India within six months under threat of civil disobedience, only made the assembly nervous: it was defeated, and Bose had to accept a hostile motion binding him to seek Gandhi's approval for his Working Committee and programme.

There followed a long and fruitless correspondence between Bose and Gandhi. Bose complained that he had been outmaneuvered by unscrupulous opponents: the hostile resolution was unconstitutional and could have been ruled out of order: he begged Gandhi to mediate and restore Congress unity. But Bose was still arguing his own case; there was no disposition to withdraw, to accept a modification in his policy. To Gandhi the disagreement was fundamental and urgent; civil disobedience in the present atmosphere must end, he said, in 'anarchy and red ruin'; violence was in the air, he would not knowingly unleash it. Neither would he agree that a Working

Committee representing both viewpoints was any solution. No, said Mr. Gandhi in the most affectionate terms, he must decline to assist: Bose had been frank about their differences: Gandhi was franker: 'How can we meet on the political platform? Let us agree to differ there and let us meet on the social, moral and municipal platforms. I cannot add the economic, for we have discovered our differences on that platform also."[18] But Bose need not worry: let him boldly formulate his policy, nominate his Cabinet, and present both to the Congress for approval.

If the Congress was to be asked to choose between Bose and Gandhi, there could be only one result – and Bose knew it. He again begged for meditation: 'If we come to the parting of the ways a bitter civil war will commence.' The Congress would be weakened and the British would reap the benefit. But Mr. Gandhi was content that their ways should part. Bose had to face the All-India Congress Committee at the end of April with the deadlock unresolved, and could only resign.

This incident has been seen by many as the beginning of Bose's fall from the heights of sacrificial patriotism. It was indeed his second turning point: the first, he would have claimed, had been the result of a British injustice: now it was the injustice of his own people, his own political comrades. For he had been democratically elected in preference to Gandhi's nominee; he was President, leader,

[18] Gandhi to Bose, April 10th, 1939.

by the will of the people, in spite of the will of Gandhi. Those who had voted for him had known his views and had deliberately chosen them. His popular mandate had been denied by intrigue, intrigue not only against himself, but against the democracy which had elected him. He had been forced to show himself to the Congress as a leader who had failed. That was the grievous injustice.

Perhaps in truth he had failed, failed where a lesser man, a less brilliant man, a less confident man might have succeeded. For there was no compromise in Bose's make-up, no middle way, no shades between the light and dark, no toleration of any opinion but his own. You either agreed with him or you were an enemy to be fought. 'I am an extremist', he had once said, 'all or nothing...' This was always his way: it was his strength and his weakness, and the undoubted cause of his downfall now.

To Bose himself, only the injustice was apparent. In bitter despair that the one chance of achieving independence which had occurred in his eighteen years of service was being rejected, he resumed the fullness of his radical views. Within a month he had founded the extremist 'Forward Bloc' in the Congress party. His aim, he said, was to consolidate all left-wing groups, and to oppose the tendencies in the Congress towards constitutionalism on the one hand and dictatorship on the other. The reluctance of the Congress Socialist Party deprived the Forward Bloc of what would have been its chief support outside Bengal. It was organised on Bose's own militaristic lines: it proclaimed his revolutionary authoritarian ideas: it gathered to itself much of the extremist enthusiasm of Bengal. But the major popular challenge to the orthodox Congress leadership which Bose had hopefully predicted failed to develop. Even in Bengal, Gandhi was eventually able to overrule him.

Nevertheless Bose's criticism remained outspoken and vigorous. The Congress he now condemned as a pernicious dictatorship not far removed from Hitler's. In July, to protest against a particular Congress move to strengthen its hold on its provincial organisation, he called for country wide demonstrations. So open a challenge could not be disregarded. In August he was suspended from Congress office for three years. He affected not to care – 'Is that all?' he said when they told him – and he was still conscious of great personal support in Bengal. But the shaft struck deep. In the following month there began Hitler's war. The Congress invited him to take part in the formulation of its war policy, but he could only see the justification of his own, and when he found that the Working Committee still did not accept it, he stalked out. He had prophesied this struggle since 1929; he had thought, momentarily, that the signing of the Russo-German Alliance would postpone it, but he was convinced that Germany would win. Yet Gandhi still relied on a British change of heart. What, said Bose, would be the good of a change of heart now? The British were moribund, their rule was in decay. Independence must be snatched from their failing grasp before their conquerors appeared. The refusal of the Congress to do this was the height of irresponsibility and amounted to consent to the continuance of British rule.

While the Congress was meeting at Ramgarh in March 1940, Bose attended an 'Anti-Compromise Conference' held in opposition, which called for an immediate all-India struggle with 'no rest or break, nor any sidetracking as happened in 1932'. The British no longer took the Congress seriously because it talked but did not act. His speeches became more violent. He maintained that he was opposed to Hitlerism as such, but the impression of German military strength was still upon him: 'I predict,' he said to Mr. Nirad Chaudhuri in June, 'that England will accept defeat and surrender by July 16th': India must free herself before the Germans came.

> With every blow that she receives in Europe the Imperialist might of Britain is bound to loosen its grip on India....
>
> Let us therefore cease talking of saving Britain with the Empire's help or with India's help. India must in this grave crisis think of herself first... It is for the Indian people to make an immediate demand for the transference of power to them through a Provisional National Government.[19]

Once war began in earnest no responsible government

[19] Speech to Forward Bloc Conference, June 1940.

could leave him at liberty. The occasion for his arrest on July 2nd, 1940, was a popular demonstration he organised in Calcutta for the removal of the memorial to the Black Hole of Calcutta victims, which was held to offend against nationalist feeling. But there were also serious charges of sedition, and when his fellow demonstrators were released, he was kept in prison.

Even Mr. Roy came to believe that, in his frustration and disgust at the blindness of the Congress to its golden opportunity, Bose began to think of himself as India's Man of Destiny. The origins of his next venture were often described in his speeches to audiences in South-East Asia:

> We were thinking what to do, what new method should be adopted. Young men were doing their bit with bombs and revolvers. We got into touch with these young revolutionaries. I knew their strength. They were real revolutionaries of high spirit. But their strength and sacrifice were not enough to achieve complete independence for our Motherland.[20]

Civil disobedience, even terrorism, was not enough. External assistance was essential for the liberation of India. Britain seemed to be tottering. India had only to be convinced of her opportunity, and to receive a modicum of military support to break through the crust, as it were, of British power. From where was this to come? That was the

[20] On to Delhi, p. 71.

question. Bose had once admired Mussolini; about Hitler he had cherished no illusions. The Axis would certainly win, but it would not give disintegrated help to India. Russia, he seems to have thought, still remembered the agony of her own revolution, and hence might understand India's need. Somebody had to be the emissary, somebody well-known who would be taken seriously. 'At last', he says, 'I decided myself to get out of India.'[21]

First he had to get out of prison. Knowing that the Government was unlikely to let him die in gaol, but with courageous determination none the less, he announced that he would starve himself to death:

> Government are determined to hold me in prison by brute force. I say in reply – 'Release me or I shall refuse to live – and it is for me to decide whether I choose to live or to die.'

His appeal was to be preserved as his political testament:

> Though there may be no immediate, tangible gain, no sacrifice is ever futile. It is through suffering and sacrifice alone that a cause can flourish and prosper, and in every age and clime the eternal law prevails - 'the blood of the martyr is the seed of the church'.
>
> In this mortal world, everything perishes and will perish – but ideas, ideals and dreams do not. One

---

[21] On to Delhi, p. 71.

> individual may die for an idea – but that idea will, after his death, incarnate itself in a thousand lives. That is how the wheels of evolution move on and the ideas and dreams of one generation are bequeathed to the next. No idea has ever fulfilled itself in this world except through an ordeal of suffering and sacrifice.
>
> To my countrymen I say – 'Forget not that the greatest curse for a man is to remain a slave. Forget not that the grossest crime is to compromise with injustice and wrong. Remember the eternal law – you must give life if you want to get it. And remember that the highest virtue is to battle against inequity, no matter what the cost may be.'
>
> To the Government of the day I say – Cry halt to your mad drive along the path of communalism and injustice. There is yet time to retrace your steps. Do not use a boomerang which will soon recoil on you. And do not make another Sind out of Bengal.'
>
> . . .I shall commence my fast on the 29th November, 1940. As in my previous fasts I shall take only water with salt. But I may discontinue this later on, if I feel called upon to do so.[22]

So eloquent a 'moral protest' could hardly fail. Having resisted forcible feeding, Bose was released after six days of

---

[22] Letter to the Governor of Bengal: November 26th, 1940.

his fast and allowed to go home. For a time he recuperated quietly: on December 29th he wrote 'from his bed' a strong letter to the Viceroy on the political situation in Bengal. Then he was in 'retreat' and would receive nobody. A few of his friends saw him on January 16th and noticed that he wore a neat beard. On January 26th, 1941, the day fixed for his trial for sedition, he was not to be found.

In the early hours of January 17th, a car had drawn up near Bose's home in Calcutta. Quietly, while nobody stirred, there had slipped out of the house a Muslim religious teacher, the Maulvi Ziauddin. His meagre baggage was loaded on to the car and he moved away as if returning to his up-country village, unnoticed. In this disguise, and accompanied by his nephew, Sisir Kumar, Bose began his escape from India. To take a train from Calcutta itself would have been to court discovery, for the stations were watched and his disguise would not have been hard to penetrate so near his home. He therefore went by road, moving at night, hiding by day, to Gomoh, 210 miles from Calcutta, where he took leave of his nephew and boarded the train to Peshawar. In Peshawar a Mr. Bhagat Ram met him and after two days took him on the next stage of his journey – to Kabul. For this there was a new Pathan disguise, Bhagat Ram becoming 'Rehmat Khan' and Bose posing as a deaf-mute to hide his ignorance of the local language.

They left Peshawar in a car and turned off the main Kabul road before Jamrud, the great fort which guards the entrance to Khyber Pass. Along a country track they jogged till the car could go no further: then, after a night in a tribal village, they set out on foot for the Afghan frontier, escorted by two armed Pathans. They passed through tribal territory, across the great loop which the Kabul River makes when it leaves Afghanistan, and spent the second night in a mosque at Adda Sharif. From here they went on to Lalpura. On the fourth day they recrossed the Kabul River and reached the main road again, far enough inside Afghanistan to avoid the demand for passports. At the river their escort left them; the friends who had helped so far could do no more. Bose, quite exhausted by the hard days of painful travel, slept near the road while Bhagat Ram tried all day for a car to take them on. At last, towards evening, they clambered aboard an open lorry which drove through the night and all the following day, on up the snowy valley to Kabul.

Half-frozen, they climbed down near the Lahore Gate and set out in search of lodgings, which they found in a lorry-drivers' inn. It was an uncomfortable night:

> A cold wind raged outside and we could not let the doors remain open. Smoke filled the cell and it became suffocating. We then managed to get a few dry logs for a fire to warm our frozen bodies.
>
> In the evening Bhagat Ram brought some candles from the bazaar for a light, and some dry bread and kabaabs. When I could not eat the bread, he brought

> me a cup of tea. I dipped the bread into it and ate it.[23]

For the next three days they sought access to the Russian Embassy. This was not easy. In Kabul they had no friends, nor was Bhagat Ram's Pushto of much use, for most people spoke Persian. Furthermore, at any moment the hue and cry might be raised in India. All must be done discreetly, they must attract no attention: any Indian might be a British agent, any Afghan a member of the C.I.D. The embassies were under guard: they could find no way to the Russian envoy and when they stopped his car in the street they could not sufficiently explain themselves. The squalid lodging and his own dumb disguise, the meagre filthy clothing, the icy weather, began to have their effect on Bose. There could be no going back, only frustration awaited him in India; but somehow, at any cost, he must leave this unfriendly country. On the fifth day, 'in sheer desperation' he sent Bhagat Ram to the Italian Legation. Here there were welcoming smiles, congratulations, and the promise of a passport.

The journey from Kabul to Rome or Berlin could only be by way of Moscow. Even now Bose had no good word for the Axis. He still hoped in the last resort to reach the Soviet rulers on his way through their country. 'I am not altogether happy', he said, 'about going to Berlin or Rome. But there is no choice.'

---

[23] Hindustan Times, February 26th, 1946: series of articles by Uttam Chand.

Bose's disappearnace became known in Calcutta on January 26th, 1941. It was probably fortuitous that at about the same time in Kabul an Afghan police agent began to inquire about the prolonged stay of two 'pilgrims' in a lorry-drivers' inn. Day after day he returned, greedier for his bribe. On February 3rd, fear of eventual betrayal drove the victims to seek asylum with an Indian, Mr. Uttam Chand. They were not mistaken. Proudly, but with trepidation for all that, Uttam Chand took them in.

Six more weeks were to pass before the journey could be resumed. Bose still failed to draw Russian attention: he chafed at Italian delays and was plotting an expedition on his own account when their plans matured. On March 18th, with a passport in the name of Orlando Massotta, and accompanied by couriers sent from Europe to fetch him, he set out for the 'Russian frontier. Many travellers have described the difficulties and delights of the forbidden road from Kabul into Bokhara: the high passes of the Hindu Kush, the gorge of Tashkurgan, the dead cities of the Afghan steppe, ancient Mazar-i-Sharif, gem of holy cities, the dreary Oxus in its reedy jungles, the squalid ferries at Pata Kesar and the heedless industrialisation of timeless Samarkhand. Bose passed through it all without pause, took the train to Moscow, and on March 28th, 1941 flew to Berlin. There had been no chance and there was now no question of appealing to Russia.

Someone asked Bose in Kabul how, in the face of religious

and communal dissension in India, the country could be united. He replied:

> So long as there is a third party in the country, that is the British, these dissensions will not end. They will go on growing. They will disappear only when an iron dictator rules India for twenty years. For a few years at least after the end of British rule in India there must be a dictatorship. No other constitution can flourish in the country. And it is to India's good that she should be ruled by a dictator to begin with. None but a dictator can wipe out such dissensions. India does not suffer from one ailment. She suffers from so many politcal ills that only a ruthless dictator can cure her... India needs a Kemal Pasha.[24]

There can be no doubt as to whom he saw in the role of India's Kemal Pasha. The revolutionary spirit had greatly increased, he thought, since 1939. This neither Gandhi, for his passivity, nor Nehru, for his subservience to Gandhi, would use. Bose's star was in the ascendant and British fortunes at their nadir. This was his moment. India must make terms for herself, lest the new masters of the world treat her no better than had the old. But India was not free to make terms. Balked of his purpose in Russia, Bose took, the task upon himself, as the advocate of a Provisional National Government now, as the self-appointed plenipotentiary of revolutionary India.

---

[24] Hindustan Times, March 9th, 1946.

4

'JAI HIND'

I am not an apologist of the Tripartite Powers ... I need no credentials when I speak to my own people. (May 1942)

BOSE could be quite confident of a warm welcome from the Germans. In the First World War their intrigues had ranged across the world to promote revolution in India and so to hold back British soldiers from the Western Front. Hitler's persecution of Communism had removed the last of the old Indian influences from Berlin in 1933, so that when the Second World War began there was no Indian Revolutionary Society such as that which had aided German plans in 1914. But by the time Bose reached Germany in March 1941, Hitler, too, had cause for thought about India. He had already decided on the invasion of Russia which was to start in June and his Army was now committed to rescuing the Italians in Libya. India was relevant to both these undertakings, for her divisions were fighting all over the Middle East and her importance as an Imperial base was growing every month. Ribbentrop received Bose thoughtfully and was glad to hear from him of the rising tide of revolution in India.

Bose's first proposals were that he should broadcast anti-British propaganda, based on news from a secret radio link he had with India, and that he should raise 'Free Indian' units from Indian prisoners of war. As a basis for the propaganda, and as a guarantee for the future, he asked for an Axis declaration of Indian Independence. Neither Ribbentrop nor Ciano, to whom Bose made the same proposals during a visit to Rome in June 1941, was ready for that. Ciano already had ex-King Amanullah of Afghanistan and the Grand Mufti of Jerusalem on his hands. 'Past experience,' he wrote, 'has given rather modest results.'[1] The German view was more specific:

> While being of the opinion that Bose must be helped in his propaganda work by putting the necessary means at his disposal, Ribbentrop considers premature any public declaration on the part of the Axis on the subject of the future settlement in India. The Führer did not receive Bose, precisely to avoid any definite commitment on the subject. On the other hand Bose has had contact with Ribbentrop and will maintain contact with the various departments in connection with his anti-British activity.[2]

Among the reasons for this attitude was the fact that, in

---

[1] Ciano's Diary, ed. Malcolm Muggeridge, p. 355.

[2] Ciano's Diplomatic Papers, ed. Muggeridge.

the secret German negotiations with Russia at the end of 1940, India had been regarded as part of the Russian sphere of aspiration when Britain collapsed.[3]
Germany was not at war with Russia until June 22nd, 1941, and could therefore not yet undertake any contrary public commitment.

Without an Axis declaration, Bose would not broadcast. But he proceeded to try the temper of the prisoners of war at once. His first idea was to form small parachute parties to spread propaganda in, and transmit intelligence from, the North-West Frontier of India. In May selected prisoners were brought to Berlin from the camp at Lamsdorf in Germany and from the large cages in Cyrenaica. Their reaction was so encouraging that Bose asked for all India prisoners in North Africa to be brought to Germany at once. This was done. The existing prisoners began to be concentrated at Annaburg Camp, near Dresden, and it was agreed that any future Indian prisoners would be sent there also.

The invasion of Russia set the parachute plot in a different light. The scale was suddenly greater. India seemed at once nearer and more remote because of the magnification of all the possibilities and chances of war. To the Germans all was already won. Bose began to plan for the day when their sweeping victories would carry him to the borders of India. He proposed now to raise an

---

[3] Sir Winston Churchill, The Second World War, Vol. II p. 520.

Indian Legion of three infantry battalions, and a company of irregulars which would form part of the German Fifth Column organisation. When the Germans launched out beyond Stalingrad into Central Asia, the Tajik and Uzbek units they had trained would accompany their forward troops. As Uzbekistan and Afghanistan were reached, the Indian Company would leap ahead of the German advance, and disrupt the British-Indian defences in North-West India. The effect of the Indian Legion, following with the Germans, would be such that Indian Army morale, and with it the whole defence system, might collapse.

Then Bose would lead his Legion into India and found on it, as the Indian Army turned on its old masers, the ever growing Army of Free India. From here too he would draw government officials and administrators, as he took possession in the name of India and founded the Congress Raj.

In September Indian recruiters were sent to Annaburg. Although the British officers and other loyalist influences among the prisoners had been removed, success only came slowly. When Bose visited the camp himself in December there was still marked hostility. His speech was interrupted, and much of what he had to say went unheard. But private interviews were more encouraging; the men's questions showed interest – what ranks would they receive? What credit would be given for Indian Army seniority? How would the Legionary stand in relation to the German soldier? Bose refused to bargain and some who might have been influential recruits were turned away. On the other hand, many of the men paid him homage as a distinguished Indian leader, several professed themselves ready to join the Legion unconditionally. Some were evidently prevented by camp opinion and the influence of N.C.O.'s from declaring themselves. Bose told his lieutenants to have the N.C.O.'s removed, and then to renew the approach through those who had already volunteered. By this means enough recruits were enrolled to found the two units in January 1942.

To begin with Bose had worked with only a secretary – his old friend Fraulein Schenkl, who had helped him produce *The Indian Struggle* in 1934. By January 1942 he had gathered around him some twenty-five Indian assistants, all carefully screened by the German Foreign Office before they were allowed to meet him. As these men arrived he had set up an office which he called the 'Indian Independence League' or 'Free India Centre'. Here he set all to work. Some planned a broadcast programme which opened as the 'secret' station 'Azad Hind Radio' in December 1941. Others joined a Planning Committee to study the social and economic problems of Free India.

Bose was a good master. His criticism was constructive, he showed great interest in individual work and was full of fresh ideas. He was generous too, and sympathetic in solving the personal problems which beset his staff. He

---

[4] *Girija Mukerjee, This Europe.*

impressed all with his concentration of purpose. 'His mind worked so much towards a single problem,' says one of them, 'that one felt embarrassed to bring up in front of him subjects of a speculative nature.' He seemed to have shut his mind to anything not of immediate importance to the work in hand. People he valued in the same way, accepting or rejecting them according to their worth in the Indian struggle. Even the great names of Indian nationalism came into the same simplicity of judgment: 'Will he live in History?' – that had always been the criterion. Unrelaxed, unrelenting, he drove his workers hard, and some were not a little afraid of him.

Although Bose's presence in Germany was not yet officially admitted – he was still referred to as Signor Orlando Massotta. His Excellency Massotta, as they called him – from the beginning of 1942 he became known to more and more people in Berlin. There were parties and functions at which the Indian community acclaimed him, and at which the greeting 'Jai Hind' was first used. He was deeply stirred by the unhesitating response, the ready allegiance. Some of the younger men volunteered for the Legion: to them he spoke of his pride in achieving at last what he had desired so long – the formation of an Army of Free India – and with emotion gave to each man a flower, all he could offer in his present exile. To them all he was now 'Netaji,' revered leader, a title he was to make peculiarly his own.

Meanwhile the Japanese hour had struck. For Bose the

swift advances of Japan in the East rendered German victories in Russia and North Africa irrelevant. Singapore, Rangoon, Calcutta – these were the keys to British dominion over India, and they were being seized one by one. The fall of Singapore was irresistible to his eloquence. He made his first broadcast from the 'secret' station soon afterwards: 'I have waited silently and patiently on the course of events; now that the hour has struck I can come forward and speak.' Here was certain proof of the collapse of the British Empire: India must rejoice. Britain was the eternal enemy; some Indians would support her but the great majority would continue the fight against British Imperialism:

> In this struggle, and in the subsequent period of reconstruction we will cooperate whole-heartedly with all those who help us to destroy the common enemy.[5]

He followed this with a 'declaration of war against England' – Goebbels was enthusiastic, though 'things aren't yet far enough (on) for us to incite the people of India to open rebellion,[6] and so, when they heard of it, were the Japanese.

In his second 'Proclamation to the Indian People' on March 13th, Bose referred to the Mission to India of Sir

---

[5] Broadcast of February 28th, 1942 (Volkischer Beobachter, March 1st, 1942).

[6] Goebbel... Diary (March 2nd, 1942), ed. Lochner, p. 68.

Stafford Cripps. A more detailed attack followed. The Mission was meaningless, how could a man of Sir Stafford's liberalism and well-known hatred of imperialism undertake so cynical a task. It was an insult to India, let the British rather adopt General Tojo's policy, now twice proclaimed, of India for the Indians, and quit. A similar campaign against the Cripps Mission was being conducted by Rash Behari Basu from Tokyo Radio. Both men thought the failure of the Mission due to the influence of their broadcasts, and so it seemed to their patrons. Infact it is improbable that their words had much effect on nationalist opinion in India; but in Tokyo and Berlin there could be no doubt.

There followed immediately the Japanese proposal for a tripartite declaration on India and their invitation to Bose. Here was solid support indeed. Bose now made his most determined and persistent effort to convince the Axis Dictators. Hitler and Mussolini considered the Japanese proposal when they met at Obersalzburg on April 29th. Their reply was negative: the moment had not yet come. Bose was in Rome and asked to see Mussolini. This, he told Ciano, was simply playing Japan's game: the Japanese would act on their own and pose as the sole liberators of India. Ciano was sceptical, but on May 5th took Bose to the Duce. His diary records what took place:

> Mussolini allowed himself to be persuaded by arguments produced by Bose to obtain a tripartite declaration in favour of Indian independence. He has

> telegraphed the Germans proposing – contrary to the Salzburg decisions – proceeding at once with the declaration.[7]

To back his new proposal Mussolini told the Germans that he had urged Bose to set up a 'counter Government' and to appear more conspicuously, Goebbels recorded the German reaction on May 11th:

> We don't like this idea very much, since we do not think the time has yet come for such a political manoeuvre. It does appear though that the Japanese are very eager for some such step. However, emigre governments must not live too long in a vacuum. Unless they have some actuality to support them, they only exist in the realm of theory.[8]

This was also Hitler's view. Bose was unable to change it. During an interview at the Führer's field headquarters on May 29th, he told Hitler that with his popularity and contacts in India he could rouse the country by propaganda from outside. Never had India been so near the brink of revolt, a mere push would send her over. Hitler replied that a well-equipped army of a few thousand could control millions of unarmed revolutionaries; there would be no political change in India until an external power knocked at her door. Germany could not yet do this:

---

[7] Ciano's Diary, p. 465.

[8] Goebbel's Diary, p. 157.

Japan was reaching her limit. He took Bose to a wall map, pointing to the German positions in Russia and to India. The distances were still immense. It would be foolish, he said, to make a declaration about India now; the world regard it as premature even from him. No, he would soon be ready to declare the independence of Egypt, which Rommel could enforce, but the time for an announcement about India was still far off.

Although his presence in Germany and his meeting with Hitler were now made public, Bose had reached the end of his hopes in Europe. A tripartite declaration would have established him: without it he realised the smallness of his scope. Even when he had founded Free India Centres in Rome and Paris, even if he raised the Legion to its full strength of 3,000 from the prisoners newly taken in North Africa, the achievement would be insignificant in a German victory. Here perhaps there was a backward glance: had he made a mistake after all in leaving India? At home he might have shared in the struggle whose climax seemed so near. Instead he was a mere client, powerless, spied upon, suspected. But there was no way back. He now accepted the leadership of Indians in the Far East. Something might be redeemed there: under the Japanese he would have control of three million Indians, already to some extent organised. He wrote a strong message to the Bangkok Conference, where his name was on all lips. The Indian Independence Movement, he said, was one: 'It is now time to link up Indian nationalists all over the world in one all-embracing organisation.'[9] Indians must not rely solely on the efforts of others; the achievement of Independence must be their own work.

Nevertheless, another year was to pass before Bose reached the East. There was still much he could do in Europe, where no slackening of effort must be allowed. The propaganda offensive went on, following closely the configurations of war and oriental politics. Bose always claimed to know more about events in India than its Government had made public and would include in his broadcasts coded instructions, as if to a wide network of agents there. He spoke of the dropping of parachutists giving circumstantial detail and calling on the Indian peasantry to assist them. He issued warnings to the Indian police and soldiers that, unless they decided for the Independence Movement, they would one day have to answer to the Government of Free India for their criminal support of the British. When in August 1942 the disturbances in India made him think revolution imminent, he opened two more 'radio stations' — 'Congress Radio' and 'Azad Muslim Radio' – to contribute to the tension. Passionately he exhorted the people at home to hold fast and fight. World opinion was on their side, they had only to ask for the help needed from abroad: he would do his best to obtain it. His own claim he made again and again: 'My whole life is one long, persistent, uncompromising struggle against British Imperialism, and

[9] *Bangkok Times, June 1942.*

is the best guarantee of my *bona fides.*' He was no Axis apologist; his concern was with India and India's freedom: when his task was done he would return home.[10]

The tone of these broadcasts was much nearer to that of Bose's own extremism than to the voice of Mr. Gandhi. But after the violent events of August, 1942, which to Bose seemed clearly to have had Gandhi's blessing, he tended to assume that there was no longer any difference of principle between the Mahatma and himself. In any case he realised that attacks on Gandhi, who was in jail and unable to answer, could profit him little, and that if his words were to have a wide appeal in India they must sound as if Gandhi – albeit the supposed new, violent Gandhi – could have uttered them.

Meanwhile the two military ventures had gathered strength. But first must be mentioned one other, an Indian unit formed under the Italians, over which Bose tried continually but in vain to assert control. The founder was Iqbal Shedai, an Indian Muslim who had conferred several time with Bose in 1941, but who had seen no advantage in cooperation with him. Instead, he had begun broadcasting from Rome with the aid of a few Indian prisoners. From this he advanced to the formation of a military unit, in spite of the Italo German agreement that all Indian prisoners should go to Germany.

---

[10] See volkischer Beobachter, May 14th, August 16th, October 8th, 1942; January 7th, March 4th, 1943; Frankfurter Zeitung December 24th, 1942.

The Centro Militare India, as it was called, existed only from April to November 1942, when it was disbanded after a mutiny. Shedai raised it from the prisoner-of-war transit camps in Italy, and from the large compounds in North Africa newly filled with Indians captured on the retreat to El Alamein. Here his propaganda was particularly successful: he arranged to divert several hundred volunteers to Italian camps where he could work on them again. In November the unit was 350 strong, and training under Italian officers was well advanced when it was rumoured that, contrary to Shedai's promises, the men were being sent to fight in Libya. On November 9th, the day after the Allied landings in North Africa, it was clear that a move was imminent. The men refused to parade and Shedai declined to intervene. On November 15th the Centro Militare India was disbanded; it was never revived.

This collapse was very much the result Bose had foreseen for Shedai's activities. He could hardly have handled things more unhappily. Bose might well have thought if he had been working for the British. But the Azad Hind *Fauj* (Free India Army) could proceed without him for, although slow progress in Russia had diminished German interest in the Irregular Company, the Legion was fast becoming a recognised regiment of the German Army.

The two civilian recruiters whom Bose had sent to Annaburg Camp in 1941, N. G. Swami and Abid Hassan, had themselves become founder members respectively of the Irregular Company at Meseritz, in Brandenburg, and of the Legion at Frankenburg, in Saxony. Swami and Hauptmann Harbig, who was to command the Company, took a group of volunteers to Meseritz, and Hassan his group to Frankenburg, during January 1942. Recruitment thereafter at the two places was similar. Lists had been made of the potential recruits for each unit at Annaburg. These men were called away in small batches and, by comfort and the example of the old volunteers, induced to enlist. There is no good evidence that violence was used; prisoners who resisted to the last were simply sent to other prisoner-of-war camps. Back-sliding, on the other hand, and counter-propaganda were harshly punished by the volunteers themselves. Several brave sepoys who joined the Legion in order to win their friends away from it suffered in this way.

Meseritz contained part of the Lehrregiment Brandenburg, the German Fifth Column Training Unit. When the Indians arrived there they found Tajiks, Uzbeks and Persians under training for operational roles similar to that envisaged for them. Harbig's first object was to make them forget that they had been prisoners. For a fortnight they were allowed to enjoy their liberty: then infantry training commenced. In due course the older recruits went on to wireless operating, demolitions and riding: there were also special mountain and parachute courses. Morale, discipline and Indo-German relations were excellent, the German officers first-rate.

Bose visited at intervals and watched progress. He was

prepared, when the Germans suggested it in July 1942, to send a contingent for front-line propaganda against Indian troops at El Alamein. Rommel was at the gates of Egypt. Hitler and Mussolini were discussing the country's future administration, and Ciano's staff had actually drafted a declaration of independence.[11] To such a moment Bose could not fail to contribute. But Rommel refused to have either the Irregular Company or the Legion in Africa: he never had considered the battlefield to be the place for the proving of Foreign Office ideas. At the Lehrregiment manoeuvres in September and on field exercises in October, the Indians were congratulated on their efficiency, But the end was near. After Stalingrad and El Alamein German interest quickly diminished, and on January 13th, 1943, the ninety Indian irregulars were absorbed into the Legion.

A vestige only was left. N. G. Swami and four men he had selected were being trained in espionage methods and equipment for work in India. This training went on. The men learnt a very high standard of wireless telegraphy, the use of secret inks, the assessment and use of economic intelligence and the operation of some of the portable transmitters which the Germans had produced for their own agents. In March 1943, Swami was given his choice of the transmitters and received the ciphers he was to use. Then, on March 24th, he and his men went aboard the motor vessel *Osorno* to follow Bose to Japan.

---

[11] Ciano's Diary: June 26th, July 2nd and 3rd, 1942.

There remained the Legion, now, at the beginning of 1943, two thousand strong. Its growth had at first been slow. In July 1942, when the supply of recruits from Annaburg had come to an end, the Germans began to threaten that it would be disbanded if it could not quickly be brought to battalion strength. This made it urgent to obtain many hundreds of volunteers from the new prisoners in North Africa and Bose worried the Italians until large contingents were arriving regularly in Germany. His propagandists would greet the new drafts – or even go to the Italian frontier to meet them – and prepare them for their first meeting with him. For he was quite tireless in this matter and at the height of his eloquence. I know, he would say, what you have suffered: I know how shattered you feel by the defeat of your British leaders. But to one who has seen as much of the world as I have, this defeat is not surprising: the British were lions, they are so no longer; they deserve no longer your allegiance or your fear:

> The English are like the dead snake which people are afraid of even after its death. There is no doubt that the British have lost this battle. The problem is how to take charge of our country. When the Englishmen are about to leave there is no point in begging independence or getting it as a present from other nations because such an independence cannot last long... We are young and we have a sense of self-respect. We shall take freedom by the strength of our arms. Freedom is never given. It is taken.

> Thank God, the nations fighting Britain are ready to help us. They know that Free India will contribute to the prosperity of the world. Consequently they are ready to help us sincerely. Now it rests with you to shoulder this noble task and bring it to perfection, or spend your life in imprisonment...[12]

Observers have told of the enthusiastic response of these prisoners, whose minds still bore the mark of recent calamity – quite unlike the tardiness and suspicion Bose had found at Annaburg among those who had been in captivity longer. Mr. Girija Mukherjee[13] has written of him 'standing very erect under a huge plane tree' and talking to the soldiers for hours. 'I saw how the whole audience was coming under his spell and how they were listening... When he had finished.. (they) had acquired new life, new animation, new excitement. Most had come out of sheer curiosity. Dozens now asked to be enrolled.' Nor is it hard to see why they did so. This authority, this singleness of mind, this study in black and white, this abhorrence of the vague or indefinite, would appeal to any soldier. It is the quality soldiers must have in their leaders in war, and many found it irresistible now.

In August the Legion moved to Koenigsbrueck, the military training centre in Saxony. Here its First Battalion manoeuvred under Bose's eye in October. Growth was

---

[12] Speech of welcome to prisoneers from Italy, June 1942.

[13] This Europe.

rapid: the Second Battalion was at full strength by the end of January 1943, and the Third began to form in February. With this expansion came a financial problem. Payment for his soldiers had originally come from Bose's monthly Foreign Office grant. Now that source was insufficient. By September 1942 Bose had had to agree to their direct payment by the Germans, and to an oath of loyalty to Hitler.

The Japanese Military Attaché, Colonel Yamamoto,[14] accompanied him at the first oath-taking parade. Five hundred Legionaries were assembled. Their German commander Lieutenant Colonel Krappe, addressed them, and the oath was administered by German officers to six men at a time. All was done with solemnity, the soldiers touching their officer's sword as they spoke the German words:

> I swear by God this holy oath, that I will obey the leader of the German State and People, Adolf Hitler, as commander of the German Armed Forces, in the fight for the freedom of India, in which fight the leader is Subhash Chandra Bose, and that as a brave soldier, I am willing to lay down my life for this oath.

Bose presented to the Legion its standard, a tricolour in the green, white and saffron of the Indian National

---

[14] See p. 16.

Congress superimposed with the figure of a springing tiger in place of the Congress spinning wheel. 'Your names,' he said, 'will be written in golden letters in the history of Free India: every martyr in this holy war will have a monument there.' It was a brave, colourful show, and for Bose a moment of pride and emotion. 'I shall lead the Army,' he said, 'when we march to India together.' The Legionaries looked well in their new uniforms, the silken banner gleaming in their midst; their drill did them credit. Yet in a sense Bose was abandoning them: hereafter they would receive promotion and precedence as soldiers of Germany: the Legion had become in fact, if not yet in name, regiment of the German Army.

The Legion standard was only one of the symbols which Bose had invented for the Legion in 1942.He dwelt upon the militance of the Springing Tiger – which they also wore on their uniforms – every time he spoke to the men. 'Freedom is not given, it is taken,' he said again and again – freedom never could be a gift, because every gift carries its obligations, its ties. There was the greeting 'Jai Hind', soon to become the password of Indian nationalism; the National Anthem – a Bengali hymn of praise to India, written by Rabindranath Tagore, which had been the theme-song of an Indian radio programme from Berlin since early in the war. Bose's assumption of the title 'Netaji' and his appointment of January 28th as 'Legion Day' served the same purpose. There must be a Legion tradition, a manufactured basis for morale which could not be produced, as in the German Army, by discipline, or as in the Indian Army, by leadership.

The German officers, unlike their comrades at Meseritz, provided none of this. Krappe was a good-natured alcoholic, a Nazi, but little inclined to strictness. Few of his German subordinates were of any higher quality: too often they regarded the Legion simply as a refuge from the Eastern Front, came to it with no special qualifications and cultivated no sympathy with or understanding of their Indian soldiers. Such men inspired little respect or affection. Nevertheless, while the Legion was small, some corporate spirit was sustained. In the general expansion, the standard of recruitment and of the German staff fell considerably. The preservation of morale was thus always difficult, and Indo-German relations never satisfactory.

There was another aspect. When soldiers joined the Legion they usually retained traces of their old military discipline, natural manners and religious feeling. Within a few weeks all this disappeared, partly because of propaganda which actually made an inducement of moral laxity. Bose's determination to abolish or ignore caste and religious distinctions also had its influence. One sepoy was heard to say: 'In India we have many religions and many gods. But here everything is Jai Hind.' 'Jai Hind' was no substitute for the wrath of the gods, and discipline rotted away.

Idleness was of course a part of the trouble. Bose and the Germans realised that, for morale as well as propaganda reasons, the Legion must be given something to do. They first planned to send it to North Africa just before the battle of El Alamein; as we have seen Rommel rejected this. Then there was a proposal to station a company in Greece: this idea was outrun by events. Bose's last instructions in Europe on the Legion's future show how far his thoughts had moved. To begin with the Legion was to have gone to war only in or near India: the only restriction left when Bose departed for the East was that it must be used against British-Indian troops. In the event its deployment on the French coast in 1943-44 was all that could be devised; it proved only a partial cure.

From January 1942, when he joined the Free India Centre. A. C. N. Nambiar, an Indian left-wing journalist who had worked in Europe for some eighteen years, was recognised as Deputy Leader. The expansion of civil activity which took place as Bose emerged from obscurity was thus from the first Nambiar's affair. Broadcasting, publications, propaganda were all extended: there were also the welfare needs of the military units and a growing list of pensioners and dependents. By May 1942 the Centre had attained an acknowledged status in Germany. It was treated as a foreign mission, which implied for its members a higher scale of rations and exemption from some of the Aliens' Regulations. Bose himself was not stinted: the Germans gave him a good house, a car and special rations for entertainment purposes. His personal allowance amounted to about £800 per month, and there was a monthly grant for the Free India-Centre which rose from £1,200 in

1941, to £3,200 in 1944. All this Bose regarded as a loan, too be repaid to Germany when India was free, and he used it liberally.

In July 1942 it became necessary for Fraulein Schenkl, who had been Bose's private secretary for more than a year, to leave the Free India Centre. The dismissal was not what it seemed. Bose had known Emilie Schenkl ever since 1934; she was now secretly his wife, and in September 1942 was to bear him a daughter. The relationship had caused him much mental stress. He may not have sought the high moral reputation which was his in India. But the reputation was there: he was said, like Kemal Pasha, to have forsworn marriage until his country was free. A mixed marriage might give rise to many misunderstandings and his German friends advised against it. At length he decided on the strictest secrecy. He acknowledged his wife only in a letter to his brother, written just before he left Germany for the Far East.

Bose waited for eight months before his passage to Japan could be arranged. No land route was open to him and at first he thought that the Italians might be able to send him by air. When this project was abandoned he turned to the Japanese. A blockade-running vessel involved too great a risk of capture: a journey by submarine was the only alternative. This he undertook as soon as the necessary naval arrangements could be made. His Japanese friend, the Military Attaché, Colonel Yamamoto, who would have been the one to make them, went home through

Turkey and Russia in November 1942.

While he waited Bose passed on to Nambiar his policy and instructions. There were plans for new branches of the Free India Centre, for broadcasting, for Indians to study German police methods and for the training of Indian seamen and airmen. As for the Legion, it must be used actively as soon as possible, the German officers and N.C.O's must be quickly replaced by Indians, there must be no communalism. Legionaries were to be trained on all the most modern German equipment, including heavy artillery and tanks: Bose would send further instructions as opportunity offered.

Christmas 1942 was spent peacefully with his wife and infant daughter Anita in Vienna. Then, after a visit to Paris in January, Bose heard that his departure was imminent. There was time for one more celebration. On January 26th, 'Independence Day' was observed in Berlin with a great party where six hundred guests drank Bose's health. Two days later he made his speech to the Legion on 'Legion Day'. To help conceal his departure he had recorded two speeches for broadcasting after he left,[15] and he referred frequently in conversation to the approaching need for long visits to the Russian Front. He hoped at first to take both Swami and Hassan with him, but there was no room and only Hassan accompanied him on board.

[15] One used on February 28th, 1943; Volkischer Beobachter, March 4th, 1943.

The secret was well kept: when Swami sailed on March 24th, he did not know that Bose had already gone.

There was no anxiety at the Free India Centre – Bose was simply on a prolonged tour. In his place and with most of his privileges, Nambiar soon settled down, assuming his master's mantle with more pomp than some of his colleagues wished to see. He was accepted with respect by the Legion, whose nerves he more than once managed to soothe in the troublesome process of replacing German officers and N.C.O's with Indians. Nevertheless, in the absence of Bose, interest and enthusiasm gradually departed, until the Indians in Europe were swept without a struggle into the maelstrom of Nazi disintegration.

5

A NEW VOICE IN ASIA

The Provisional Government is entitled to and hereby claims the allegiance of every Indian. (October 21st, 1943)

Subhash Chandra Bose and Abid Hassan left Kiel in a German U-boat on February 8th, 1943. They made a wide sweep out into the Atlantic, sailed down its whole length past the Cape of Good Hope to a meeting place four hundred miles S.S.W. of Madagascar. Here, on April 28th, they were transferred by rubber dinghy to the Japanese submarine I 29 which took them across the Indian Ocean. From Sabang, at the northern tip of Sumatra, they went by air to Tokyo with Colonel Yamamoto, now head of the Japanese-Indian liaison group, the Hikari Kikan, who had come to meet them. They reached Tokyo on June 13th after a journey of eighteen weeks.

There had been no other passengers on this the longest of Bose's journeys. He accepted with serenity the silence and discomforts, the momentary excitement when the captain thought they were sighted, the long cramped hours of danger. The time was passed in reading, making notes, working on a new edition of *The Indian Struggle,* talking to Hassan of all the new things to be done in the Far East. For there were many problems awaiting solution. He knew something, but not all, of the events of 1942: he knew that there had been raised a force of sixteen thousand men, but it seemed that the leader had lost patience just when he might, by perseverance, have obtained all he asked. Perhaps the trouble had been short-sighted political leadership: who cared if Indians did contribute to some Japanese purposes, so long as they were serving their own? Rash Behari could not be expected to grasp this, much less hold his more complicated colleagues to the point. His political experience had been in the somewhat specialised realm of terrorism – no place to learn political *finesse* or the art of impressing the Japanese. 'You are not a Government,' they had said, 'you are not a State, you have nothing to offer that we have not first given you: how then can you make treaties?" This was all partly true and it had to be faced; there was no sense in waxing indignant with the Japanese about it.

Bose would approach them differently. First he would show them that the movement could be important, not simply as a source of military intelligence and fifth columnists in Burma, but in their whole political and propaganda effort. Names, cries, slogans were of more significance at this stage than action – even military action. There must be a Provisional Indian Government recognised by the Axis, as the Japanese themselves had proposed in 1942.[1] That would give them someone to deal with. There must also be definite, dynamic, Indian leadership. Bose must mobilise under his Government all Indian resources in the Far East, money and men, so that he would have financial independence and an Army worth the name. Nobody could then prevent him from taking over in due course the government of India itself.

His welcome in the Far East was assured: the turbulent past, the still-mysterious escape from India, his negotiations with the Dictators and his achievement in Europe would guarantee that. But more than these things – his name and the promise of his coming had been with the eastern communities from the very beginning of their Independence Movement. He had been named by Mohan Singh to Fujihara in 1941. They had talked of him in the first civilian discussions in Singapore and again in Tokyo. There had been his stirring message to the Bangkok Conference, and its invitation to him. *The Indian Struggle* had been republished in Malaya in August 1942. There had been hopes and rumours of his coming throughout the critical weeks at the end of the year, and finally the promise of his arrival had been used in February 1943 to induce wavering officers to remain in the I.N.A. and to silence civilian criticism.

So soldiers and civilians were ready for him, and they welcomed him boisterously. The moment was his. His

---

[1] Goebbels' Diary, p. 157

personal enthusiasm, his vitality, his authority and his world view won him the real allegiance of Indians in East Asia. He swept people off their feet; there were few who could stand back and consider whether he was taking them in the direction and by the means which their leaders in India would have approved. Nor was that any longer an issue. He proclaimed his authority, they acclaimed it. The few whose minds resisted could not help seeing in him an arrogant autocrat who thought dictatorship desirable in India and who planned to wield it himself. But these soon learnt to hold their peace.

Bose was received by Tojo on the day after his arrival. The Japanese Premier was frank; whether India were invaded or not, she would come under Japanese control on the defeat of the British. But Japan had no demands to make on her beyond the necessities of war and intended her to be independent. Any action Indians could take themselves would be helped and appreciated by Japan; such action was in their own interests. Bose was encouraged in his project of a Provisional Government which would take control of Indian territory as the Japanese forces moved on; he then heard Tojo make a declaration about India in the Diet:

> Japan is firmly resolved to extend all means in order to help to expel and eliminate from India the Anglo-Saxon influence which are the enemy of Indian people, and enable India to achieve full independence in the true sense of the term.[2]

[2] June 16th, 1943 (on to Delhi p. 11)

To one who had waited upon the European Dictators for nearly two years in vain, this was most satisfactory. Bose did not fear the Japanese; no more than the British could they rule India without Indian consent, particularly if he had a strong Indian National Army. Japan, he said, was India's greatest friend: this was an epoch-making declaration, which would live in history.

The world has yet to reconcile the ceremonious charm and ant-like industry of the teeming Japanese with the barbaric savagery of their soldiers in war. Bose, visiting Japan for the first time, liked what he saw of these disarming people, and was impressed by their vigour and discipline. Within a few days he had heard all that Rash Behari could tell him of the League and the I.N.A., and had discussed Japanese policy towards them with the War Department. He studied Japanese relations with the governments of Manchukuo and Nanking-China, and their arrangements to grant 'independence' to Burma and the Philippine Islands. On June 19th he held a press conference, and followed it with two broadcasts to publicise further his presence in the Far East. He appealed once more to the people at home who doubted the merits of the Axis powers: if India did not trust the Axis, let it trust him: for 'if the wily cunning and resourceful British politicians have failed to cajole and corrupt me, nobody else can do so.'[3] Let there be no more thought of compromise with England: it was economically impossible for her to give up India and madness on India's

[3] Broadcast, June 24th, 1943.

part to expect it. But the three Axis powers had mortally wounded her and India was grateful for this and for offers of direct assistance. Indian liberty must, however, be won with Indian blood. Only so would Indian strength suffice to preserve it. The purpose of his escape from India had now been fulfilled: he knew the international situation at first hand: the Axis, particularly Japan, was ready to help India; all Indians in Axis-controlled countries were organised as one, to bring assistance to those at home. Now let India do her part:

> Civil disobedience must develop into armed struggle. And only when the Indian people receive the baptism of fire on a large scale will they qualify for their freedom.[4]....
>
> India shall be free – and before long. And a Free India will throw open the prison gates so that her worthy sons may step out of the darkness of the prison cells into the light of freedom, joy and self-fulfilment.

This was indeed a new voice in Asia. It remained to bring it to bear on the Indian communities. By June 27th Bose had realised the urgent necessity of a visit to Singapore, and had postponed projected study visits to China and Manchukuo. He reached Singapore on July 2nd and received a tumultuous welcome.

---

[4] Press Statement, June 19th, 1943.

There followed a week of public functions and private consultations commemorated annually as 'Netaji Week' while the War lasted. Bose met and assessed the military and civilian leaders one by one. Few of them had met anyone of his quality before. All were dazzled, flattered. To each he was the authentic leader, long awaited, who would remove all doubts, answer all questions. On July 4th, in the presence of League representatives from all Japanese Asia, he accepted the Presidency of the League and the allegiance of the Indian National Army. All Indians outside India, he claimed, now acknowledged him as leader in the independent struggle, and his efforts were in harmony with public opinion in India which he knew well through his secret agents. Japan was a worthy ally and he guaranteed her sincerity. All fighters for freedom inside India and without, must now unite under the Provisional Government of Free India which he would set up, to prepare and strike in time with Japan, the final revolutionary blow:

> We have a grim fight ahead of us – for the enemy is powerful, unscrupulous and ruthless. In this final march to freedom you will have to face hunger, thirst, privation, forced marches and death. Only when you pass this test will freedom be yours.[5]

On the next day Bose reviewed the Indian National Army and announced its existence to the world.[6] This, again, was

---

[5] Speech at Singapore, July 4th, 1943.
[6] On to Dehli, p. 37, July 9th, 1943.

the proudest day of his life: here was the Army whose approach would raise the final rebellion and mutiny in India: let the battle-cry be 'Chalo Delhi', 'To Delhi', until the victory parade was held in the Red Fort of India's ancient capital. There were two tasks for the Army: to fight for freedom, and then to stand as the defence force of Free India. It must become a first-class modern army of superb morale, its officers fit to form the General Staff of Free India. If you follow me...' he said, 'I shall lead you to Victory and Freedom.' The parade was followed by another on July 6th at which Tojo himself took the salute. Then on July 9th, sixty thousand people stood to hear him in the pouring rain:

> There is no nationalist leader in India who can claim to possess the many-sided experience that I have been able to acquire.[7]

The struggle in India would not suffice to expel the British. He had come to organise help from outside. All the resources of the three million[8] Indians in East Asia, he told them, must now be mobilised. The slogan would be 'Total mobilisation for a total war.' His aim was three hundred thousand soldiers and thirty million dollars.[9]

---

[7] Ibid, p. 32.

[8] This figure which Bose usually qouted was a considerable exaggeration for the number of Indians in Japanese Asia: even two million would probably have been an over-estimate, after the exodus from Burma in 1942.

[9] 1 Straits Dollar =2s. 4d.

Everywhere Bose met adulation, near adoration, devotion which moved him so that sometimes, simply in answer to the popular mood, he would make claims and promise which his most sanguine admirers deplored.[10] But his audiences cheered the more. He toured the prisoner-of-war camps and won two thousand volunteers, he spoke to Indian meetings everywhere, he conferred constantly with the Japanese. In August he was at the Burmese Independence celebrations in Rangoon. There followed visits to Bangkok and Saigon. There were more speeches, interviews without number and long meetings with Japanese commanders and government officials; broadcasts too – at every opportunity. He seemed tireless, taking little sleep and working far into the night.

He followed the international situation closely and, as in Germany, used it in his broadcasts to his own best advantage. Of particular value to him was the disastrous famine in Bengal during the summer of 1943. In August he made an offer of 100,000 tons of rice to be shipped under suitable guarantees to Indian ports as a gift from the League. The offer was ignored, and this gave him further opportunity for vehement attacks on the Indian Government and on the new Viceroy, Lord Wavell. The Allied victory in North Africa, the occupation of Siciliy and the landings in Italy were dismissed as too remote to concern India, who need only look at the Japanese standing on her eastern frontier to be sure of

---

[10] S.A. Ayer, Unto Him A Witness: see pp. 247-248.

British defeat. The official British policy of silence regarding the I.N.A. exasperated him. "If only,' he would say bitterly, 'they would abuse us.'

Within six weeks Bose had a clear grasp of the main problems. He saw that the most important territories were Malaya, Burma and Sian. Malaya had a rich Indian population of 800,000; Burma a less wealthy one of 600,000. These must be his main sources of money and men. Siam also had its place as the home of 55,000 Indians, as a major source of supply for the I.N.A. and as the link between the other two. He appointed personal representatives at once in Burma and Siam with special tasks. Indian efforts in Burma wanted coordination and control: in Siam the League was internally divided and needed a firm hand. To the smaller communities in China and Indonesia which he could not yet visit, he sent senior Army Officers to start the collection of money and recruits.

It was clear, too, that he must assume personal command of the Indian National Army: this he did on August 8th, proclaiming the fact on August 25th in the first of his 'Special Orders of the day'.[11] He had already discussed with the Japanese the Army's role in the proposed Imphal campaign. Field-Marshall Count Terauchi, the commander in South-East Asia, had been reluctant to have the I.N.A. appear at all. Its soldiers, he said, had been demoralised by

[11] See Appendix II, No. 1.

defeat in Malaya; they could not stand up to the rigours of a Japanese campaign, and would have an irresistible compulsion to cross over to their old friends and easier circumstances. He proposed that the Japanese Army should do all that was necessary to liberate India, that Bose himself should assist by enlisting the goodwill and cooperation of the Indian population, that the main part of the I.N.A. should be left in Singapore, and that only espionage and propaganda groups should be used in the field.

So frank an appraisal had been a shock; this was the fifth-column role in its plainest terms, and even Mohan Singh had rejected it. Bose wanted to expand his Army to the utmost, and to throw as many men into battle as possible. The triumphant Japanese march to India would then also to a significant extent be an Indian victory, which would qualify India to take her independence at once. With characteristic insight he approached the matter as one of face. 'Any liberation of India secured through Japanese sacrifices,' he said, 'is worse than slavery.'[12] He talked about the national honour of India, insisted that Indians must make the maximum contribution of blood and sacrifice themselves, and urged that the I.N.A. be allowed to form the spearhead of the coming offensive. Terauchi at last consented to the employment of one regiment[13] as a

---

[12] Shah Nawaz Khan, *My Memories of the I.N.A. and its Netaji*, p 265.

[13] A Japanese regiment of three battalions was equivalent in strength to a British brigade.

trial. If this regiment came up to Japanese standards, the rest of the Army would be sent into action.

Upon his promise Bose based his plans. Having established a Supreme Command Headquarters, reformed the 1st I.N.A. Division and sent it to North Malaya for training, he set about the major task, that of morale. Morale was all-important, far more important to the I.N.A. than to other armies, for the I.N.A. not only had to face an enemy more numerous and better equipped than itself, but it had to win that enemy over. I am convinced, he said, that the very appearance of the I.N.A. on the Indian frontier 'will be a clarion call to the people.... and to the Indian Army.'[14] But this was only conceivable if every member of it was of superb spirit, utterly confident in his power of leadership and his mission. Instead of this the I.N.A. was slack, idle and ill-disciplined. Desertion and pilfering were rife, there was disloyal talk. Bose spoke plainly: such behaviour must cease. Let the lukewarm and chicken-hearted declare themselves and go; he would not keep them. For those who remained he would do his best: there would be pensions for the families of the killed, care for the wounded, rewards for the brave. He increased I.N.A. pay, improved its rations, and N.C.O's, showed the most detailed interest. He would join its soldiers without warning at their meals and his door was always open to its officers. For these his entertainment and conversation were liberal.

---

[14] Speech at Kuala Lumpur, September 5th, 1943.

He would invite them to play badminton – his daily exercise – and lend them towels or a change of clothing, treating them as equals and comrades. His Army was nearest of all to the heart of the Indian struggle; he sought by every means to bind it to himself.

Personally he gave an example of boundless, flawless confidence. Photographs of his inspections of the I.N.A. at this time showed him striding along, his eyes sternly to the front only rarely moving aside to take in some detail, his face set in an expression of haughty determination, his staff smartly in step behind him. The heroic pose, the insistence on being 'Supreme Commander,' the immaculate uniform, the invariable field boots – which cannot have been comfortable in a hot climate – these were intended to make Netaji so powerful a focus of loyalty and fighting spirit of the I.N.A., that the dark reminiscence of its foundation would vanish and all India succumb to its shining temper.

During September the picked men of the 1st Division came together as 'Subhash Regiment' under Captain Shah Nawaz, formerly of the 1/14 Punjab Regiment, one of the best young officers at Bose's disposal. There was hard training for the trial regiment until it began to move to Burma on November 20th. The other regiments were refilled rapidly with new volunteers and with recruits from the civilian centres which now began to spring up in Malaya, Siam, Burma and South China. The training structure was supported on the one hand by Officers' and

N.C.O.'s Training Schools, and on the other by the Boys' organisation, the Balak Sena. Women were to play their part as nurses and soldiers in the Rani of Jhansi Regiment founded in Singapore.

Bose had accepted the earlier I.N.A. obligation to provide battle and strategic intelligence for the Japanese, but he intended to exercise personal control. Hitherto Indian espionage had failed. Of the one hundred and thirty Indians sent into India through the Japanese outposts in Burma during 1942, none had returned; from the group of parachute agents dropped in March 1943 nothing had been received. Only the short-range networks operated in the broad frontier zones by Indian master-spies who kept their men closely controlled, had produced results. These networks, still operating from Hikari Kikan outposts along the Chindwin and in Arakan, were strengthened and reinforced. Agents for them had been drawn from spy schools in Rangoon and Penang, and from special service groups included in the I.N.A. by Mohan Singh. The role of these groups was now redefined: the 'Bahadur Group' would operate behind the enemy front, carrying out sabotage, espionage and the subversion of Indian troops. The 'Intelligence Group' would work similarly in the battle area and the 'Reinforcement Group' would collect Indian prisoners and pass them, after indoctrination, into the I.N.A.

From the spy schools Bose required a direct wireless link with India as soon as possible. Swami, who had followed him from Tokyo in July, went to Penang, and he himself carried out a careful inspection of the schools in Rangoon. Neither was much impressed with the standard of technical training, but Bose saw possibilities in the group run by S.N. Chopra, a schoolmaster from Batu Pahat, in Penang. The Japanese accepted the proposal to form a submarine party under Chopra, which would include the four men and some of the equipment brought from Germany by Swami. The agents were to report by wireless from the Punjab, from Bombay and from Bengal, while Chopra coordinated their work from Delhi. In October Bose briefed the men himself. He gave them lists of informed and sympathetic people to be met in their areas, and advised them on employment and disguises. The chief object, he said, would be to pass back military and economic information. Political work they might undertake in time, but it was not easy for the inexperienced, and the process of proving their *bona fides* to secret revolutionary groups might give them away. He therefore issued no lists of Forward Bloc leaders – he did not know in any case, he said, who was still out of jail.

Bose warned his agents that they must not run too many risks. They were working at present mainly for the Japanese and only indirectly for India. In case of danger they should lie low. Let them not lose patience, he said, there would come a time when the value of their work would justify every risk: for that moment they should save themselves. Chopra's party spent a month perfecting its wireless technique under Swami and learning the ciphers he provided. It left by submarine on December 8th and disembarked on the Kathiawar coast, between Bombay and Karachi, fourteen days later. It was at large in India with its wireless sets for less than two months.

THE PROVISIONAL GOVERNMENT

> Just as the peacock emblem now flies over Government House in Rangoon – so will the tricolour soon fly over the Red Fortress of Delhi.[15]

With these words Bose had hailed the granting of independence to Burma by the Japanese on August 1st, 1943. He had been in Rangoon again for further celebrations at the end of September, and had made an Indo-Burmese occasion of his visit to the tomb of Bahadur Shah, last of the Moghuls, who died in exile there. On October 17th he spoke in honour of Filipino independence. Now, in his turn, he prepared to inaugurate the Provisional Government on October 21st.

Although Tojo had agreed to this necessary development in June, Bose had fought many a battle with the Hikari Kikan in Singapore before he obtained local and detailed Japanese approval. His association with Yamamoto was already less cordial, it was to deteriorate further as he learnt to rely on Tokyo for support. But for the moment differences were in abeyance. Bose drafted his proclamation and formed his

---

[15] Press Statement (*On to Delhi,* p. 52).

Cabinet. This to begin with was simply constructed: he could not risk Japanese confidence by including members of the discredited old regime – even if they were prepared to accept office – and there were few others of the requisite calibre ready to abandon their own affairs. He appointed at first only, four ministers, styling himself 'Head of State, Prime Minister and Minister for War and Foreign Affairs.' There were also eight military representatives, and eight civilian advisers representing the League Territorial Committees.[16]

Mr. Ayer, the Minister of Propaganda, had told how the Proclamation was drafted before dawn on October 20th.[17] Bose took a handful of blank paper and started writing swiftly in pencil, sheet after sheet. There was never a backward glance or a correction; the manuscript went to the typist page by page as it was finished, and when it was typed there was not a word or a comma to alter. He wrote his statement on the Proclamation in the same swift, absorbed way, his eyes never leaving the paper. 'It was nearly six a.m. by the time he completed it; he had been sipping black coffee since midnight.' Coffee was the symbol of night work: his staff could tell how late he would sit up by the number of cups after dinner.

Ayer has given other glimpses of his private life: he was a heavy cigarette smoker, chain-smoking if there was

---

[16] See Appendix II (2)

[17] S.A. Ayer, *Unto Him a Witness*, p. 163.

anything to tax his nerves and smoking every cigarette to the last puff. His doctor would grumble – too much tobacco, too much betel nut, too much badminton – and he was always ready for a cup of tea. Nevertheless, apart from the constant hospitality he dispensed, he lived frugally, devoutly. In his personal luggage was a little leather bag containing a rosary, a small 'Gita', and his spare reading glasses. Often when in Singapore he would commune with the missionaries of the Ramakrishna Mission or, late at night, he would drive to the Mission, 'there change into a priestly silk *dhoti*, shut himself up in the prayer room, rosary in hand, and spend a couple of hours in meditation.[18] In person he was meticulous, in manner precise, thorough in all he did. His daily work would absorb him so that sometimes he would forget his meals. He loved animals and would spend leisure hours visiting his pets; in Rangoon later on there were monkeys, goats, rabbits, ducks and geese, and a pony; only cats he disliked. He appears in private as a calm, considerate person, teasing his servant daily about the price of bananas, or the chauffeur about his speed, careful to put the humblest guest at ease.

The ceremonies of October 21st took place in the Cathay Cinema at Singapore. Bose opened them with a major speech. He claimed that in forming the Provisional Government he had 'the fullest support, not only of the civil population of India, but also a large section of

---

[18] S.A. Ayer, *Unto Him a Witness*, p. 269.

Britain's Indian Army'. He had not the slightest doubt that when India's frontier was crossed and the national flag planted on Indian soil the real revolution 'that will ultimately bring about the end of British rule in India, will begin.' In gratitude he offered Japan's Government the price of ten military aircraft. The Proclamation[19] was made in the presence of Yamamoto at the afternoon session. It was a colourful, impressive scene: the hall hung with banners, slogans, national flags – Bose himself and his Cabinet, imposing in their uniforms – the platform lined with microphones, dumb symbols of power in the world outside: the I.N.A. guards of honour: Japanese courtesies, and greeting from the diplomats and political leaders of the East. All combined to give a sense of reality, of substantial achievement, which the assembly had not seen before. To this was added the strongest emotional appeal. The Government was no puppet – the gift of ten aircraft, the offer of rice for Bengal, spoke for themselves. It would be, said Bose, like the Provisional Government founded by Kemal Pasha in Anatolia after the First World War. For the present its scope would be limited, military affairs must dominate, but when the time came it would assume the 'functions of a normal government operating in its own territory'. Then in an atmosphere charged with emotion and himself hardly able to speak, Bose took the oath:

> In the name of God, I take this sacred oath that to liberate India and the thirty-eight crores of my

[19] On to Delhi, p. 131, See Appendix II, (2).

> countrymen, I, Subhash Chandra Bose, will continue the sacred war of freedom till the last breath of my life.
>
> I shall remain always a servant of India and to look after the welfare of thirty-eight crores of Indian brothers and sisters, shall be for me my highest duty.
>
> Even after winning freedom, I will always be prepared to shed even the last drop of my blood for the preservation of India's Freedom.[19a]

The members of the Cabinet took a similar pledge, standing before him each in turn. A choir sang the National Anthem, the same poem of Tagore which had been sung in Germany, now newly translated into Hindustani, and set to music at Bose's command by a young Indian soldier. All scrambled to their feet: Bose, Yamamoto and the Cabinet stood at attention: there were cheers, slogans, acclamations. Almost, it seemed, the day of freedom had dawned. The delegates looked round in wonder, and tried to capture something of the essence of that moment to carry back to their people at home.

At midnight on October 23rd the Provisional Government declared war on Britain and the U.S.A. The Cabinet had not been unanimous about the inclusion of the U.S.A. Bose had shown impatience and displeasure – there was never any question then or later of his absolute authority,

---

[19a] Appendix II, No. 2

the Cabinet had no responsibility and could only tender advice. Over some weeks came recognition of the Government: from Japan, Burma, Croatia, Germany, the Philippines, Nanking, Manchukuo, from what was left of Fascist Italy, from Siam but, to Bose's disappointment, not from Vichy France.

Recognition was one thing, legitimacy another. The only sphere of government was the League and the only subjects were the members of the League, yet even for them this must be without prejudice to any allegiance they might owe by reason of domicile. Until it entered some part of India, the Provisional Government was a government of the future. It made no laws, had no territory, no extra-territorial rights, could not confer citizenship or exercise protection. The claim Bose made for it was nevertheless specific:

> The Provisional Government is entitled to, and hereby claims the allegiance of every Indian. It guarantees religious liberty, as well as equal rights and equal opportunities to all its citizens.[20].

There were brave words and a bold claim, among the bravest and boldest that this courageous man ever made. But he knew well on what his authority rested. The Japanese had held the league responsible for the behaviour of the Indian communities, it had thus been able to

---

[20] The Proclamation: On to Delhi, p. 135, See Appendix 11(2).

exercise sanctions – for instance in Singapore by the issue of ration cards. Beyond that it could call on the services of the Japanese security police: and such calls would be answered because it was in the Japanese internal to maintain the authority of the League. The Provisional Government took over this position. Netaji controlled his subjects just as Rash Behari had controlled League members not through any allegiance of theirs or any sovereign right of his, but by authority delegated from the Japanese.

The introduction a little later in Malaya of an 'Oath of Allegiance' to the Provisional Government and to Bose as its leader made no legal or practical difference, but the oath was a propaganda point which Bose had wanted to use in Germany and which he valued now. The Malayan Indian community was told:

> The privilege of owing allegiance to our Government will be extended only to members of the League, as any Indian who is not a member of the League cannot be considered a true Indian.

The oath was printed on a small blue card which was signed in the presence of the League Branch chairman who issued it:

> I.... a member of the Azad Hind Sangh, do hereby solemnly promise in the name of God and take this holy oath that I will be absolutely loyal and faithful

> to the Provisional Government of Azad Hind, and shall always be prepared for any sacrifice for the cause of the freedom of our motherland, under the leadership of Subhash Chandra Bose.

The Cabinet required no change in the main league structure. Bose worked through department heads, now called Ministers, and a military staff. But he was a stronger man with a Cabinet than without it, and a better figurehead. The Cabinet took a broader view of Indian nationalism than had the League and the moral effect was great. It was also the personal fulfilment of Bose himself, that which would ensure his acceptance whatever he might or might not achieve. He had a title, an office, however illusory. He was 'Head of the State,' and although Mr. P.K. Menon cried: 'What, then, is the state of his head?' this was something which the mass of Indians could grasp, a better assurance of their security than any they had known since Britain's ended.

The League was now far better organised than in its first period. In April, Lieutenant-Colonel Chatterji, an officer of the Indian Medical Service, had been commissioned by Rash Behari to reconstruct League Headquarters. Bose had endorsed the work of this excellent organiser and built the Provisional Government on what he had made. There was a General Secretariat and eight departments: Finance, Publicity and Propaganda, Health, Training, Recruitment, Reconstruction, Education and Women's Affairs. Gradually, ministers were appointed for all these. Bose found it necessary to tighten up League discipline: he suspended all elections for the duration of war, and ordered the expulsion of anyone not whole-heartedly cooperating, or making counter-propaganda. For this purpose he accepted and strengthened the League's internal security system; he was to deal with offenders himself, directing many of the investigations personally.

Now, as always, money was the greatest single problem. Bose was drawn in two directions. He realised that he could not do without Japanese finance, and often said that all help offered must be accepted for India's sake, but he knew the strong feeling among his followers that Japanese money must not imply Japanese dictation. Some Japanese assistance was indeed his due. The Japanese must naturally continue to maintain the prisoners of war whether they were in the I.N.A. or not; that they would be doing in any case. He aimed, however, to pay for all the civilian activities of the League, including the recruitment and training of civilians for the I.N.A. By October 1943 these expenses amounted to about a million local dollars (£116,700) a month and Chatterji saw that the bill would increase five-fold when the new recruitment and training projects developed. Income had not approached this rate, less than two million dollars in all having been subscribed up to July 1943.

Thus Netaji was always demanding money from his audiences. At first donations flowed in freely from rich and poor, but the early eager generosity did not last and his persuasion gave way to threats. 'I shall wait for one or two more weeks, and I shall see,' he said on October 17th, 'and after that all the steps that I have to take in the name of India I shall take.' On October 25th he addressed the merchants of Malaya with severity:

> Legally speaking there is no private property when a country is in a state of war... If you think that your wealth and possessions are your own you are living in delusion..... Your lives and your properties do not now belong to you; they belong to India and India alone.....
>
> I have every confidence that if you realise this simple truth – that we have to achieve independence by any means... and that we are now a free people in a state of war, you will realise that nothing belongs to you, that your lives, properties and everything are no more your own.
>
> If you do not want to realise this simple truth then you have another path clearly chalked out for you... the path taken by the Englishmen. They lived as rulers once here, but now they have only one place left here and that is prison. If you choose, you can go to the prisons and keep company with the Englishmen. But remember this: when the war is over and India becomes independent, you shall have no room in Free India.

Bose had heard that some of the rich Indians of Malaya were murmuring that he was harassing them, and that they were thinking of changing their nationalities or of avoiding payment by some other means. Let them think again, he said:

> I have to liberate India and I shall make India independent by all means and at any cost... If you want to evade the issue say plainly that you do not want independence; then as I have already told you, a different party lies ahead of you....
>
> So long you as you say you are Indians and you want to claim and make money in East Asia as Indians you cannot shirk performing the duties which devolve on you as free Indians. Do not think that it is left to your option to perform your duty or not...
>
> I stand here today representing the Provisional Government of Azad Hind which has absolute rights over your lives and properties... I have said that we have to get Indian independence by all means and at any cost and that we have to carry out Total Mobilisation voluntarily if possible, by compulsion if necessary... If you do not choose to come forward voluntarily, then we are not going to remain slaves on that account... Everyone who refuses to help our cause is.... our enemy.

But it was no good: Bose required more than petty cash and recognised that he must make a systematic levy on

Indian property. This Chatterji was told to devise: there resulted the 'Boards of Management for Raising Funds', to which from the beginning of 1944 Indians had to declare their assets. Levies of from ten to twenty-five per cent were imposed and collected with progressive vigour.

Another matter on which Bose had set Chatterji thinking was the administration of Indian territory as it came to be occupied. After the I.N.A. sets foot on Indian soil, 'it will take', Bose had said, 'at least twelve months – and perhaps more – to liberate the whole of India.'[21] What he called the 'Reconstruction College' was set up in Singapore under an Indian ex-magistrate, to train administrators in civil affairs and relief work. The Cabinet met several times in the first week of its life to consider this and other problems. Sub-committees were formed to study the abolition of communalism in Free India – 'national unification' as it was called – medals and pensions for the I.N.A., the design of Provisional Government banknotes for use in occupied territory. The design of currency notes and medals was settled at once, and orders were placed for them in Tokyo during November. National Unification was less immediate and the report was not produced until much later. It was eventually agreed that Hindustani should be the common language of India,[22] that 'Jai Hind' should be the common greeting that the Congress tricolour should

[21] Broadcast, October 2nd, 1943.

[22] Bose had always held that the dstinction between Hindi and Urdu was artificial. He advocated the adopted of the Roman Script, as a means of integration and to simplify India's relations with the rest of the world.

be the national flag and the Tagore poem the National Anthem.

BOSE REPORTS AGAIN TO TOJO

Bose left Singapore by air on October 25th to attend the Greater East Asia Conference in Tokyo. He called on Tojo on November 1st. He knew now the awkward possibilities of the Hikari Kikan in Malay and tried for firm Tokyo decisions on all subjects in which he hoped for progress.

To Tojo he spoke confidently as to an equal. He complained of Terauchi's attitude and asked that the 1st I.N.A. Division be employed as a whole in the 1944 offensive. He wanted to form two more divisions in Malaya, to secure control of the Indian spy schools and a cessation of secret Indian activity under the Hikari Kikan. He wished to move his own headquarters to Rangoon and asked for the Andaman and Nicobar Islands – the only Indian territory held by the Japanese – to be handed over to him. He sought an assurance too that as the Japanese marched into India the occupied regions would be put under his control. There were other matters – the production of banknotes and the old unsettled questions of abandoned Indian property.

Tojo dealt with few of these matters himself. He promised an early decision on the transfer of the Andaman and later consideration for the status of occupied territory in general. He had no objection to the banknotes, and ruled that Indian property abandoned after the outbreak of the Pacific war should be administered by the Provisional Government. On the remaining questions he promised Bose his support, but referred him for detailed discussion to the War department and to his military commanders.

The Conference took place on November 5th and 6th in the Diet building. Bose took his place as an observer and not as a full delegate, because he could not commit India to a part in the Co-Prosperity Sphere. The speech he made after Tojo and the delegates had finished was nevertheless a personal success. The Co-Prosperity Sphere, he said, was a venture of world significance. It was from regional organisations of this sort that an eventual world order could be built. There was world interest, too, in Japan's struggle with Britain and the U.S.A.:

> Unless Anglo-American Imperialism is wiped out in India it will be difficult, perhaps impossible, for the suppressed Islamic nations to overthrow the British yoke and recover their lost liberty.

All, including India's fate, depended on a Japanese victory.

> If our Allies were to go down, there will be no hope for India to be freed for atleast a hundred years.... For India, there is no other path but... uncompromising struggle against British Imperialism. Even if it were possible for other nations to think of compromising with england, for the Indian people at

> least it is out of the question. Compromising with Britain means to compromise with slavery and we are determined not to compromise with slavery any more.

Japan could be assured therefore of India's determination. The battles would be bitter, the cost heavy, heavier for India than for the others represented there: they had only to retain freedom. India had to win it. But he was full of confidence in India's destiny and Japan's invincibility. Life and death did not matter: it was enough that India would be free and the menace of Anglo-American imperialism removed for ever from East Asia.

Tojo responded with the announcement that Japan would shortly be ready to hand over the Andaman and Nichobar Islands to the Provisional Government as proof of her readiness to help. Events showed that there was no intention of transferring the administration of the islands, which were an important naval outpost, so long as war continued, neither did Japan have any right under international law to do so.[23] Bose was not deceived as to the fact, but used the specious fiction as best he could, renaming his territories the 'Shahid' (Martyr) and 'Swaraj' (Independence) Islands respectively to mark their new status. He obtained reluctant naval consent to a formal visit to the islands and to the appointment of an Indian Chief Commissioner pending completion of the transfer.

---

[23] Oppenheimer's *International Law*, vol. II, p. 341.

Further than this the Navy would not go.

From the Army Chief of Staff, General Sugiyama, Bose secured agreement that in the 1944 offensive the I.N.A. would rank as an Allied Army under Japanese operational command. Its movements and role must therefore rest with the Commander-in-Chief in Burma. Sugiyama consented to the raising of the 2nd Division, to the planning of the 3rd and to the training of cadets for the I.N.A. in Japan. The Japanese would remain financially responsible for the ex-prisoners of war in the I.N.A. and Bose would find the money to pay his civilian recruits. There was no shortage of equipment, which could be supplied almost indefinitely out of captured British stocks.

Bose left Tokyo on November 18th, 1943, returning to Singapore by way of Nanking, Shanghai, Manila and Saigon. The journey was something of a triumphal progress: there had been no foreign statesman in Tokyo who had approached Bose in political stature or personal force and this his hosts had warmly acknowledged. He had been invited to address a Japanese mass meeting; he had been shown academies, cadet colleges, war factories; he had received flattery and deference from the Japanese and other national leaders; had been received by the Emperor. Now, very much the international statesman, he visited the other capitals of the East. From Shanghai he broadcast an appeal to Chiang Kai Shek to make an honourable peace with Japan by which foreign troops could be withdrawn from

China. 'There is no reason', he said, 'why you should wait till the end of this war for peace.' China could start her national reconstruction now with the kindly help of Japan. Bose said later that he had met representatives of Chiang Kai Shek during his visit to Nanking; this may have been the reason for his belief that a negotiated settlement was possible.

After a state reception in Manila, Bose visited Terauchi's headquarters in Saigon on November 24th. It was decided that the 1st Division and his own civil and military headquarters would move to Burma in January 1944. The Indian community in Saigon was assembled to greet him. He assessed its contribution to his funds at twelve million piastres and, when the leaders demurred, exclaimed, much as he had done in Malaya: 'All your wealth would not buy back one life lost in battle. I have full jurisdiction over you and can order you to the front.'

TO BURMA

Bose returned to Singapore on November 25th and began to implement the arrangements he had made. The move of the Provisional Government was not to involve the main League Headquarters in Singapore which would still cope with the 'rear areas'. He planned simply to take his Cabinet to Rangoon and to superimpose it upon the League Headquarters for Burma, relegating Burma League affairs to a new minor department. The move of Supreme

Command Headquarters could not be similarly reduced, but as only one regiment had yet begun to leave Malaya, there was no great urgency.

The 2nd I.N.A. Division was formed in December 1943, and enough men were already coming from the recruit training centres to justify early plans for the 3rd. But all was not well at the centres themselves. In November there had been a serious mutiny in Singapore attributable to unaccustomed discomfort and discipline, and perhaps, also to the poor physical standard of the recruits. This, and the generally high desertion rate, argued ill for future plans and it had already been thought necessary to issue a warning in I.N.A. Routine Orders that 'desertion and joint action are punishable by death in the I.N.A. as in other armies'. Bose considered the matter with his Cabinet and launched a campaign to promote corporate spirit and raise morale, but there was no real improvement until the middle of 1944 and that did not last long.

Chatterji's Boards of Management, whose inauguration Bose had approved on his return, were meanwhile hard at work. Their activity in Java and Sumatra was commenced during a five-day visit which Bose made to the two islands in December. The brief tour, crowded with public speeches to as many Indians there as possible and private interviews with the rich, produced about one and a half million guilders in cash and promises. Although this was far short of the official target it was taken as a sign of the health of the League.

Bose was to visit the Andaman in token of possession and to pay a state visit to Siam on his way to Rangoon in January 1944. But before he left Singapore he at last yielded to requests from the I.N.A. that he should interview Mohan Singh and consider his employment. Mohan Singh had been ill for some months and when Bose met him he was still very weak. Yet it was easy to see what he had been and what he might become again. He spoke to Bose of his motives and actions in 1942. Bose was strangely unsympathetic, showing no consciousness that the movement was at all indebted to Mohan Singh and suggesting that he had been undiplomatic and had lost his head. The former leader said he would be glad to serve under Bose if a suitable post were vacant, and there was talk of a position in the League. But Bose left the thing indefinite. There were difficulties; he must not seem to condone what had occurred in 1942. Furthermore, Mohan Singh had a mind of his own, he would not fit easily into Netaji's encourage, and might make trouble if he were restored to power. Bose had him moved to healthier surroundings in Sumatra and improved his amenities, but made no further contract.

On December 29th Bose was received by the Japanese Admiral at Port Blair in the Andaman Islands. He stayed in the former residence of the British Chief Commissioner, received the freedom of Port Blair from its mayor, toured the island's defences, and saw the famous prison where many of India's early revolutionaries served their sentence.

The Admiral, in agreeing to the appointment of an Indian Chief Commissioner, told Bose that for cogent strategic reasons there could be no complete hand over during the war, but that if the Commissioner was prepared to cooperate; some departments of civil administration could be transferred.

A few days later, in Bangkok, Bose told Lieutenant Colonel Loganadhan, another senior officer of the Indian Medical Service, that he was to be Chief Commissioner of Port Blair. Loganadhan took up the appointment on February 22nd. There remained for Bose another triumphal week as the state guest of the Siamese Government, before he faced his task in Burma. The Siamese were at their best, charming, hospitable, generous, eager to do honour to one who, none dared doubt, would soon march invincibly into India. They feted him with full hearts and he savoured a moment of royalty and unmixed confidence which was not to come again.

6

THE SUPREME COMMANDER

For the present, I can offer you nothing except hunger, thirst, privation, forced marches and death. But if you follow me in life and death..... I shall lead you to victory and freedom.[1]

THE decision to launch an offensive in Burma was not finally taken by the Japanese until January 1944. General Mutaguchi, commander of their forces in North Burma since April 1943, had been convinced that Imphal should be attacked when he saw the success of General Wingate's first Chindit Expedition in country he had previously thought impenetrable. His insistence led to planning in the second half of 1943. The objects of such an offensive were to forestall any British invasion of Burma in 1944 and to establish the Japanese defences on the frontier mountains, a stronger line than that of the River Chindwin where they had rested in 1943. The idea would be first to overwhelm the British in Arakan, involving all their reserves in a battle for Chittagong and the gateway to Eastern Bengal. Then, during April, Imphal and Kohima

[1] Speech to the I.N.A., Singapore, July 5th, 1943.

could be mastered at leisure, without danger of their being reinforced. The monsoon would descend in May and end operations. It was not thought that the British could organise new defences east of the River Brahmaputra, so that when the rains ceased, the whole of Assam and East Bengal would lie open to the Japanese. The linked plans were approved in Tokyo during January 1944, and Mutaguchi received his orders in February.

The Indian National Army was to assist these operations in two ways: there was to be an espionage and propaganda group with each Japanese division, and an independent role for the Subhash Regiment. This role was left for Bose to discuss with the Japanese, but the special groups were being formed and trained well before he reached Burma. As reinforcements arrived from Malaya the existing group in Arakan had been built up to a strength of some two hundred and fifty men. For the Imphal attack there were formed three more such units, each with elements from the Bahadur, Intelligence and Reinforcement Groups: these were sent to join their Japanese divisions for training in December 1943.

Bose arrived in Rangoon with the key members of his headquarters and Cabinet on January 7th, 1944. Government reorganisation took him most of January, and as it advanced he discussed with the Japanese Commander-in-Chief, General Kawabe, the coming invasion of India, for already the Subhash Regiment was preparing to move forward.

Kawabe suggested that the Regiment be split up into small parities for attachment to all the Japanese formations taking part, in the manner of the special groups already deployed. Bose was firm. Kawabe did not perhaps know that the performance of the regiment was to be a test of the battle-worthiness of the whole I.N.A. It must therefore retain its identity, he said, and this could not be done if it were used in units smaller than a battalion. Indeed, Bose was anxious that the I.N.A. should be the spearhead of the whole advance into India: 'The first drop of blood to be shed on Indian soil should be that of a member of the I.N.A.'[2]

The Commander-in-Chief told his staff to find tasks on which all three battalions of the Subhash Regiment could be safely left to themselves. But there could be no question of the untried I.N.A. being used as a spearhead. Bose must not delude himself. There were to be three thousand of his soldiers in the offensive; the Japanese strength in Burma was 230,000, his part could hardly be decisive. It is possible that, in offering to split the Regiment over the whole Japanese force, Kawabe thought he was offering more and not less than employment as a unit. But Bose was pacing leagues ahead with the vision of one, then two whole divisions in action, and five more which he would raise from new Indian prisoners. He saw his national flag planted at Imphal, Kohima, even on the banks of the Brahmaputra, and the people of India

[2] Shah Nawaz, My Memories of the I.N.A. and its Netaji p. 75.

welcoming him with open arms. The Subhash Regiment would be his advance guard. On January 24th he accepted two trial roles for it: the First Battalion was to form part of the force opposing the British West-African Division in the Kaladan Valley, while the other two were to relieve a Japanese battalion in the guarding of routes over the Chin Hills.

There were many matters now demanding Bose's attention; the drive for money and recruits to be intensified, civilian camps and schools to be inspected, the propaganda campaign to be renewed. But he spent whole days nevertheless with the Subhash Regiment, reviewing, watching it at exercises and on parade, talking to its officers, exerting his magic on it in a way that he had not attempted before. These were his comrades, the men by whose means he would uphold the rights and honour of India. Everything depended on their achievement in battle; they must absorb all his feeling of confidence, feel the whole of his personal force. On February 3rd he bade them farewell:

> Blood is calling to blood. Arise! We have no time to lose. Take up your arms. There in front of you is the road our pioneers have built. We shall march along that road. We shall carve our way through the enemy's ranks, or, if God wills, we shall die a martyr's death. And in our last sleep we shall kiss the road which will bring our Army to Delhi. The road to Delhi is the road to Freedom. On to Delhi![3]

[3] On to Delhi, cover.

The regiment left for the front during the next three days. Netaji watched the trains move away and could not restrain his tears as the officers took their leave. But the news was good. The offensive in Arakan, launched on February 4th, quickly cut off the 7th Indian Division in the Mayu Valley. Among the reasons for success was the reconnaissance and subversion of an Indian outpost position by Major L. S. Misra, the I.N.A. Commander in Arakan. Bose called this an 'active and important' part in a great Japanese victory.

At about the same time messages were received from Master Chopra's party of spies despatched by submarine in December. This was a further cause of confidence. It was no accident, said Bose to the Japanese, that the first success had come from the agents he had briefed. Secret work must be related to the political situation in India: the essence was the right choice of men and right instruction, and only he could guarantee these. In the face of such dramatic evidence Japanese objection to Bose's control of the spy schools and networks were withdrawn. Bose now asserted his authority in Rangoon and sent Swami to do the same in Penang.

Prisoners of war in Japanese hands often discovered the wisdom of firmness and even obstinacy in dealing with their captors. The Japanese respected courage, and courage they certainly found in Bose. They despised disloyalty, and this was a taint from which the I.N.A., in their eyes, could never free itself. Hence their respect for their leader, and the contempt in which they were to hold the requests and opinions of his military commanders. Bose showed no fear of them and sometimes little respect, indeed his readiness to quarrel with them over the slightest infringement of his rights was one of the pillars of his reputation. His relations with General Isoda, new head of the Hikari Kikan, were full of strife. In April 1944, for instance, the Hikari Kikan printed some propaganda leaflets directed at Indian troops; they were signed by the Japanese commanders in the areas for which they were intended, and were never shown to Bose. The same sort of leaflet had been used in 1943, but when Bose saw these he treated Isoda to such a flow of invective that the General was never wholly at ease with him again.

It was many months before Bose knew that the Arakan battle had ended in shattering defeat for the Japanese, and his militant mood remained. During March, and the 2nd and 3rd Regiments of the 1st Division prepared for their progress to Imphal, he again strove by speeches, inspections and personal contact to foster morale and heighten confidence. The move northwards from Rangoon began at the end of March. Once more there were farewell speeches: Major Misra was recalled from Arakan to tell the men of I.N.A. successes, to receive from Bose a decoration for gallantry and to join in the leave-taking as the troop trains began their long journey to Mandalay. But there was less emotion. Japanese offensive was going well and nobody expected that these men would have to fight. They were to line the route at Bose's entry into Imphal and assist in the formation of the new divisions there.

The other task waiting at Imphal was the establishment of civil government. None of the men trained at the Reconstruction College in Singapore had yet reached Burma, for Bose had not thought that they would be required until he was in Imphal, but when he saw General Mutaguchi in Maymyo on March 1st, he learnt that there would be no Japanese Military Administration in the areas of India about to be entered and that some responsibility would fall on him immediately. The General asked for a civil affairs group to move forward on March 8th when the Imphal offensive was to be launched. Bose thus found himself compelled to raise hurriedly in Rangoon the nucleus of a service which he had intended to staff gradually with trained men. Nor was his Civil Governor available. He sent for Chatterji who arrived in haste on March 16th to find himself 'Chief Administrator of Occupied Territories'.

Bose envisaged two phases of civil administration. First there were to go on the heels of the military advance sections of his Azad Hind Dal, the Free India Party, which were to perform urgent tasks such as the handling of refugees, the feeding of newly occupied areas, the restoration of essential public services, the maintenance of law and order and reconciliation of the Indian population. Then, as soon as an area ceased to be operational, a provisional provincial administration would take over, and this would last until the future government of Free India was settled.

Before the revival of democracy the Azad Hind Dal would have assumed its true function in India, to exert 'the leadership of a political party which is clear as to the principles of revolution'.[4] This was the party with the 'clear ideology, programme and plan of action' with which Bose saw the future to lie when he wrote *The Indian Struggle*. He gave it a code of discipline, ranks and a distinctive uniform. Like the Indian National Congress it would base its political strength on social service and relief work, things which would demand workers of skill, experience and integrity. It was thus more than unfortunate that it should have to be formed in a hurry. Bose recruited anyone he could find to form the team of about seventy which left for Maymyo on March 8th.

Japanese troops and I.N.A. irregulars crossed the Indian frontier on March 19th. Two days later Tojo stated in the Diet that the Provisional Government would administer occupied Indian territory. For his part, Bose issued a call to the Indian people to cooperate with the invaders and prepared proclamations as Supreme Commander and as Head of State. Then, on March 24th, together with General Kawabe, he attended a full conference between the Provisional Government and the Japanese Army on the problems of the occupation. Discussion soon centered on the chairmanship of the joint Indo-Japanese labour and

---

[4] Speech to cadets at Rangoon.

supplies boards through which Japanese were to obtain their requirements after Bose's administrations took over. It was a stormy meeting. Bose would not agree to Japanese chairmen and the point was never settled.

In fact the Japanese certainly intended to control India as effectively as they already controlled Burma; such an aim was essential if they meant to continue the war. The Dal found in Maymyo Japanese economic missions preparing to go to India, and some of its leaders saw a document in which the Japanese purpose was quite plain. Bose was told, but as always he refused to worry about Japanese intentions in India, counting on the I.N.A. and his own political influence to check their designs.

On April 7th 1944, the Imphal campaign being fairly launched and his own troops either involved in it or moving towards the front, Bose took a small headquarters to the little hill town in Maymyo near Mandalay. The fall of Imphal was expected in three weeks at the most. There his work would begin: first civil government, then the direction of a new campaign at the head of a vastly expanded I.N.A. This would be the climax of his whole life: the work would be endless, the strain greater than the greatest he had known. It was good therefore to escape for a time from the surging militance of torrid Rangoon, into coolness and peace.

He had little cause to feel dissatisfied with the way in which the Indian communities had responded so far to the demands of action. Even the Azad Hind Dal, hastily prepared and hurried to the front, looked as if it might do what was required of it. Low morale and bewilderment would be removed by victory, he could set all right at Imphal. There had been one blow. Just before leaving Rangoon he had dismissed Colonel N. S. Bhagat[5] from the command of the 2nd Division in Malaya for insubordination and disloyalty. From his first association with it Bhagat had been unhappy about the I.N.A. Drafted early to a Japanese labour camp in the South-West Pacific, he had been recalled to help Mohan Singh and had eventually consented to do so in the hope that he might be able to restrain him. He had remained in the Second I.N.A., hoping again to exert a moderating influence. Bose gave him the task of raising the 2nd Division and had him watched. In April he was called to Rangoon and handed a letter. You have been disloyal and defiant, said Bose, your conduct cannot be overlooked. Bhagat remained in protective custody until liberated by the Indian Army.

This disappointment was incidental; there had been many achievements; Bose had just declared the Legion in Europe to be part of the I.N.A., had appointed Nambiar to be a Minister in the Provisional Government: his Chief Commissioner had been installed in the Andamans; his first heroes from Arakan had been decorated; his troops were on Indian soil. Now Imphal seemed very near. In Maymyo Bose made his proclamation to Indians in

---

[5] His Indian Army rank had been Major.

liberated territory. 'The Provisional Government of Azad Hind is the only lawful Government of the Indian people. The Provisional Government calls upon the Indian people.... to render all assistance and cooperation to the Indian National Army and to the civilian officials appointment by the Provisional Government.[6] The Government guaranteed the safety of Indian life and property, but would severely punish those who collaborated with the British or hampered its work. Let the Indian people cooperate also with the Japanese Army, the trusted ally of the Provisional Government,' he said, ... and thereby help in preserving and safeguarding your newly-won liberty.'

Chatterji's provisional administration of occupied territory, the draft laws and ordinances, the proposed appointments, were now checked over. These appointments were important because Bose intended the officials of the provincial administration to graduate to provincial governorships as he moved on into India. All was drafted in great detail. Japanese banks would not operate. Bose had set up his own, the Azad Hind Bank, to handle his currency and other financial problems. Government departments were named, relations between the Provisional Government and successive provincial governments defined and the district and village administrations described. Provisional government stamps were being

[6] Azad Hind Gazette, No. 2, dated April 30th, 1944: Appendix II (5).

printed, simple banknotes would soon be ready. Lieutenant-Colonel Chatterji had worked hard, and with the best available Indian and Japanese advice. In Maymyo also, Bose held public meetings, telling the audiences of the little hill station about the Indian struggle, about total mobilisation and of his purposes now. On April 21st he announced to such a meeting the capture of Kohima by 'Indo-Nipponese' forces.

Operational news of this kind he received from Mutaguchi and his staff who were still in Maymyo. Mutaguchi was completely confident and not at all worried by the great distance which now separated him from the battlefield. The Commander had launched his army and saw no need for a personal grasp of the battle, which was going well. 'My officers do everything,' he said to a visitor who caught him in his garden. 'I just tend my roses.' Bose had urged him, in an earlier discussion of the campaign, not to cut the Imphal-Kohima road. If the escape route remained open, the British would withdraw as they had always done. But no, to Mutaguchi Imphal was a lake in which there lay fish. 'I intend,' he said, 'to net it.'

This confidence was echoed everywhere. The fall of Imphal was a foregone conclusion. All were convinced of Japanese victory. The League in Maymyo staged satires on the desperate situation of the British-Indian Army, and Indian audiences laughed while bulletins such as this were put into the mouths of British officials:

> The Japanese have retained the initiative in their advance through Manipur. The I.N.A. troops are advancing up the Kaladan and have occupied Paletwa, Tiddim, Tongzang, Palam and Fort White have fallen into the enemy's hands. Our 17th Division is in full retreat. The road Imphal-Silchar has been cut. The situation is serious but not critical.

But the time was coming when General Mutaguchi was to admit that the fish in the Imphal lake was a crocodile which had broken his net. As April wore on it became clear that the 2nd and 3rd I.N.A. Regiments would see action before they entered Imphal. Bose was glad of this, it would increase his stake in Japanese victory. Then on April 25th, just before the Japanese Army Headquarters[7] moved to the front, Mutaguchi admitted that there had been a hitch. By now Bose, also, had received reports from the battlefield. Colonel M. Z. Kiani the I.N.A. Divisional Commander, wrote from his headquarters some thirty-five miles from Imphal, pleading that, since the whole of his Division was now going into action the 1st (Subhash) Regiment should rejoin it. Shah Nawaz, commanding two battalions of the Subhash Regiment in the Chin Hills, told of the hardships his men were suffering. The ground was difficult, rations were poor and scanty, there was much malaria and no medicine, there were no pack animals and half the men

[7] A Japanese Army was equivalent to a British Corps. General Mutaguchi had three divisions under his command in N. W. Burma.

were being used as porters on the long mountainous communication line. Bose put these matters to Mutaguchi, who confessed that severe supply and transport difficulties were affecting his whole force. But he promised to let the Subhash Regiment join Kiani on the main Imphal front as soon as possible.

It was to be many months before there came to Bose any realisation of disaster. With the Japanese Army Commander no longer in Maymyo, Netaji found it difficult to communicate with his troops, much less to further their requests. He was not without means of his own to remedy the shortage of supplies. A Supply Board was set up by the League in Rangoon to obtain what was needed, and the Supply Minister, Lieutenant-Colonel Alagappan, was told to provide the I.N.A. with local produce through the League Headquarters in Mandalay. Then, in mid-May, Bose sent Chatterji, Alagappan and A. M. Sahay, his Government Secretary, to Tamu, partly in order that they might be at hand when Imphal was entered and in any case to buy up supplies, relieve I.N.A. difficulties and bring back an accurate report. But this report did not reach him until the end of June.

Meanwhile the monsoon had broken. On May 21st Bose returned to Rangoon where he could at least obtain news of the front – he could fly almost as quickly to Imphal from there in the eleven-seater aircraft, *Azad Hind*, which the Japanese had just given him, as from Maymyo. Besides, he must explain to the League the delay in operations, and use the tension of the moment to obtain even more support in recruits and money for the I.N.A.

Rangoon was still full of confidence. Young Indians anxious to be present in the still imminent hour of triumph – or for less dramatic economic reasons — continued to flock to the training centers. On May 29th Bose collected some five million rupees' worth of cash and valuables at a public meeting. One merchant was so moved that he gave his entire property; from many others Bose accepted humble donations of a necklace, gold earrings or a few rupees. The Zeyawaddy Sugar Estate, near Toungoo, owned by an Indian firm, was handed over to him by its manager: Bose regarded it thereafter as part of Free India and its profits as Provisional Government Revenue. It was all sorely needed. The I.N.A. in Burma now cost two million rupees per month, the estimated cost of reconstruction in the occupied territories was rising and the value of the Japanese Rupee falling fast. Thus more and more money had to be raised. Bose had recently induced Mr. N. Raghavan, a leading member of the old Council of Action, to enter the Cabinet, and he now made him Finance Minister.

Besides going through six weeks' accumulated business, reviewing the troops most recently arrived from Malaya, and watching the 4th I.N.A. Regiment leaving Rangoon, Bose dealt personally with the case of a Tamil recruit at one of the Rangoon schools who had died after field punishment. There was clear evidence of high handedness and cruelty. Bose presided at the Court of Inquiry exonerated the Medical Officer, reprimanded and removed the Commandent. The affair worried him; he had been careful to prevent any recurrence of the forceful persuasion of Mohan Singh's regime and this was the sort of incident that he could not afford. He made a thorough inspection of all the Rangoon schools to reassure himself.

It was also primarily for a matter of discipline that he flew to Singapore early in June. At the end of March a party of agents who had once belonged to a Muslim Spy School in Penang, now disbanded, had surrendered in India and broadcast from Delhi. The men had been despatched by submarine after training under Japanese arrangements and it was quite clear that their only motive had been escape. During the Japanese security investigation in Penang, it came to light that Captain Durrani, a former officer of the School, had been on leave in Penang while his old pupils were under training there. The Japanese strongly suspected a connection. The truth was that Durrani not only instructed the men to surrender, but gave them intelligence to pass on to the authorities in India. He had been arrested for interrogation but had given nothing away.

In Rangoon Bose received a short report on the case from Swami and decided to make his own enquiries. He took no responsibility for the incident because Swami had been refused access to the party before it had sailed, but he soon assured himself of Durrani's guilt. In cold rage he confronted him at a secret midnight arraignment in the

Bidadari Concentration Camp. Durrani, who had suffered ten days of Japanese third degree, was weak and dazed. Bose would take no denial. 'You should be grateful to me,' he said, 'that I have saved you from the Japanese firing squad, and that you will be shot by Indians. Of this such as you should be proud.' Durrani protested his innocence and was taken out by senior I.N.A. officers who did their best to extract a confession. There was a second interview at which Bose said that a confession would be obtained before Durrani's execution, by one means or another.

Further efforts were made next day when Bose had gone; there were long interrogations which gradually moved towards torture. The 'finger pressers' and the hideous "water treatment" were administered at least four times, until the victim was in an almost continuous state of collapse. For his part in the escape and his fortitude afterwards, Durrani was awarded the George Cross in 1946. It can be accepted that Bose did not specifically sanction torture, but the thought of treachery could rob him of all control and of any concern for one he believed guilty of it. He cannot escape responsibility for what happened to Captain Durrani.

Bose may have had less to do with another matter of discipline which had come to a head about a month earlier. On April 22nd, Mr. K. P. K. Menon, who had taken no part in League affairs since his resignation from the Council of Action in December 1942, was arrested by the Japanese Security Police. Menon's stalwart attitude towards the

Japanese, whom he distrusted, and towards Bose whom he suspected and despised, was well-known; the bitter remarks which he freely uttered about both had circulated widely. 'You say Bose is a man of action,' he once said, 'so is my pet ape; man of action indeed, he acts first and thinks afterwards.' He particularly abominated Bose's belief in dictatorship for India: 'Netaji?' he cried –'Netaji!' (ne'er do well).

Such behaviour was intolerable both to the Japanese and to Bose. Menon, a man of sixty, was interrogated over a period of two months, and sentenced by a military court to six years' rigorous imprisonment for lack of faith in Japan and for calling Bose a Fascist dictator. Bose absolutely refused to intervene.

While he was in Malaya, Bose received a report from Swami on the spy schools in Penang, and reviewed the League and I.N.A. organisation. The boards of Management were working well; the campaign for recruits, funds and League membership was continuous. But in comparison with Burma results had been poor. Bose sent for all League chairmen in Malaya, Java and Sumatra and for some of the richer merchants, and obtained thirteen million dollars in cash and promises. He warned the 2nd Division, now in the North Malayan Training Camps, for a move to Burma in July and August, and visited the 3rd Division being formed at Johore. The Divisional Commander told him that he despaired of ever turning Tamil labourers into soldiers. Bose turned on him.

The quality of the leadership, he said, was the main factor. Good officers would succeed: let them see to it. He inspected the troops on training, telling them that the Division would be fighting in Burma by the end of the year.

The Penang Spy Schools had at last been grouped together under Indian control. In May Swami had despatched a party of his own planning to South India and had arranged with the Japanese Navy for others to be sent as submarines were available. But Bose was now thinking of direct access from Imphal: the problem of working up revolution in India would be far more immediate and the opportunity better than ever before. He took Swami with him when he returned to Burma on June 29th.

There the Imphal campaign still seemed to be going well, if somewhat more slowly than had been anticipated. News was slow to reach Rangoon. On June 16th I.N.A. Headquarters had replied to requests sent by Kiani from the front in mid-May. But the 1st Division had been in action and there was great optimism. Everyone had been 'thrilled to read about the bold action of the 2nd Guerrilla Regiment from April 24th to May 6th'[8]. The Japanese in Rangoon spoke highly of the I.N.A. in battle and there were other reports of Kiani's leadership and of the wonderful work of his men. Sahay had returned from the front and told of Japanese enthusiasm for the 2nd

---

[8] The attempted attack on Patel airfield, see Appendix III.

Guerrilla Regiment. He said less of the crucial administrative difficulties which had been seen even in May, and Chatterji, who had dealt with some of them, was lying sick in Maymyo. Even on July 10th, when Bose was told that the Japanese were abandoning their Imphal campaign, he seems to have had no inkling of the magnitude of its disaster.

So, to begin with, everything in Rangoon was again triumphal and, as the rains poured down, flooding away ever more certainly Japanese chances of success, the League celebrated Netaji Week and Bose contemplated a government reorganisation on the continuing assumption of victory. This was the League and Bose himself at the peak of their prestige, confidence and eloquence. A death sentence imposed by an I.N.A. court martial was commuted to imprisonment, there were Government Receptions, a message of congratulation from the Foreign Minister of Burma, Thakin Nu, an investiture at which Bose pinned his highest award for bravery on to the tunic of a disabled Sikh officer, an I.N.A. parade at the tomb of Bahadur Shah, last of the Moghals, and numberless League ceremonies.

Bose issued a statement on the year's progress. What had been achieved was far more than he had expected, the financial objective of a year ago had been reached and only training facilities limited the intake of recruits. But there could be no relaxation, the fight must go on, reinforcements and supplies must be sent to the front, total mobilisation must be hastened. Some problems would now require more attention, the creation of the revolution in India, propaganda to the Indian Army and administrative backing for the I.N.A. In particular the administrative task was developing. To deal with it the Cabinet would be divided into three committees, one for each of the three spheres of activity – the base in East Asia, the liberated areas, and British-occupied India. Base organisation was most important. A new Ministry of Manpower, to coordinate recruitment and training, would share the burden with the recently established Supplies Ministry, the Finance Ministry and the new Revenue Ministry.

The anniversary was also marked by carefully worded broadcasts on the war situation and the situation in India[9]. The Allied invasion of Europe did not disturb Bose any more than American success in the Pacific. The march to Delhi might take two more years, but he had no doubt 'that we shall be able to liberate India' provided that there were no compromise between Mr. Gandhi and the British, which he admitted would make his task as liberator much more difficult. He despised Allied propaganda, scorned its tow agents the '*B*luff and *B*luster *C*orporation' and the '*A*nti-*In*dia *R*adio', and refuted arguments and statements which he said they had made about him. Their propaganda was false, he had redeemed all he had promised. 'India shall

[9] The speeches and statements of this week were collected under the title Blood Bath, from which the extracts on this and following pages are taken.

be free this time'; he had the strength and organisation to accomplish it, strength which came, not from superior rations and equipment, but faith and sacrifice, heroism and fortitude. When she was free,

> all those who are now in the service of the British Government and are efficient in their work will be taken over by the new Government ... provided they were not pro-British at heart, and ... had not gone out of their way to harm the independence movement.

Soldiers of the Indian Army would be received on the same terms, and their Indian Army service would be allowed to count for their I.N.A. pensions. Let the British now accept the 'Quit India' resolution and give effect to it and 'I guarantee that not a single Japanese soldier will set foot on Indian soil'. Yet:

> The British who spilt the blood of innocent freedom-loving Indians and tortured them inhumanly ... must pay for their crimes. We Indians do not hate the enemy enough. If you want your countrymen to rise to heights of superhuman courage and heroism – you must teach them – not only to love their country – but also to hate their enemy.

The ringing, confident tone is absent, however, in the message Bose broadcast on July 6th to Mr. Gandhi, newly released from prison in India. Here he is once more full of defence, apologetic and anxious to convince: 'I can assure you, Mahatmaji,' he said, 'that before I finally decided to set out on a hazardous mission I spent days, weeks and months in carefully considering the pros and cons of the case.' There could be no justification for calling him a traitor: he had risked all in leaving India, and he had done so for his belief that Indian nationalism must have outside help. His record surely proved his sincerity and good faith. He had nothing to gain from the Axis: he had already obtained in India the highest distinction that could be offered to him. Nor was he a simpleton to be deceived: he had not and would not give anything away of India's interests and honour.

The change of heart in Japan he had seen with his own eyes: 'an Asiatic consciousness' had seized the souls of her people and her present policy towards Asia was 'rooted in sincerity'. As for the Provisional government:

> Once our enemies are expelled from India and peace and order are established, the mission of the Provisional Government will be over. It will then be for the Indian people themselves to determine the form of Government that they choose and also to decide as to who should take charge of that Government.

The Provisional Government was the servant of the Indian People, as he was and all his fellow-workers, and it would have no demands to make for itself: 'There are many among us who would like to retire from the political field ....' Meanwhile, until in one way or another the British quitted India, the fight would go on. It would inevitably end in 'Our Victory'.

By this Bose no longer necessarily meant the victory of Japan or of the Axis. His triumph would be the expulsion of the British from India, and that he would share with Mr. Gandhi and the Indian people. All he now hoped for from Japan was time, two years of time, for that end to be accomplished by the I.N.A. and her forces in Burma. After it, whatever the outcome of the war, at least the British could never re-establish themselves in India. He began to envisage in fact the sort of situation that developed in 1946 in Indonesia, where it proved impossible to oust a nationalist government set up with Japanese assistance before the Allies could occupy the country.

No uncertainty about Japan's victory would have been voiced in Rangoon. It would in any case have been bad for I.N.A. morale, and Bose was seeking to raise the confidence of his following. During Netaji Week every possible spectacle was staged for the Indian community of the Burmese capital. The investiture had been a moment of emotion: 'By honouring such a brave officer,' he had said, 'I am honouring myself, my Army and my Government.' Then, on July 10th, there was a public recognition of the 'new comrades,' the soldiers – fewer than a hundred – who had been captured from the Indian Army in recent fighting. Public confidence was sustained somehow through July. All was activity: recruits and money, he claimed, were pouring in. He introduced a special title, 'Sewek-e-Hind,' for those who donated their whole property, and conferred it on several in Rangoon.

While he must have realised by now that the Imphal campaign had failed. Bose did not yet understand that it had turned into a military catastrophe of the first magnitude. Letters from the front, sent under the Japanese eye, could give no hint of this. Chatterji's report revealed serious administrative difficulties which had existed in May, but there was reasonable hope that these had been remedied by the Rear Headquarters of the 1st Division which had been at work when he left the forward areas. The trouble had been that when the Japanese called the 1st Division to the front, they had already outrun their administrative plan, which was based on the capture of 'Churchill rations' by mid-April. Provision for the I.N.A. thus had to be improvised by a Japanese Administrative Service already unable to supply two of its own three divisions. In consequence, rations, transport and ammunition for essential fire support were lacking. The Hikari Kikan became, not a vehicle of supplies but a purveyor of excuses: too often it actually diverted to the Japanese material intended for the I.N.A. Chatterji did what he could to set things right laying out some £50,000 in local purchases. He recommended to Bose that the Hikari Kikan be abolished, that supply and transport difficulties be referred immediately to as high a level as possible and that the I.N.A. undertake far more of its own administration in future.

But no remedy could any longer affect the Imphal campaign. The decision to suspend it was made public on July 26th, the day of Tojo's resignation for another cause. August saw the full horror of disaster. The Indian Army following up the Japanese retreat met 'pitiful, starving and utterly demoralised I.N.A. soldiers, crawling up to our troops to point out others of their comrades too weak to move. With the hundreds of bodies of Japanese dead'[10] were found many of the I.N.A. who had died of starvation. On August 12th there came to Bose from mandalay requests for food, clothing, blankets and boots. The messenger had seen some of the survivors, and his account made Bose realise for the first time that general disaster had overtaken his 1st Division. He was appalled: his whole energy was at once thrown into the work of salvage. Already the I.N.A. in North Burma had set up staging camps, medical and rest centres and a meagre transport service. Now all spare stores and supplies were sent from Rangoon, vehicles were collected, clothing and boots procured and a new emergency hospital formed. Bose sent his own medical officer with all the other doctors who could be spared. On August 19th there came a pathetic appeal from – Colonel Kiani that he should intervene with the Japanese to save hundreds of sick men stranded by

[10] Fourteenth Army report.

floods on the withdrawal route. Bose was helpless, for the Japanese in Rangoon were equally out of touch with the situation and could do nothing.

Bose did not yet leave Rangoon himself: there must be no appearance of precipitancy, the Japanese would allow no admission of what had occurred nor must the Indian public suspect. In his Special Order of the Day on August 14th,[11] he talked only of the suspension of the campaign and of a tactical withdrawal. The British forces had been better equipped, but 'we defeated them in every battle. Our units with their better training and discipline...soon established their superiority over the enemy, whose moral deteriorated with each defeat.' The courage of his I.N.A. heroes had earned the praise of all and was a sure basis of confidence. The British at Imphal had only just been saved by the rains, but they would surely succumb when, with better weather, the new mighty offensive was launched. At the same time there were rewards for those who had done their duty.[12]. On August 28th Bose announced a new decoration for those who killed or captured British soldiers. He held an investiture on September 8th of some of the decorations announced in April and July, and proclaimed September 21st as 'Martyrs' Day' in memory of some of the 1943 parachute agents executed in India.

---

[11] Appendix II, No. 6.

[12] Fifteen awards, including posthumous promotions, had already been announced; twenty-four more were published in October and sixteen in November; thirty-three more awards were made in 1945.

This was all for the public. In private Bose did not disguise his anger at the behaviour of the I.N.A. He knew that there had been hundreds of desertions and blamed the leaders. Early in September he delivered a bitter, scathing address to all I.N.A. officers in Rangoon. It was the loose conduct, luxury and corruption of the officers, he said, that had been responsible for the state of morale in which desertions were possible. The disaster had been a clear failure of leadership. He upbraided them for placing their own comfort before that of their men, for peculation and treachery, demanded repeatedly that any officer who did not want to fight should leave the I.N.A. at once, and dismissed them after two hours of angry words.

Bose may well have been right in asserting that the general standard of his officers was low, but to attribute to them so large a share of blame for the Imphal disaster was to over-simplify, to forget their origin and the manner of their training. Those of the rank of battalion commander and above had formerly been officers of the Indian Army: some of them, the most senior, were pre-war graduates of the Indian Military Academy, one had been to Sandhurst. But few of the platoon and company officers in the 1st I.N.A. Division had been trained as officers at all: most of them had been promoted direct from the ranks by Mohan Singh. A very few had received a three-month course at the I.N.A. Officers' Training School, where instruction was based, apart from minor Japanese help, on the British training manuals of 1940 and 1941. What quality of leadership could be expected of officers such as these in the battles of 1944?

Of this Bose took little account: rather it was anger and a puzzled sense of personal failure that were uppermost in his mind as he learnt more and more about the campaign. He had put forth his whole spirit to inspire these soldiers, but it had not been enough. Of the six thousand men he had sent to the Imphal front, at least 1,500 had deserted or been captured. The effect of the I.N.A. on Indian Army morale, on which he had counted heavily, had been insignificant. What was the answer to this problem of faith and fighting spirit? His Second Division was now gathering in Burma: would it have the same tale to tell? He talked to some of its officers at dinner one night. What did they think, he asked, should every soldier be told to shoot any man he thought was going to desert, regardless of rank? No, they said, such an order would be open to misinterpretation: let the causes of desertion rather be established and removed. Bose thought he knew the causes - the Japanese failure to supply and maintain the I.N.A., their failure to cooperate in battle, and above all his officers' failure to inculcate in training the right nationalist fervour and will to fight. Perhaps he too had failed in not insisting that the Japanese allow him to the front: he would see that they did not deny him this again.

In such a mood, bitter against the Japanese, sorrowfully disappointed with his Army, discontented with his own part, he set out on September 18th for North Burma and at last began to see for himself. He met all the Indian commanders and such of the Japanese as had not already been replaced. He visited the I.N.A. camps and hospitals where four-fifths of the survivors were detained. Everywhere he saw suffering and heard pitiful tales of the retreat: everywhere, too, his presence was welcomed, for there was about this dedicated man an awe and a passionate sincerity which could inspire devotion and love.

7

DEFEAT IN BURMA

The story of the I.N.A. in the Japanese campaign of 1944 is long, intricate and closely interwoven with the actions of the Japanese regiments and divisions with which its soldiers campaigned. That story will one day be told. But although he followed it as well as Japanese Intelligence would allow, Bose had very little part in it and the barest outline will suffice here.

The Japanese employed three divisions in the Imphal offensive, rather more than one in the linked operation in Arakan. With each of the Imphal Division there were one hundred and fifty to two hundred irregulars of the I.N.A. special groups, organised in small parties to act as guides, interpreters, propagandists and spies, as the invaders probed forward through the vast, mountainous jungle. The force in Arakan had a similar group of about two hundred and fifty. These parties were of some nuisance value to the Japanese, shouting propaganda or confusing orders in encounters with British-Indian troops, leading them sometimes into Japanese ambushes and spying out their defence positions. On four occasions propaganda played some part in the capture of bodies of Indian soldiers, bodies of never more than platoon strength. One such incident, the subversion of an outspot platoon of the Gwalior Lancers in Arakan, may have contributed to the initial surprise achieved there by the Japanese. There were also atrocities: at Lamtong on about March 19th, a prisoner was bayoneted to death by two Indians under Japanese instructions. There was nothing else. For the most part the I.N.A. agents did what was expected of them when under the Japanese eye, but deserted as soon as there was a reasonable chance of escape.

The exploits of the I.N.A. regiments were more varied. Three were involved, the 1st (Subhash) Regiment with a strength of about three thousand men, the 2nd and 3rd Regiments each two thousand strong. One battalion of the 1st Regiment reached the Kaladan Valley on March 24th, as the 81st West African Division was withdrawing, and suffered a few casualties in two or three days of skirmishing with the rearguards. It remained there intact, without further encounter, until September, posting a company at Mowdok in the Sangu Valley, on Indian soil, during the monsoon.

The other two battalions, under Shah Nawaz and his Regimental Headquarters, maintained up to two companies in the Chin Hill Villages, Haka and Falam, from the beginning of March. There were three or four clashes with the British-led Chin Levies and one small expedition to capture a British patrol-base, before the monsoon broke. At the end of May six companies, by then reduced to about half-strength, were taken to reinforce the Japanese at Kohima. None of them reached Kohima: only Shah Nawaz and a few of his staff went further than Ukhrul, and then only for reconnaissance.

The 2nd and 3rd regiments, under the I.N.A. Divisional Commander, were in action on the left and right flanks respectively of the Japanese force on the Tamu-Palel road, during May, June and July. The 2nd Regiment was sharply defeated in the first action it undertook, an attempt to attack the Palel airfield; it remained thereafter on the defensive, slowly wasted away by battle, disease, desertion and starvation until, when withdrawal began, scarcely six hundred of its men remained. The 3rd Regiment did not reach the front until the end of May when the rains had begun. It saw little action, but suffered as much as did the 2nd Regiment from disease and starvation. A fuller account of the career of these two regiments will be found in Appendix II, *Yamamoto Force and the 1st I.N.A. Division.*

Shah Nawaz ordered the withdrawal of his force from Ukhrul on June 20th, with the idea of joining the rest of the division, but he was involved in a disaster which put such action beyond him. Even on June 4th the Japanese had been calling his regiment "Malaria Unit": now things were much worse:

> By this time all administration services had completely broken down. Doctors had no medicines left to treat anyone and most... were themselves suffering from malaria and dysentery.[1]

Millions of huge flies feasted on the dead. Rations ran out completely: even at Tamu and Kalewa the men continued to starve to death. About four hundred sick were carried to Teraun on the Yu River and left to await water transport, the marchers went on, but it was a month before all the sick could be collected and by then two hundred had died. Only five hundred out of the two thousand men he had taken to the Chin Hills in February remained with Shah Nawaz when he reached safety on September 8th.

The I.N.A. Divisional Commander ordered his regiments to withdraw on July 18th. The appalling conditions in which the Japanese retreated are well known. Although fifty thousand of their men, more than half the total force, lay dead, they were still a fighting force. But the I.N.A. had little cohesion left and it was shown scant sympathy, instead of 'Comrade Indian,' the Japanese mode of address became 'Oh Shameless Indian'. Relations deteriorated fast. The Indians stole without scruple from Japanese stocks, and on at least one occasion the Japanese bayoneted to death I.N.A. soldiers as enemy spies. Nearly all were unfit when they started to withdraw: throughout the march disease and starvation took their daily toll.

---

[1] Shah Nawaz, *My Memories of the I.N.A. and It's Netaji'* p.106.

The full account of dead and missing could not be compiled until the regiments were at rest stations in September and October. It made sorry reading. The I.N.A. Division had started out for Imphal six thousand strong; only two thousand six hundred returned, and of these about two thousand had to be sent at once to hospital. During the campaign 715 men deserted, about four hundred were killed in battle, about eight hundred surrendered, about fifteen hundred died of disease and starvation.[2]

All this and more Bose came to know as he motored through the steamy, waterlogged plains of Upper Burma in September, 1944 visiting the hospitals and rest camps from Mandalay to the Chindwin. Even the sympathetic Fujihara, who spent the campaign as General Mutaguchi's liaison officer with the Japanese force of which the I.N.A. Division was a part, was disappointed. 'As a revolutionary Army', he says, 'its morale was high and it was quite well organised; but the standard of its tactics, training and leadership was low.... It lacked, in particular, offensive strength and tenacity.' He does not mention equipment, but it lacked that too. The I.N.A. in action had no wireless sets, no telephones, no transport, no weapons heavier than light machine guns. Its soldiers wore old British Khaki uniforms in which they were easily distinguishable from the Japanese and British-Indians, who were inconspicuous jungle green. Nevertheless, Fujihara concedes something:

[2] Official figures given by G.H.Q., New Delhi, in 1945-46.

the 2nd and 3rd I.N.A. Regiments did assist the Japanese force to hold out on the Palel road at a time when its collapse would have been very serious. That is the most that can be said. To Bose, the I.N.A. performance brought shattering disillusion. He had failed not only to turn his men into heroes, but also to disturb the loyalty of the Indian Army. Field-Marshall Slim has told how the Indian reception of I.N.A. deserters was so hostile that orders had to be issued in Fourteenth Army for them to be welcomed more kindly. The axiom of Indian Army demoralisation had vanished; the dream of an I.N.A. standing 300,000 strong on the banks of the Brahmaputra was ended.

There were other lessons. First, the Azad Hind Dal, instead of a *corps d'elite* of independence workers, was a scratch collection of artisans of no standing at all. This would not do. The Dal, said Bose, 'will be organised on the lines of the S.S. Party in Germany, or the Communist Party in Russia'. He ordered its purging and redirection to start at once. Second, it was no good relying on the Japanese for supplies or artillery support in battle. The regimental commanders said that the Japanese had betrayed them. Bose saw the matter more clearly. His army had been involved in a general failure of Japanese administration and supply. The impotence of the Hikari Kikan and the embitterment of its relations with his commanders was the inevitable consequence. There had been no rations for it to obtain. There was not a gun uncommitted or a round of ammunition to spare by the time the I.N.A. arrived. The Hikari Kikan could not admit this without loss of face and so kept putting off the I.N.A. commanders to the point of crisis. Bose resolved to take care of these matters in future himself and to eliminate the Hikari Kikan as an authority between th I.N.A. and the Japanese commanders. He would form a 'War Council' to organise military administration and to negotiate with the Japanese higher staffs.

At this point, on October 9th, there came an invitation from the new Japanese Premier, General Koiso, for Bose and Dr. Ba Maw to visit him in Tokyo. Bose returned to Rangoon and, on October 14th, held a conference of his regimental commanders to discuss the case against the Hikari Kikan. He hoped at first to take these officers with him, but this proved impossible. Having inaugurated his War Council of Eleven officers, he left for Tokyo on October 29th with Chatterji and Kiani: between them these two could present a graphic case against the Hikari Kikan.

Again Bose found the Japanese authorities in Tokyo sympathetic, and became convinced that I.N.A. difficulties in the field were not of their making. It was racial and military arrogance at lower levels that had been the cause, and he might have dealt with it if, Like Dr. Ba Maw, he had access to Tokyo through a Japanese ambassador. In addition, therefore, to his proposal on I.N.A supplies and fire support in battle, he asked for the establishment of diplomatic relations between Japan and the Provisional Government. Japanese agreement to this was announced on

November 26th: the Ambassador, Mr Hachiya, was nominated at the end of December.

The Japanese also accepted that the function of the Hikari Kikan should be reduced to simple military liaison. Political matters would be the concern of the Japanese Ambassador to the Provisional Government and military orders would come from the Japanese military commanders direct. From this stemmed other agreements: the I.N.A. would not be subject to the Japanese military code of law, but to its own, even in respect of offences against the Japanese Army. There was a clear understanding too on its strength. Bose's army now numbered about 33,000, some 16,900 in Burma, 13,750 in Malaya and 2,000 staffing the recruit training camps, whose capacity was 15,000. The Japanese accordingly agreed to strengths of 35,000 under arms, for whom they would pay and 15,000 in training, for whom Bose would continue to provide.

The supply system was to be considerably changed. Hitherto all supplies had come from the Japanese; although the I.N.A. had undertaken distribution. In future only the staple rations – rice, sugar, *dhal* – were to come from the Japanese: Bose's supply organisation would provide the meat, fish and vegetables. For this the Japanese undertook to pay him ten million rupees per month from March 1945. So rapidly was the value of the Japanese rupee falling – in the frontier areas of Burma the exchange rate with Indian rupees was already twenty to one – that even this vast subsidy had to be doubled by the time the first payment was due.

The speeches which Bose made in Tokyo at this time[3] gave little indication that there was a darker side to his official conversations. His broadcast addresses to the peoples of India, China and U.S.A.; but it is only in the last of these, and in a long speech at Tokyo University, that any feeling of approaching disaster can be discerned. To India, he spoke of his visit as a means of strengthening Indo-Japanese cooperation at a critical time, and of the coming offensive in Burma: to China he spoke again of Japan's change of heart since 1937: to Japan herself of his will to fight on in the common struggle and of the solidarity which now existed between him and the Japanese nation. 'You can rest assured we will be with you in fair weather and in foul...' Nothing of this was new, these were the propaganda phrases he had used hundreds of times. But to the U.S.A. he addressed a serious defence of himself and of the new Asian nationalism that was being fostered by Japan. We are making for ourselves with Japanese help, he said, what you failed to help us achieve before the war; real national independence. Burma and Malaya do not want the British back, China does not want Chiang Kai Shek and the Philippines do not want you:

> I want to tell my American friends that Asia is now surging with revolutionary fervour from one end to the other.... we are men as much as you are. We want

[3] Collected in *Said Subhash Bose*, by Amar Lahiri.

> our freedom and we shall have it by any means. You had an opportunity of helping us, but you did not do so. Now Japan is offering us help and we have reason to trust her sincerity. That is why we have plunged into the struggle alongside of her. It is not Japan that we are helping by waging war on you and on our mortal enemy – England. We are helping ourselves – we are helping Asia....

He could not yet speak with freedom, but he could and did say what would have been the foundation of his defence had he survived.

The speech at Tokyo University was likewise in the nature of testament, for in it he set out again his political beliefs and redefined his attitude to most of the problems of India. He accepted Gandhi's leadership and described his differences with him – the old quarrels about non-violence and the future. India must be industrialised because only so could she obtain the modern army necessary to her defence and to do this she must open herself to foreign assistance. After defence came the fight against poverty and illiteracy. These could never be removed by private initiative and must be the concern of the State. That implied socialism powerful enough to carry out quick and drastic reform, an authoritarian regime 'that will work.. as the servant of the masses and not of a clique'. Caste and communalism would present no problem in such a State. Free India would combine the good points of National Socialism and Communism – national unity and the ideally planned economy – and avoid the pitfalls, capitalism on the one hand, and over-emphasis of the economic factor in human life on the other. He no longer wanted a new party to support the authoritarian government because he now felt that the nationalist movement, in India was identified with the interests of her people.

In foreign affairs, Bose advocated internationalism: not that of the League of Nations, which had failed because its leaders had tried to use it for national ends, but in regional systems based on common interests and culture, which would gradually extend until a world order came into being. This was Bose's real view. He had often said the British Commonwealth must develop into an association of free nations or disintegrate: provided that Japan's hegemony was disinterested, the Co-Prosperity Sphere was one of the regional organisations which might help in building world peace.

But in November 1944 the prospects of the Co-Prosperity Sphere were diminishing. This came home to Bose particularly when he had to agree that the 3rd I.N.A. Division should remain in Malaya and take part in its defence. He had pretended to a certain optimism about the next campaign and until his departure for Tokyo had been talking of the movement of the 3rd Division to Burma on the heels of the 2nd. But when he saw the wider pattern of disaster being traced in the Pacific and the frequent, concentrated air attacks on Japan, when he heard that not only were there no reinforcements for Burma but troops were being drawn from it for use elsewhere, it was clear to him that the Japanese were doomed. At most, he thought, they might hold out long enough in the Pacific for a new invasion of India from Burma.

Before he left Tokyo Bose asked to be allowed to approach Soviet Russia. He believed that the alliance between Russia and the West would not outlast the war in Europe – he had already lectured I.N.A. officers on this – and that Russia might therefore be willing to sponsor him next. To the Japanese he suggested that, as an unofficial intermediary with no face to lose, he might be able to improve their relations with Russia. The Japanese declined.

A week of storms delayed Bose's arrival in Malaya until December 14th. One of the first people he met in Singapore was his Chief Commissioner in the Andamans who had returned for consultation, unwell and bitterly disappointed at the failure of his administration. The only department taken over was that of Education: the Japanese had prevented or hindered all other work and had continued their harsh oppression of the islanders. The worst feature of this had been their spy mania. Fifty-five Indians had been executed and thirty-three imprisoned as British spies up to September 1944 and in October two hundred were under arrest and investigation. Savage torture and family blackmail supported this rule of terror, of which the educated were the main victims. The Chief Commissioner had been quite enable to stop it, though his personal influence may have been felt in a few individual cases. Whatever might be said in Tokyo, the local Japanese would part with none of their authority. Bose, who had been intending to appoint a new Chief Commissioner, changed his mind. The Andamans were too exposed for the new strategic situation: the Provisional Government must write off its commitment and turn to what was more worth saving.

Malaya held other disappointments. To increase the administrative independence of the I.N.A., cart and animal transport companies had recently been formed. Bose had hoped to move these, and the existing artillery and A.F.V.[4] battalions, to Burma in time for the next battle. The Japanese now said that this was impossible, both because of transport difficulties as the Allied air offensive in South-East Asia gathered strength and because every man would be needed for the defence of Malaya. The Japanese would solve the I.N.A. problems of transport and fire support in battle themselves. In Malaya the I.N.A. was to take up defensive positions in the areas it happened to occupy.

The state of the League all over East Asia reflected the growing realisation of certain Allied victory. There were fewer new members: at Singapore in May nearly ten thousand had enrolled, in November only five hundred and sixty. The flow of recruits was drying up: there were

Euipped with 1941 British Bren-carriers.

already two thousand deserters at large in Malaya, and two hundred men were disappearing from the training camps every month. The Malayan collections in April had totalled over $2,000,000, in November $617,000; even the thirteen million dollars promised to Bose in June had not been paid in full: in Singapore $72,000 was outstanding in promises on one fund alone: There had been difficulty in enforcing assessments – people persisted in concealing their assets and delaying payment, now that time was so clearly on their side.

Bose made one more attempt to revive interest. He spoke to senior I.N.A. officers on December 16th, examining all the new problems. He then toured the country. His soldiers were sacrificing their blood, he would say, his demands on the civilians were legitimate, let the rich and secure pay for their safety. In Penang he ordered the arrest of a defaulter – the example proved profitable at once – and discussed with Raghavan new ways of raising money. While Bose visited Sumatra in an effort to gather some of the unpaid dues, the 'New Year Gift to India Fund' was opened. 'Keep what is required for your needs', says Raghavan... and give the balance for the service of our Motherland.'[5] On his return Bose threatened ten people in Singapore with arrest.

There followed severe measures against defaulters by the Board of Management.

---

[5] Speech in Singapore, January 4th.

> It is regretted that you have ignored our letter of 20th January requesting payment of five hundred dollars being your unpaid balance to the Azad Hind Fund. Please note that the above amount must be paid within three days. This is a final warning to you.
>
> I am ordered to return your present cheque for one hundred dollars and to demand from you payment of your arrears amounting to three thousand dollars within one week.. Failure to do so will result in your being called up here to answer for your action.[6]

Many letters of this sort were sent out in the ensuing weeks by the Singapore League, each of them backed by the threat which Bose had many times uttered but which he was now to carry out.

Meanwhile Chatterji had been left to discipline the League in Bangkok, where dissension and defeatism were bringing its work to a halt. There was reluctance not only to pay but also to collect assessments. Bose addressed a public meeting himself on his way back to Rangoon on January 11th. His speech was direct and bitter: those who opposed him should say so openly, they could then be put into concentration camps with the British and their property could be confiscated; if they wished to remain free they must pay their assessments. Bose left with the Japanese Security police a list of ten persons for immediate arrest,

---

[6] Letter dated January 16th and 17th.

and eighty others for varying degrees of surveillance and pressure: in the following two weeks the ten were arrested. Chatterji's task was thus made easier. He obtained over three million ticals in promises on January 19th, and had actually collected one-third of this sum by February 8th when his reorganisation of the League was complete.

THE SECOND CAMPAIGN

By this time I.N.A. troops had been disposed for action on the banks of the Irrawaddy, to which the Japanese had gradually withdrawn in the last three months of 1944. At first it had been planned to use two regiments of the 1st I.N.A. Division and the whole of the 2nd Division on the river line. In the event only the 4th Guerrilla Regiment, which had not yet been in action, was available in time: it was already deployed in Myingyan. The sorry remnants of the three Imphal regiments, too weak even now to provide a contingent for the front, were withdrawn in December to Pyinmana. Two regiments of the 2nd Division waited in Rangoon for their heavy equipment and for the rest of the Division from Malaya.

As Bose had directed, everything possible was done to raise the morale of these fresh troops. They were protected from contact with the Imphal survivors and encouraged by glowing accounts of I.N.A. heroism in battle, by the grant of medals and accelerated promotion and by stricter discipline. Above all the danger of any more mass desertions must be removed: the new arrivals were kept in ignorance of the 1944 surrenders and fed on stories of the execution and ill-treatment of members of the I.N.A. by the British. It was planned to examine the morale of every man before the 2nd Division moved to the front. Commanders were to certify as to the 'spiritual fitness' of their men before taking them into an operational area. Every soldier would be given the chance of staying behind if he did not think himself fit, and his doing so would not affect his military prospects!

Yet, on November 27th, before any move had taken place, it had been found necessary to issue this order in Bose's absence:

It has been noticed that desertions in the Azad Hind fauj are on the increase day by day, which is most deplorable for a Revolutionary Army... Commanders must lay special stress on spiritual development of the troops, in order to prevent any further desertions.

In December battalion commanders were asked for the names of men they thought unreliable: one hundred and fifty were removed from the 4th Guerrilla Regiment alone and sent to the rear. Meanwhile, as we have seen, Bose was hearing of the desertions in Malaya, and determining afresh that the disgrace of 1944 would not be repeated.

The front in Arakan had remained static through the monsoon of 1944 while the main battle was fought out at

Imphal. For in Arakan, because of the innumerable brimming streams which flow into the sea to the west, and into the Mayu and Kaladan Rivers across every natural route inland, the monsoon restricts movement much more severely than in North-west Burma. The British had pulled out of the Kaladan Valley, leaving only one division to hold the Mayu Valley and the coastal village of Maungdaw. The Japanese followed up the withdrawal to the limit, but they now had to spare a whole division from this area to reinforce their Army in North Burma. Only three weak battalions, a mere delaying force, were left to face the British.

In December the Japanese were quickly swept away. The Mayu Valley was cleared and the West Africans once more moved into the lower Kaladan. Akyab was occupied on January 1st and by mid-January Myohaung, east of the Kaladan River, was in danger. The British advance continued without pause, gathering up the I.N.A. as it went. Fifty I.N.A. soldiers had 'escaped' by mid-December: by the end of January, out of the original one hundred and sixty, only forty remained to find their way across the hills to Rangoon.

In North-Western Burma it was the British who followed up a retreat, driving their enemy back to the Irrawaddy. The Japanese were hardly ready on their river defence line when, on January 14th, the British crossed it at Thabbeikkyin, fifty miles north of Mandalay. At this point the Japanese concentrated, thinking to hold the main thrust of the British-Indian 4th Corps. Such was the deception that General Slim had devised. He had led his enemy to believe that the whole of the 4th Corps was ready to support the crossings at Thabbeikkyin, whereas in fact he had moved it to the southern flank of his advance to cross the Irrawaddy at Nyaungu and seize Meiktila.

Bose had reached Burma on January 12th, eager for participation by his 2nd Division in the new victories which the Japanese still planned. The 1st and 2nd Regiments were to move from Rangoon in February and the 4th Guerrilla Regiment was ordered to hold the I.N.A. sector – from Nyaungu, for about twelve miles southwards – until the rest of the division arrived. The Commander, Major G.S. Dhillion, formerly a lieutenant of the 1/14 Punjab Regiment, received this order at Myingyan on January 29th. He obeyed with all speed, began the move four days later and was completing it, well in advance of any other I.N.A. move to battle, when the spearhead of the British thrust to Meiktila crossed the river just to the north of his regimental area.

The Japanese had not worried about Nyaungu. They knew that a British column had been moving towards it, but thought that it was only of brigade strength and probably heading for Yenangyaung. Dhillion had thus received no particular warning. He was told to send covering troops across the river and to co-operate with the Japanese company on his right. But his regiment numbered barely 1200 men, a sadly inadequate force for twelve miles of river bank. He had posted a battalion at Nyaungu, another at Pagan and the third with his headquarters nearby. The digging of the main position began on February 8th: next day the I.N.A. patrols were forced back across the river and a small British party was seen on the eastern bank.

The crossing of the Irrawaddy by the 7th Indian Division began on February 14th. A British infantry company crossed silently before dawn about a mile northeast of Nyaungu and established itself, but the embarkation of the rest of this battalion was delayed and its assault craft did not begin to approach the eastern bank until well after daybreak.

Medium machine-guns on the extreme right of the I.N.A. battalion at Nyaungu and in the Japanese company position opened up at about 6.10 a.m. Many of the boats were soon out of control and drifting downstream past the I.N.A. trenches for which they made prefect targets. There were many casualties, although some of the craft returned to the western bank and many men escaped by swimming. But the set-back was incidental, a second battalion crossed withtout loss later in the morning further upstream and by the end of the day two more battalions were safety ashore. About a hundred survivors of the I.N.A. at Nyaungu surrendered.

At Pagan, too, the initial crossing had failed. But as the soldiers were preparing the cross again, they saw a boat, flying a white flag, put out from the Japanese bank. In it were two I.N.A. emissaries who said the Japanese had left Pagan and that the I.N.A. there wished to surrender. One hundred and forty of them did so and the new crossing was unopposed. Dhillon rallied what was left of his regiment on February 16th but the situation was beyond him. The Indian Army had established itself in Nyaungu and Pagan: he could only withdraw with his survivors to the new I.N.A. divisional area at Kyaukpadaung, thirty-five miles to the south-east on the road to Meiktila.

Japanese troops were now rushed northwards from Yenangyaung to bar the way to Meiktila and to destroy their enemy in his weak and difficult moment of river-crossing. The 2nd I.N.A. Infantry Regiment, which was arriving under Lieutenant-Colonel P.K. Sahgal (formerly a captain in the 2/10 Baluch Regiment), was ordered to patrol to the west and north from a defensive base on the western slopes of Mount Popa, a steep, isolated 5,000-foot mountain, eight miles north-east of Kyaukpadaung. The Japanese meant to hold this area strongly and entrusted it to their 72nd Independent Mixed Brigade at Yenangyaung. On February 17th Saghal saw the commander, who guaranteed him fire support from Japanese artillery, and supplies

At this point, on February 18th, Bose left Rangoon with a retinue of Japanese and Indian officers to tour the front. There had been another state visit to Siam and more triumphal days in the Burmese capital. He had initiated a far-flung secret project to penetrate the obscurity of the operational zone by infiltrating wireless agents behind the enemy. Swami, still in touch with some of his emissaries in India, was training a special party to sabotage the American pipeline in North Burma. There had been spectacular celebrations of Bose's birthday on January 23rd. Somewhat to his distaste he had been weighted against gold, over twenty million rupees had been collected, and a company of young men and women had pledged themselves in blood to form a suicide squad in his service. There had been moving farewells and exhortations to the 2nd Infantry Regiment as it left for the front and the promotion of four of his officers to be the first Indian major-generals on 'Army Day' February 4th. Bose had done his best to secure increased supplies and equipment for the I.N.A. from the Japanese and had given every man leaving for the front the chance to withdraw – if he thinks he is incapable of going...' for any reason at all. Surely now his Army would stand, surely his own presence at the front would remove any doubt which might remain. Thus, in elation and new confidence, Bose inspected the veterans of Imphal at Pyinmana and hearing of a battle at Nyaungu, pressed on to Meiktila with Shah Nawaz, now to command the 2nd Division.

At Meiktila all was confusion, with the Japanese making desperate efforts to improvise some defence under frequent and heavy air attack. The British had broken out of the Nyaungu bridgehead, their advance to Meiktila might come at any time. Bose heard with indignation of the desertions at Nyaungu and wished to set off at once for Kyaukpadaung where Dhillion was said to be reforming his regiment. But although it seemed that the British were by-passing the Japanese strongpoint on Mount Popa, there was no certainty and Shah Nawaz was sent first to discover what was going on. He carried with him a sharp message for Dhillion:

> 'I have heard with grief, pain and shame of the treachery shown by Lieutenant Hari Ram and others. I hope that the men of the 4th Regiment will wash away the blot on the I.N.A. with their blood.

Bose also wrote at this time to an officer of the I.N.A. Police in Mandalay, a note which shows his close control of the campaign against deserters:

> According to my information the men who recently deserted from Mandalay... are still in Mandalay area. These men must be arrested and sent down to Rangoon under escort. If you cannot arrest them, they must be shot at sight. Please do everything possible to arrest them or to shoot them.

While Shah Nawaz was away Bose visited the I.N.A. hospitals at Kalaw and Taunggyi, and ordered their removal to Zeyawaddy where they would be out of danger if Meiktila fell.

At Popa village on February 22nd Shah Nawaz found Sahgal well in control of the Headquarters of the 2nd Division and of such troops of his regiment as had arrived.

Dhillon, goaded by the shame of Bose's displeasure, was collecting stragglers; on February 18th he had hoped to gather as many as five hundred of his twelve hundred men, but scarcely four hundred came in. 'It has been a bad show,' wrote Shah Nawaz in his diary, and Sahgal: 'There s no discipline left and morale is gone. They are a source of nuisance to me also because they wander about and give away my positions.' Shah Nawaz saw nevertheless that Dhillion had been given an impossible task at Nyaungu, and this impression he reported to Bose in Meiktila on February 25th.

Bose was now quite certain that he ought to go to Mount Popa himself. This time he said, nothing would divert him: what did the danger matter? It was obvious that the Japanese could not hold Burma and his only wish was to die fighting the British. This seemed the moment. Had he not promised that he would lead the I.N.A. to victory or death? If the march to Delhi was over for a time, his soldiers must create such a legend of heroism and determination that their countrymen would be inspired to raise the banner of revolution again in India. Human lives were an inconsiderable price to pay for such a shining tradition. In the early hours of February 26th Bose stood arguing with his officers. It was a moonlight night, the dark mass of Mount Popa could be discerned momentarily on the north-western horizon against the flash of gunfire or the blaze of a bomb. Shah Nawaz lost his patience:[7]

[7] Shah Nawaz, *My Memories of the I.N.A. and Its Netaji*, p.144.

'You are proposing to risk your life', he said, in effect, 'just to show your personal courage; but this is selfishness and you have no right to do it; your life is not your own, it is a precious trust for India, held in our keeping: we are responsible.' Bose was still determined: 'You have no need to worry,' he returned lightly. 'England has not made a bomb that can kill me!' When it seemed that the argument would never end, his officers schemed to delay his departure until insufficient darkness remained for the journey. Bose kept losing his temper, but the car was not ready in time and he was still in Meiktila at dawn.

There had been several heavy air raids on February 25th: the twenty-sixth opened with another. As the bombers receded, a Japanese Liasion Officer came to say that a British armoured column was sixteen miles away. There was nothing to stop it driving on to Meiktila, he said; the road to Mount Popa was probably cut and there might even be blocks on the Rangoon road. To die fighting at the head of the I.N.A. was one thing, to be trapped with the Japanese in Meiktila quite another. Bose decided to get away if he could. Shah Nawaz has described the episode:

> 'I.... filled up the car with grenades and ammunition...' When we entered the car and started off (at about 9 a.m.) Netaji was sitting with a loaded Tommy gun in his lap. Raju (Bose's doctor) had two hand grenades ready. The Japanese officer was holding another Tommy gun and had a loaded Bren... We were all ready to open fire simultaneously. The

> Japanese officer stood on the foot-board of the car to be on the lookout for enemy aircraft.[8]

They fled the twenty miles to Yindaw without incident and hid until nightfall. There were many alarms, the sky seemed full of enemy planes and the villages of British spies. Were their movement known? Were these aircraft even now seeking for 'the notorious Bose, head of the Indian National Army, Japanese puppet and traitor? There came to all the sense of isolation that follows the fugitive from air attack, the feeling that enemy eyes are peering through the thin screen of foilage overhead.

Bose reached Pyinmana on February 27th and ordered the formation of a new fighting regiment from the remnants of the 1st Division encamped there. This new 'X' Regiment was to hold a defensive position at Yezin, a few miles to the north: the remaining 2,500 sick and convalescent soldiers would retire to Zeyawaddy, south of Toungoo. Bose stayed for two days with his troops at Pyinmana, moving among them constantly, helping in the new organisation and considering the Yezin position with his officers. He would now, he said, fight his last battle here, to the last man and the last round.

On March 2nd urgent summons came from headquarters in Rangoon. There, the most shattering news awaited him. Five staff officers from the 2nd Division Headquarters at Mount Popa had deserted: surrender leaflets signed by

---

[8] Shah Nawaz, *My Memories of the I.N.A. and Its Netaji*, p.146.

them had been dropped on I.N.A. positions: further mass desertions seemed certain. Bose was stunned: for days, sick with shock, he kept to his room. He spared himself no pang; the blame was his: his men could refuse him nothing; such a disaster could never have happened had he been to Mount Popa himself to be diverted by the fears of others. There had been no danger, he knew that now; it had been weakness to listen to those so reasonable arguments and to be thwarted so easily.

This was Bose's only real moment of defeat and he had to face it in the cloak of loneliness he had always worn. There had rarely been anyone to share his life: Dilip Kumar Roy, his brother Sarat in the early years, and the woman whose secret letters he would sometimes receive from Vienna. Now all drew strength from him: there was no one with whom he could talk freely in the moderating terms of friendship: he had for himself only the rosary, the tiny Gita he carried, the inner silence. The moment passed as such moments do, leaving him purged and calm. No misfortune could touch him now. He appeared serene, withdrawn, unaffected by the constant news of Japanese reverses in March. Only the thought of treachery would move him, and this could loosen the hinges of his mind: he said he would take his own life if such a thing happened again.

A similar hysteria pervaded the two Special Orders of the Day[9] in which were embodied Bose's official reaction to

---

[9] Appendix IJ, Nos. 8 and 9.

the desertions. He had already authorised the death penalty for desertion, and had ordered the I.N.A. Police to list 'undesirable officers' who might still have escaped suspicion. Now he announced the observance of the 'Traitors Day' on which I.N.A. units would compete in doing public dishonour to the deserters, and brought in a measure which had been in his mind for a long time:

> Every member of the I.N.A. – officer, N.C.O. or sepoy – will in future be entitled to arrest any other member of the I.N.A. no matter what his rank may be, if he behaves in a cowardly manner, or to shoot him if he acts in a treacherous manner.

He renewed his offer for anyone unwilling to work or fight properly to leave the I.N.A. and ordered a thorough purge of all against whom there was suspicion. Several officers were relieved of their commands during the inquisition of the next few days and a number of 'unreliables' still living as free men in Rangoon were locked up. To the field commanders were sent the names of doubtful individuals serving under them, so that they might be removed. No less did Bose try to encourage his men with new aggressive ideas and personal letters. He forgave Dhillon for the Nyaungu fiasco and won his heart by promotion and two messages of confidence:

> We all feel happy and proud. I have no doubt that you and your Regiment will, through your good

Appendix II, Nos. 8 and 9.

> work and sacrifice, wipe out the sin committed by a few traitors.

It was all of no avail. In March the I.N.A. operated under increasing difficulties, and, except for a few, had no stomach for the fight. There was no wireless communication, there had been no replacement of the equipment lost at Nyaungu, there was no telephone line between Divisional Headquarters and the regiments, there was not even a despatch rider for a regimental headquarters – one operation order contained special instructions for a motor-cycle to be procured for use by the 4th Guerrilla Regiment in emergencies. 'We are a Revolutionary Army', Bose had said – as if the revolutionary spirit would make up for material deficiencies. And so his soldiers were sent into battle with no communications, with little transport, with few support weapons and far too little ammunition. They were left without boots and with their clothing in rags. Small wonder they deserted in droves. They would have done so even if they had possessed the patriotic fervour attributed to them by their leader. But now for the most part there was no patriotic fervour, only fear, shame and a dumb longing for home.

There were several small actions by the I.N.A. during March as Japanese attempts against the British bridgeheads were launched and thwarted. Dhillon's regiment suffered heavy casualties in actions near Taungzin on March 15th to 17th, in which it showed persistence and gallantry. The 2nd Infantry Regiment was relatively unengaged, while the 1st Infantry Regiment, employed on security patrols far from the fighting, saw no action at all. Late in March one of Dhillon's battalion commanders deserted. This would make no difference, he said, 'we will sacrifice our lives to maintain the honour of the I.N.A.'

But the Indian Army was now ready to clear Mount Popa. After a day of heavy air attacks on April 2nd, a strong force moved from the north towards the village of Legyi, where the 2nd Infantry Regiment was entrenched. It was clear that a full-scale attack would develop next day. During the night three officers and some N.C.O.'s deserted. In the morning, said Sahgal, there was 'great alarm and despondency... Everybody appeared to feel that the enemy had full information about our dispositions, and as he was in such overwhelming strength, our case was hopeless.'[10] Just after midday a force of tanks, armoured cars and lorried infantry with strong artillery support began to attack Legyi. There were two more attacks in the afternoon. Then the administrative area was overrun. Sahgal ordered a counter-attack but the two platoons concerned deserted. A second counter-attack after nightfall was successful, but Sahgal then heard that virtually the whole of his 1st Battalion, including the Commander, all company commanders and about three hundred men had deserted. The remainder could not face another attack; Sahgal withdrew them on his own initiative during the night.

---

[10] P.K. Sahgal, *Report on the Legyi Operations,* I.N.A. C.M. document.

Nothing was left but retreat and disintegration. The remnants from Mount Popa moved southwards on April 12th, to be overrun, rounded up or driven to surrender as the Fourteenth Army's drive through Burma overtook them. Not all gave in without a fight. A party of six hundred under a Captain Bagri was surprised by British tanks. The story goes that Bagri and about a hundred of his men perished in a last desperate charge with hand grenades and bottles of petrol. But it made no difference. At the end of April only fugitives remained at large: on May 13th Shah Nawaz, Dhillon and about fifty men surrendered at Pegu; the story of the 2nd I.N.A. Division was over.

The last word comes best perhaps from a Japanese: Captain Izumi, the Liaison Officer with the 4th Guerrilla Regiment, reported to his superiors on April 8th:

> The commanding officers (regimental and divisional commanders) who have been favoured with Chandra Bose's personal confidence, and assisted by letters and interviews with him, are devoted to upholding the honour of the I.N.A. and full of enthusiasm for the war. However this is not the case with those of battalion and company commander's rank..
>
> The Regimental Commander, and his subordinates... recognises the power of the Imperial Army in its night fighting, its vicious pincer movements, and its close combat fighting. Their demands for material

> assistance, guns, planes, etc. are exorbitant as one might expect from their past record, and they are suited neither to the rough life of the trenches nor to the violence of a night operation.
>
> Generally speaking they are unsuited to defensive warfare, and though they take the offensive on their front, they worry so intensely about the general war situation, that it is no exaggeration to say that a gallant and dashing attack by the I.N.A. is only a beautiful dream. However, there are some units of the I.N.A. that have lived up to the very highest standards of conduct in battle.

THE END IN BURMA

While the retreat and disintegration of the I.N.A. had been proceeding, the Fourteenth Army had swept on towards Rangoon. By April 15th the 5th Indian Division was approaching Yezin, where two battalions of 'X' Regiment were to fight to the last. Just in time, orders reached their commander to withdraw to Yeni and support a Japanese stand there. But in this and other withdrawals the marching I.N.A. were outpaced by the mechanised British columns and by April 24th there was no course but a hard retreat through the hostile mountains and along the Salween Valley to Moulmein. This was what all the Japanese in Central Burma now tried to do and the 'Breakout Battles' of May and June resulted.

The Japanese Ambassador to Bose's Government, Mr Hachiya, had reached Rangoon in March. Bose discovered that he had no 'credentials', and refused to receive him until they were produced. He had thought out his own problem again and again. Japanese failure was accepted. 'I know we have lost in Burma,' he had said when Shah Nawaz came to take leave early in March, 'but that should not dishearten us... We have to continue fighting to uphold the honour of India.' He refused to allow the I.N.A. to be used against the Burmese National Army of Aung San after its revolt from the Japanese on March 25th. When one of his Ministers suggested that he too should turn on the Japanese, he replied simply that the Indians in Malaya would pay a heavy price if he did. To his intimates he would say that he had enough of politics and that his happiest moment would be when he laid life in the cause of his country.

His solace, as so often, was work. First there were about a hundred women of the Rani of Jhansi Regiment to be returned to their homes outside Burma; he was responsible for them to their parents he would say. He also tried to secure the gradual evacuation of the two to three thousand unfit men from Zeyawaddy and Rangoon to Siam. For the rest, as long as the Japanese will to hold Rangoon lasted, he intended to fight to the end in Burma. He permitted no lowering of Indian morale – as late as April 17th he ordered an urgent investigation into the activities in Rangoon of a group of Muslims, whose clever lampoons, privately circulated, may now have come to his notice. The large I.N.A. camps outside the city, which contained six thousand soldiers, were organised to help in the last battle.

Then, on April 20th, it became clear that in spite of their assurance the Japanese were leaving the Burmese capital. Indian resistance could now achieve nothing. It was already too late to evacuate the mass of the I.N.A., but two 'suicide companies', each two hundred and fifty strong, formed from the intact 1st Battalion of the Subhash Regiment, were marched off to Moulmein. Bose decided to send out the rest of the Rani of Jhansi Regiment home with some of the civilian workers from Siam and Malaya, and pressed the Japanese for transport. Only on April 23rd was he told officially of the Japanese withdrawal: Dr Ba Maw was going with them; what, asked the Japanese, was Bose going to do? Bose had no doubt, but the initiative came from his Cabinet. He left by road with a few ministers and senior officers, about fifty League workers and the last contingent of women on the night of April 24th.

Major-General Loganadhan was left to preside over the I.N.A. surrender in Rangoon. The chief members of the Government, the other three major-generals and Swami departed with their leader. 'I do not leave Burma of my own free will,' said Bose in his last massage, 'I would have preferred to stay on here and share with you the sorrow of temporary defeat.[11] But his advisers had overruled him, he

---

[11] Appendix II, No.11.

had other responsibilities in Siam and Malaya which nobody else could fulfil, and for Indians this defeat was only an incident in their struggle. 'Go down as heroes,' he said, 'go down upholding the highest code of honour and discipline.'[12]

Loganadhan's authority in Rangoon lasted until May 4th when the first brigade of the 26th Indian Division landed from the assault craft which had brought it up the Rangoon River. On May 3rd the senior British prisoner in Rangoon Jail had, as representative of the Allies, already ordered the disarming and concentration of the I.N.A. and this was in progress when the first soldiers arrived. So the Indian Independence Movement in Burma came peacefully to an end, its leaders behaving with dignity and giving what assistance they could to the British commanders. It was inevitable, nevertheless, that stern action would be taken. Seven hundred and fifty of the ex-Indian Army Officers and men were shipped to India for investigation in May. They were followed, as the months passed, by many thousands more from Rangoon, and then from Malaya and Bangkok.

[12] Appendix II, No.10.

8

INDIA SHALL BE FREE

Never falter in your faith in India's destiny. There is no power on earth that can keep India enslaved. India shall be free and before long. (August 15, 1945)

'There is no doubt,' Bose had said to the Indian prisoners in Germany, 'that the British have lost this battle.' Now, while he and the pitiful, stricken remnants of his Army of Free India were making their escape from Burma, the Allied victory in Europe became complete. Yet Bose was saying much the same thing in Siam, with one meaning for the Japanese and another for his own people. He continued confident of victory, India's victory, her emancipation from British rule; on Japan's prospects he no longer gave an opinion. For Nambiar, watching the disintegration of all organisations in Germany, including his own, there was no such relief from despair. The Free India Centre and the broken pieces of the Legion vanished in the bog of German disaster and his world narrowed to the village, the house, the room where he was arrested.

In 1943 Nambiar had taken over a growing concern for which he could still envisage eventual success. He had been able quickly to establish the authority he had inherited. The Free India Centre came easily into his hands; he expanded its broadcasting service, which stood at two hours per day, and added, in August 1943, weekly transmissions to America and to Ireland over the official German radio. He dealt successfully with a wave of mutiny which swept over the Legion when it was being moved to Holland in April; he established at long last a Free India Centre in Paris, and secured from the Germans numerous additional privileges for members of the Centre in Berlin. He sponsored the printing of Free India stamps, some of the Free India medals were struck, and Free India passports were issued to replace the British documents which most Indians in Germany still retained.

But the Centre was managed with increasing difficulty as the bombing of Germany rose to a climax. At the end of August 1943, the broadcasting section went to Hilversum and the general office followed when in November its building and Nambiar's house were destroyed. Nambiar himself remained in Berlin as Bose's official representative. On his appointment as 'Minister of State' in the Provisional Government in March 1944 he was told to press for the appointment of a German Ambassador in return. The Germans were willing, but the Japanese, who, no longer because of their greater victories but because of their lesser defeats, thought themselves the senior Axis partner, refused.

Bose kept in touch with Nambiar by periodic letters sent in a submarine or a Japanese diplomatic bag, by rarer messages through the secret radio in Afghanistan and by occasional radio-telephone conversations. He was most critical of the broadcasts from Germany, seeking always to enliven them and to keep them in tune with events in India, on which he provided his own commentaries. His criticisms were personal and detailed: this speaker should improve his voice, that announcer be transferred to another programme; there must be no weakening, the march was still to Delhi. He kept Nambiar supplied with material on his own progress, and the Germans provided monitoring reports of the Far Eastern broadcasts.

In September 1944, the progress of the allied Armies made it necessary to move the Free India Centre to Helmstedt in Western Germany. The move was carried out at leisure, and with some care to ensure the continuity of broadcasting.

The Indian Legion had remained in Holland only until August 1943, when it was moved to South-Western France. There its three battalions were at first widely dispersed for coastal defence north and south of Bodreaux. As more Germans troops arrived, the Legion was brought together and given the peninsula between the Gironde Estuary and the sea as its defence sector. Life was pleasanter for the Indians than it had been in Holland, the winter less severe than in Germany and the supply of Red Cross parcels undiminished. The men soon settled down.

There was collective training with German units, field firing and numerous courses. The Legion hockey team, after many local successes, beat a strong German Army side in Berlin. In October 1943 the first Indians were promoted to officer rank. They were given preliminary instruction in tactics and deportment; there was careful *camraderie* by the German officers and punctilious respect from the German N.C.O.'s. To the men themselves their honour was real: India would understand and applaud.

But this was not all. With the departure of Bose the whole basis of Legion service changed. Bose had told the Legionaries that they would fight the British in India or, at worst, in North Africa. Before he left he had told Nambiar simply to find employment for them against British-Indian troops. The first indication of this change had reached the Legion when it was ordered to Holland. Nambiar explained the move as 'training in coastal defence' but was unable to prevent a serious mutiny before the move ended. In France, even at such an extremity of the Western Wall, this pretence was soon revealed and there grew up in the Legion a sense of insecurity, of abandonment. There were murmurings, counter-propaganda. Legionaries listened to the B.B.C. at the houses of French friends and at least one of the German Officers, an anti-Nazi, was deliberately subversive. 'Why are you in the Legion?' he would ask the men. 'And what are you going to do when the British catch you?' Contacts were made with the French Resistance and a few of the Indians later escaped to serve with it, but for the moment active disloyalty was too risky.

If there was an immediate effect, it could be seen perhaps in the deterioration of Indo-German relations in the early half of 1944. When, in March, the Legion was warned that Allied invasion was imminent morale fell sharply. There were more French contacts against the day of need. Any excuse was seized upon by the Indians N.C.O.'s for protest and the German officers, who understood little of what was going on, dared no strong action against them. Rommel visited the defences in April and in May Nambiar was sent for. He found the men despondent and full of complaints about discrimination and the slowness of Indian promotion. It was only partly, he felt, the war situation that was to blame; action would soon cure. Neither Krappe nor his superiors, wanted to use the Legion in battle, but they agreed under pressure to a trial: one company, the 9th, was sent to Italy at the end of May.

This was not the first body from the Legion to be sent to Italy. A party of ten men for front-line propaganda tasks had preceded it in January 1944 and a second smaller group had gone there for espionage in May. The first group was employed on broadcasting, on packing propaganda leaflets in mortar bombs for firing into Indian unit areas and on tracking down escaped British and Indian prisoners of war for the Germans. This latter role continued almost to the end of the war. The second Group was intended for the winning over of Indian soldiers in action, a task which, so seldom accomplished in the friendly jungles of Burma, was nearly impossible in the hills of Italy. The three attempts made were half-hearted and came to nothing, the group being returned to the legion early in 1945.

The story of the 9th Company can be quickly told. It was sent into action against the Poles; the first reconnaissance party deserted and then the whole company refused to take up its position, maintaining that Poles were not in the contract. The Germans withdrew it and sent it back to the Legion.

Meanwhile the Allied invasion of France in June 1944 had given the main body of the Legion its first opportunity of action. For most of the seven weeks that passed before the Allied breakout from the invasion area, it remained in position on the coast. Then, towards the end of July, it was used with German troops in security columns against the French Resistance around Bordeaux. There were raids on arms stores and suspected distribution centres in which the Indians behaved like their German comrades and attracted to themselves some of the odium which attached to them. This phase passed as the Allies swept across France and on August 11th the Legion began a slow retreat by road and rail to Germany. It passed through the Belfort Gap just as the American Seventh Army reached it, and reassembled at Hagenau, north west of Strasbourg.

There had been several hundred casualties *en route*, including about two hundred and fifty desertions. A few men were killed in a rearguard action with American tanks, many more by the Maquis in skirmishes or in reprisal for Legion behaviour towards the French during the withdrawal. Others remained with French friends in the South-West, some displaying much courage and initiative in service with the Maquis.

In September the Germans decided to transfer the Legion to the Waffen, or Armed S.S. Krappe had warned his superiors of trouble if this were done, and he was right. The Legionaries thought that they might now really be sent into battle and that the German cadre would be increased. There was typical indiscipline when the SS uniforms arrived and Nambiar had to send a representative to quieten the men. He found the Legion moving across the Rhine to Oberhofen; it was frightened and once more full of grievances, one of which was that the Germans were confiscating the souvenirs it had brought back from France.

At Oberhofen it settled down again, appeased by being allowed to retain its old Legion badges, by other concessions relating to the S.S. uniform, by new promises of promotion, and by the award of medals to 1,100 out of the 2,450 remaining Legionaries. Bose had once again written to ask that the Legion should be sent into action. There had been a plan to send it to North Italy in November, but Himmler decided to keep it, and in December moved it to Heuberg – in the direction, it must be noted, of the 'National Redoubt' which Hitler at one time planned to hold to the last with his S.S. and foreign troops. Here, on the approach of French forces in April 1945, the Legion disintegrated. Many of the soldiers escaped into Switzerland, others surrendered to the French, others for a time went into hiding. By the beginning of July all but two hundred of the 3,115 Indians who had been in the Legion had been accounted for by the Indian Army authorities.

At the end of 1944 Nambiar had been encouraged by Bose to enquire if the Russians would accept Indian political refugees from Europe. The Germans could not, the Japanese would not help him and he found no way of asking the question. In February and March 1945, the Indians of the Free India Centre thought of surrendering to the Russians, but times were already too uncertain and none tried it. The staff dispersed a week before the Americans reached Helmstedt on April 12th. At Bad Gastein in Austria, Nambiar received a last message from Bose. If the Legion could not be sent into battle, he said, let it be moved to a region where the Russians and not the British would find it. But all was now over. A mere handful escaped, some to reappear in India when it was safe to do so: some are doubtless still behind the Iron Curtain, alive or dead.

As he covered the weary marches from Rangoon into Siam, we find Bose discussing eventual sanctuary in Russia for himself also. He was utterly cast down, but practical concern for his companions gave him the continuous activity his mind craved. The little cavalcade of twenty-one vehicles had safely reached the Moulmein road early on April 25th, a day ahead of the advancing Fourteenth Army, but by the time it crossed the River Sittang three or four days later, all but two of the trucks had been destroyed by air attack or abandoned in the mud.

The fugitives moved at night. When dawn came they had to find a safe place of concealment where they could spend the day. Was there drinking water? Was there food? Was the transport well dispersed and hidden? At every halt Bose moved among his people attending to all these things, counting heads, seeing that the weak and footsore were cared for and that the worst cases were carried in what lorries remained. He would direct work at the ferries, labouring with his own hands to bring the vehicles to safety. There were a few casualties, only one Indian of the party was killed, but nearly all the baggage and the Government files and records were lost.

Bose had covered the last ten miles to the Sittang River on foot. East of it he made three long night marches before the Japanese found enough lorries for his whole party – and he would not ride while any of his people marched: 'Do you think,' he burst out at the Japanese walking with him, 'that I am Ba Maw of Burma that I will leave my men and run for safety?' There were times of stress when his Indian companions also tried his temper, but the outbursts were rare; his tirelessness, his determination to share in the common suffering and his personal courage impressed them all.

Moulmein was reached on May 3rd. From here, after a pause, about half the party went on by train, half by road. The railway journey was not without its hazards: the trains could only travel by night and movement was slow. Bose set off as soon as his various parties were on the move again, visiting them at halts on the way to Bangkok. He reached the Siamese capital on May 15th, arranged for the reception of the stragglers from Burma and reassembled his Cabinet.

The graver implications of Axis defeat had now to be considered. Bose still said that Japanese recovery was possible and that in any case there was plenty of time and territory to be taken. Japan could only be brought low by direct invasion and, in spite of American successes in the Pacific, that was still far off. His view was that the Japanese should draw in their scattered forces to a more compact defensive area. Only delaying forces should be left in places like Java and the major strength concentrated in China and Japan. He saw the immediate danger to Malaya, and envisaged an eventual withdrawal of the 3rd I.N.A. Division to join the 1,300 survivors of the I.N.A. from Burma who were now gathering in Siam.

But, for the long term, if the Allies beat down Japanese resistance, Russia was his only hope. The Indian struggle would of course go on: India would still need help from outside. Bose realised the basic enmity of Russia towards the West and saw her influence rising in Eastern Asia, whose nationalist movements she had partially penetrated even before the war. It might even be possible for him to preserve the Provisional Government in Moscow; much would depend on how quickly and how openly the breach with the Anglo-Americans developed. But the Japanese were jealous of Russian influence in the Co-Prosperity Sphere and had never allowed him access to the Russians in Tokyo. The growing danger of war with them was not likely to make the Japanese any less sensitive and he must be very careful of his approach now. Referring therefore to the inner ring of Japanese defence. Bose proposed in June that he be allowed to set up a 'safe deposit' government within it, in Manchuria. If they allowed this, he thought,he would be certain of continued activity to the limit of Japanese resistance and then of flight to Russian territory if he had not been able to arrange something better. Again the Japanese refused.

Meanwhile he had made in Bangkok on May 21st 1945, a speech which contained a hidden appeal to Moscow. The conflict between the Russians and the West, he said, had already begun at San Francisco:

> The time is not far off when our enemies will realise that though they have succeeded in overthrowing Germany they have indirectly helped to bring into the arena of European politics another power — Soviet Russia – that may prove to be a greater menace to British and American Imperialism than Germany was. The Provisional Government of Free India will continue to follow international

> developments with the closest interest, and endeavour to take the fullest advantage of them. The fundamental principle of our foreign policy has been and will be – Britain's enemy is India's friend.

As her hostility towards Britain came to qualify her for the title of India's friend, Russia would, he felt, easily sense what was expected of her.

For the Provisional Government in Bangkok, finance had again been critical. League funds in Siam, already depleted by supply purchases for Burma, could not support the influx of soldiers and the re-establishment of the Provisional Government. Raghavan was summoned from Singapore with all available assets, Ayer tried to borrow from the Siamese Government, Chatterji was sent to raise money in Saigon and Sahay despatched for the same purpose to Hanoi. There was a second motive to this dispersion of key ministers. Nobody could say where in Japanese Asia the Allies would strike next. Bose was trying to guard against the simultaneous capture of the whole Cabinet and to provide in each area where an Allied attack might come an authoritative spokesman for Indian interests. Others were detailed to play this part in Malaya and Siam.

In his speeches from Bangkok Bose called again on the Indians of South-East Asia for increased effort and heightened morale. 'We may not travel to Delhi,' he said, 'via Imphal, but we shall get there all right.' The British were no longer of any account without American support, the tide of opinion was turning in India itself, even in the Indian Army 'at heart large sections sympathise with the I.N.A.' Far more would do so when, in Burma, they came to realise that the Provisional Government and Indian National Army were not puppet organisations as they had been told, when they heard the national greeting 'Jai Hind' freely used, and the National Anthem freely sung. He had bidden the Indians of Rangoon to contact the Indian Army and 'carry on the good work'. This they would do – and as prisoners his I.N.A. soldiers would help: the British would not be able to mishandle or muzzle them, he had already threatened reprisals if they did.[1]. The defeat in Burma would prove to be a blessing in disguise:

> This is not rhetoric – nor is it propaganda. It is the plain and unvarnished truth. And those who doubt the truth of this statement have only to wait and see. The ways of history – like the ways of Providence – are often mysterious... for the fulfilment of our objective, it was perhaps necessary that the British Indian Army should come into Burma and see the I.N.A... The British Indian Army have now seen us with their own eyes. What is the result? There is no longer any talk of a puppet Army – of a Japanese Indian Force or 'J.I.F.'. Even enemy propagandists now talk, at last, of an I.N.A.[2]

---

[1] Appendix II, No.12
[2] On With the Fight, p.15

Bose's eloquence flowed on: America, he said, could never control Europe from across the Atlantic; Britain could no longer play power politics there. Neither Britain nor America could 'produce a plan of social reconstruction, which will be acceptable to the nations of Europe.' Hence, he said, the inevitable victory of Communism in the long run. Nothing could now stand between India and her liberty: the final battle would still be fought in 1946. He came close to saying that the fate of the Japanese also was immaterial. In private he told his Cabinet that the Japanese were far from beaten, but that if defeat came, the records of the movement would be preserved and every man would remain at his post.

At this point the Viceroy of India, Lord Wavell, announced new proposals for a political settlement in India. Bose believed more than ever that negotiation with Britain was against India's interests. There were so many new factors: the growth of nationalism in South-East Asia and the disappearance of European prestige, Burma's taste of freedom, the renewed sympathy of America with Indian aspirations. These things would force the British to reconsider their position and the reconsideration would be done not by the Imperialist Churchill Administration, but by the Labour Government which would surely replace it in July; by Cripps, Attlee, Bevin, the men he had met in 1938. A renewal of the Indian struggle now would turn the scale. Bose prepared a series of broadcasts intended, like those against the Cripps Mission in 1942, to prevent political agreement. Bangkok Radio was no longer working and on June 18th he flew to Singapore.

Here we must glance briefly backwards at the political situation as it had developed in India. 1942 had been a year of rebellion, 1943 a year of disaster. The Bengal famine of that year hardened both the communal deadlock and the political one, for the Congress accused alike the Muslim League Ministry in Bengal and the Viceroy's Government in Delhi of causing it. In October 1943 came a new Viceroy, Lord Wavell, and with him an energy and a common touch which had perhaps been lacking in his office. The urgency of India's vast economic problem was realised afresh and new constructive measures for its alleviation appeared likely to lead into a new political atmosphere. Indeed Lord Wavell's appeal in February 1944 for cooperation and a new start seemed capable of acceptance everywhere. But Mr. Gandhi had not moved from the position he had taken up in 1942, and his continuance in prison made this clear to the Congress Party at large. Mr. Rajagopalachari, alone of those with influence in the Party, took the moderate view - but he had broken with Gandhi two years ago and now stood alone. The Muslims, meanwhile, were becoming ever more firmly consolidated in the Muslim League under Mr. Jinnah, who was determined on the partition of India and would not treat with a Viceroy who saw union as a geographical necessity.

This was the state of affairs when, on May 6th, 1944, Mr. Gandhi was released from prison on grounds of health.

It was soon clear that even in the present more hopeful atmosphere, his conditions for cooperation were still substantially those on which Sir Stafford Cripps' negotiations had foundered. But he seemed disposed to try once again to reach agreement with Mr. Jinnah, in order that Britain might be faced with a united demand in India, and a series of meetings between the two men began at Bombay on September 9th.

The discussions lasted a fortnight. Gandhi proffered a formula which was closer to Jinnah's mind than any he had previously proposed. Sir Reginald Coupland has summarised it as follows:

1. The Muslim League was to endorse the Indian demand for independence and to cooperate with the Congress in forming a provisional government for the 'transitional period'.

2. At the end of the war a commission would demarcate those contiguous areas in N.W. and N.E. India in which the Muslims are in an absolute majority, and in those areas a plebiscite of all the inhabitants would decide whether or not they should be separated from Hindustan.

3. In the event of separation, agreements would be made for defence, commerce, communications and other essential purposes.

4. "These terms shall be binding only in case of transfer

> by Britain of full power and responsibility for the governance of India.'[3]

To Bose this meeting of minds represented two dangers, a danger to his own activity outside India and a danger to the position of the Congress within. He had not followed and did not understand the prodigious growth of the Muslim demand for Pakistan and saw these discussions with the eye of 1938, when he himself had tried to argue with Mr. Jinnah. The All-India authority of the Congress Party could, he thought, still be maintained and any agreement with the Muslim League meant a reduction of that authority and a sharing of eventual supreme power. If such an agreement were to lead to an actual political settlement Bose's own position would be in danger. As lately as July 1944, he had shown concern over the implications of a compromise solution:

> As long as there is no compromise between Mahatma Gandhi and the British Government we have no reason to feel anxious. In any case the war has to be fought and we will go on fighting even if Mahatma Gandhi makes a compromise, but there is no doubt that our efforts will be considerably lightened... If there is no compromise (4th July, 1944)
>
> The only other alternative plan (to mine)... is that of Mahatma Gandhi embodied in the 'Quit India'

[3] *India — A Restatement* p.237

> resolution. If that plan succeeds, our plan and our activities will be set at naught. On the contrary, if Mahatma Gandhi's plan fails – as it has failed – then all hopes of Indian independence rest entirely on the fulfilment of our plan. (*12th July, 1944*).

The long and the short of it was that Bose's liberation of India would depend on his being able to win the Indian Army and people over to his side when the Japanese invasion took place. The tenser the political situation, the easier that would be. If there were a compromise settlement, he could never again pose as the liberator of India.

In this his interests coincided with that of the Japanese: if there were a settlement in India, then the Japanese could expect not only a more efficient and concentrated Indian war effort, but an immediate increase in the forces opposing them in the field as troops were released from Internal Security duties in India. But we may believe that this was to Bose a secondary consideration. He was following an independent and coherent line of his own. He resisted compromise now for the old reasons —mistrust of the British, mistrust of the Congress leadership, his belief that independence could not be won that way. The possibility of an accord between Gandhi and Jinnah which might permit a compromise, threw him into a panic. Unable, himself, to act because of preoccupation with the I.N.A. survivors of the retreat from Imphal, he ordered his Propaganda Minister, Mr. Sivaram, to start a full-scale effort against the talks and against Gandhi. Sivaram resigned rather than carry out what he regarded as an infamous plan; he was by now convinced that Bose's object was to establish himself as Dictator of India with Japanese support and that his policies were bound to create unrest and dissatisfaction at home.

Without Sivaram this particular campaign could not proceed. In fact it was quite unnecessary. Jinnah could not bring himself to trust Gandhi to keep his agreement when power had once been transferred and insisted that the British should referee and enforce the division of India. The talks thus broke down without any assistance from Bose, and the communal deadlock became more rigid as the months went by. It was public opinion in Britain which in the end demanded and obtained a new political initiative. In June 1945 Lord Wavell took to India proposals for an interim arrangement to cover constitution-making and the final transfer of power. It was proposed to reconstitute the Viceroy's Executive Council so that all the members except the Viceroy and the Commander-in-Chief would be Indian politicians. When this was done it was hoped that responsible government could be resumed in the provinces where, owing to Congress non-cooperation, it was now suspended. In order to obtain agreement Lord Wavell was to hold a conference of party leaders and provincial premiers and ex-premiers, who would give him lists from which he could select the members of his new Council.

It may fairly be said that from the return of Lord Wavell with these proposals, it was abundantly clear – and in most circles in India this was accepted – that the question was no longer whether Britain was to hand over power, but how quickly this could decently be done. Bose, ranting at the British for making the new offer and at the Congress for considering it, was a voice out of tune alike with nationalist sentiment in India and with that of his more responsible followers in Malaya. He pictured the proposals as one more British trick, intended this time to relieve the war-weary population of Britain from the need to find more men for the remote Japanese war. The last drop of Indian blood and treasure was to be exacted, and the abandonment of the independence struggle, in return for a 'few jobs on the Viceroy's Executive Council'; it was 'Swaraj for the Viceroy', but for nobody else. Britain's failure to grant an amnesty to all political prisoners and her refusal to legislate during the war were proofs of insincerity. Furthermore, a settlement would deprive Indian nationalism of the American backing it had won while the active, bitter struggle against Britain was making news and of possible help from new friends like Soviet Russia. The Anglo-American victory over Germany had made no difference: the correct recipe for independence was still resistance within India, armed struggle without and 'diplomacy in the international field'. Indian nationalism was on the threshold of victory, let it give nothing away. The British were in a hurry: Lord Wavell wanted agreement before the British General Election on

July 5th, so as to win votes for the Tories. Let India not be deceived; if she must bargain let her wait for the Labour Government.

What was to be the central issue in the Conference which the Viceroy summoned at Simla was soon clear. Equal representation in the Council was proposed for Muslims and Hindus. The Congress, as an inter-communal body, claimed to nominate Congress Muslims to the Muslim seats, the Muslim League recognised no Muslims but its own. This fundamental disagreement was quickly realised by Bose who did his best to sharpen it. The Congress, he insisted was a national organisation, not a sectional one. The Viceroy was favouring the Muslim League, so that when the new Council began to work, the League members, as well as those nominated to represent the minorities, would support him. The Congress Councillors would then be powerless to prevent the vivisection of India to the British and Muslim advantage:

> At this critical hour the destiny of India lies in your hands. Now is your time for starting the 'Quit India' campaign all over the country, and thereby making it impossible for anyone to arrive at a compromise.

Bose was certain that this would be the verdict of the Congress as a whole, if the members of the Working Committee – itself unrepresentative of leftist Congress opinion – dared to consult it.

When the Congress leaders decided to attend the Simla Conference, Bose made the point more fully. The Working Committee was not empowered to take decisions and negotiate for the whole of the Congress. It was ignoring the All India Committee and doing what was contrary to the whole policy, and tradition of the Congress. Let them think again before they hurled another half-million Indian soldiers into Britain's imperialist war to fight their own kith and kin in the I.N.A. For there was no doubt that the I.N.A. would fight for Malaya, its base in East Asia, even as it had done for Burma.

Night after night Bose's voice could be heard, arguing, condemning, exhorting. Mr. Raghavan and his other Ministers made their broadcasts too, but they disagreed with their leader's intransigent view, confiding rather to the judgment of those who were negotiating, and their tone was therefore more moderate. While the Congress leaders had been silent, Bose's right to speak for India could be conceded: now that there seemed to be a conflict once more between his opinion and that of Mr. Gandhi, Mr. Gandhi's was preferred. But Bose need not have worried: the talks broke down. For the last time he voted himself a triumph.

The Indians of Singapore had again celebrated 'Netaji Week' in July. There had been mass meetings to mark Bose's two years of leadership, sports meetings, an I.N.A. Review, processions on the grand scale. The rich were herded together once more to hear new demands for money: Bose ordered the arrest of five of the defaulters warned in January, and the arrests were carried out by the Japanese Security Police. More demand notes went out from the League. A man who had promised ten thousand dollars sent only half: 'I regret that our instructions are not to accept part payments. Netaji made it very clear that promises must be fulfilled in a day or two. It is incumbent on you to pay your promised amount at once.' Kuala Lumpur was similarly visited, five defaulters being arrested there also.

On July 8th Bose laid the foundation stone of a memorial to the I.N.A. dead, on the Singapore water front. A few days later he went on a tour of Indian communities in Malaya, visiting with particular interest the units of his 3rd Division which had been disposed in North Malaya since the autumn of 1944. The Divisional Commander had agreed with the Japanese on the localities for which the I.N.A. would fight. But his task had not been without difficulties. Desertions and unrest in his command had continued. On the one hand both officers and men were secretly trafficking with the Communist-led anti-Japanese guerrillas who were coming more into the open, on the other he was being continually pressed by the Japanese to allow his troops to be used against the guerrillas. This pressure he had resisted and Bose now supported him, but there resulted a straining of relations which would have been serious if invasion had come.

Hardly had he returned to Singapore, where Bose's

business was still mainly financial, when there broke out which appeared to be a grave mutiny at the I.N.A. Training Centre in Seremban. Anxious to discover for himself the real significance of this, Bose accompanied the soldiers and armoured cars sent up from Singapore to restore the situation. It was a tea-cup storm, an officer not so much corrupt as comfortable. But Bose was keenly interested and he was still at the guest house in Seremban when, in the early hours of August 11th, he learned that Russia had declared war on Japan. He was without his wireless set and received the news briefly by telephone. He did not let it disturb what he was doing and went on with the careful and detailed investigation of an officer's motives and conduct, hiding his head, as it were, in work. Next day he was annoyed at a message recalling him to Singapore: 'How does it affect us?' he said. 'We shall have to go on whatever happens.'[4]. Nevertheless his thoughts were not entirely with his people in South-East Asia. He followed the news of the Russian advance into Manchuria: 'I wonder,' he said, 'where the Japanese will make a stand.' Was this another remote chance for him? Did it bring him nearer to a Soviet sanctuary?

The phone call had not been to do with Russia's progress. At about 2 a.m. on August 13th two of his advisers arrived from Singapore to tell him that Japan was about to surrender. It was a hot night; he was sitting in his vest

---

[4] This account of Bose's last days relies heavily on *Unto Him a Witness*, by S.A. Ayer, pp. 49-54.

under a fan. For a moment he said nothing, then: 'So that is that. Now, what next?' And later: 'Well, don't you see that we are the only people who have not surrendered?' Where indeed did the Provisional Government stand? Had Japan expected it to declare war on Russia two days ago? Strange, he had not thought of that. The talk wandered on until the messengers went to bed. Bose's first reaction was then to summon Swami and Raghavan from Penang. 'Now we have got to think out what we shall do,' he said quietly to Ayer as they sat on the verandah outside his room. Ayer was anxious that he should have some sleep – but there was to be little rest that night – 'It doesn't matter. We shall have plenty of rest from tomorrow on.'

Bose reached Singapore on the evening of August 13th. He conferred immediately with his civil and military chiefs, and agreed on instructions to be sent to League branches. There were further conferences on the fourteenth: routine matters such as the disposal of funds and the temporary administration of the I.N.A. were easily settled. Bose issued a Special Order warning his people against rumours.[5]. Hachiya sent him formal notice that Japan was to surrender. The Cabinet discussions went on: the I.N.A. would be surrendered as it stood – there could be no disagreement about that – and all records would be destroyed but the Ministers talked on endlessly; what should their leader do? Again Bose himself would not decide, said he was inclined to stay and face surrender with

[5] Appendix II, No. 13

the rest, and allowed pressure on him to be gone – somewhere, anywhere – to come from his advisers. August 14th wore on. In the afternoon he had a tooth out: in the evening he saw a play about the Rani of Jhansi staged by the women of the Regiment. Most of the work was done, all possibilities had been faced and there was still no final decision.

But it is probable that Bose's mind was made up. Had he not written: 'There is nothing that lures me more than a life of adventure... in search of the Unknown'? Now again there was the lure of adventure that had so often mastered him. Even as in 1940 death had seemed better than passivity in prison, so perhaps now, in the very crisis of uncertainty, he could not bear to sit idle. The British had won their war and would presumably have their will of India, but the right course for India was still the same – resistance within, armed struggle without and international diplomacy. Must these last two elements now really be abandoned, or could he find some way of keeping things going? The Japanese had again in the last month rejected his request for contact with Russia but might there not be chance in the confusion of the next few days to seek asylum there? How far had the Russians got? How soon would they be in Dairen? The Cabinet resumed its discussions on the fifteenth: in the afternoon the radio announcement of surrender came from Tokyo. The last Order of the Day[6] was written, the final broadcast prepared.

---

[6] Appendix II, No. 14

As might have been expected there was little advice to be obtained from the Japanese in Singapore. Numbed by their country's fate, and each officer faced with the urgent problem of honourable suicide, the defeated could well be excused their contemptuous indifference to Indian affairs. Some committed suicide singly or in the mass, some accepted with bewilderment their Emperor's decision, none cared how the surrender of the I.N.A. should proceed. During the evening Bose made his broadcast. Late that night, under strong pressure from his Cabinet, he decided to leave and approach successively higher Japanese headquarters, until he found a commander who would give him some guidance. That, at least, was his official purpose. In fact he would seek refuge in Russian territory and resume the struggle from there. The Cabinet sat until dawn on August 16th. Bose appointed a committee to carry out his last instructions, and made Major-General Kiani official representative of the Provisional Government in Singapore. There remained the choice of companions for the new venture. He wanted to take as many of his Ministers and chief soldiers as possible, but not all would come. Kiani had declined the honour, Raghavan, Swami and Thivy were in North Malaya and, when the plane was ready to leave at 9.30 a.m. on August 10th, had still not arrived. Bose took therefore Mr. Ayer, Lieutenant-Colonel Habib-ur-Rehman, who was I.N.A. Chief-of-Staff, and one other officer. He left orders for some to follow as they reached Singapore, and hoped to pick up others on his way.

At Bangkok Bose conferred with his I.N.A. Major-General Bhonsle, with General Isoda and other Japanese: they advised him to approach Southern Army Headquarters. The party which left for Saigon on August 17th to do this was somewhat larger. Besides Isoda and Hachiya, there were Abid Hassan, another officer and a second civilian Minister. In Saigon it appeared that no orders on the surrender of the I.N.A. had been received from Tokyo. As he told him General Isoda offered Bose one seat in an aircraft bound for Tokyo via Dairen in Manchuria. There was another heart-searching conference: should Bose go on alone? He must not seem to be running away – once more he had to be persuaded: there was no sense in his being captured: if there was only one place, he must take it. The Japanese had waited for the answer: when he pressed them, they allowed one more seat for Habib-ur-Rahman, and promised to send the rest of the party on as soon as possible.

It was a hurried, bewildered parting for which nobody was quite ready. 'Jai Hind' he said as he shook hands with those he was leaving, 'I will see you later.' The plane, a twin-engined bomber carrying senior Japanese officers, took off at 5.15 p.m. and landed at Tourane in French Indo-China later the same evening. The flight was resumed next day. Taihoku in Formosa being reached at about 2 p.m. on August 18th. The passengers had lunch while the plane refuelled. At about 2.30 p.m. just after it had taken off again, the plane lost part of its port propeller. It caught fire, dived steeply and crashed. With other survivors, Bose and Habib-ur-Rahman struggled from the wreckage. Bose's clothes were on fire and his companion beat out the flames. But Netaji had head injuries in addition to terrible burns on his face and body and even before he was taken to hospital he seems to have realised that he would not recover.

Habib-ur-Rahman was near his bedside throughout the day, while life slowly ebbed. Bose rallied from time to time as drugs administered to him by doctors took effect; sometimes he fainted away with pain. It was clear that nothing could save him. He spoke quite calmly and, although his lips were grotesquely swollen and it was difficult for him to speak, he called for an interpreter and dictated a message to Field Marshal Terauchi. A few minutes before the end he spoke to his companion: 'Habib,' he said, 'I feel that I shall die very soon. I have fought for India's freedom until the last. Tell my countrymen "India will be free before long." Long live Free India.' Presently he asked for morphia. Shortly afterwards, between 8 and 9 p.m. a violent shiver shook his bandaged body; then it stiffened and he was gone.

Habib sought to have the body embalmed or transported to Singapore, but this was now beyond the Japanese. There was no other course; the remains were cremated at Taihoku on August 20th and the ashes taken to Tokyo some weeks later by Habib-ur-Rahman. Funeral rites were observed at the Reokoju Temple on September 14th.

News of Bose's death did not reach the outside world until August 21st when the facts of the accident were broadcast from Delhi. The nine senior officers and ministers who were by then trying to follow him stopped, stunned and confused, where they happened to be. Everywhere Indians mourned, for a time half-believing that some miracle would cause him to reappear when least expected, that this was some new strategem of disappearance; and even now, as the years pass, some still look for him, or see him momentarily, disguised as a *Sanyasi* roaming through the hills and villages of Free India. But it is humanly certain that he died on August 18th, 1945, in the Nammon Ward of the Japanese Military Hospital at Taihoku. Had he survived and reached Dairen, he would have tried to place himself and as many of his faithful friends as possible under Russian protection. This was still something he had to do for India, his last and decisive contribution to her freedom – a freedom that others had already won.

EPILOGUE

Let them wait until February 4th, 1946, and then start criticising us if our timetable goes wrong. (July 12th, 1944)

THE sudden end of the war with Japan in mid-August 1945 was as much a surprise to the scattered British and American forces in South-East Asia as it was to the Japanese Army. The invasion of Malaya, planned for late September had to be mounted in haste as a peaceful but cautious occupation of Malaya, Siam, Indo-China, Java, Sumatra and other Allied territories. Such an improvisation could not be immediate and when it took place the recovery of prisoners of war was necessarily its first object. Thus before the arrival of Allied troops the retiring Japanese were able, if not to sow, at least to allow to be sown, the seeds of the political unrest which has burgeoned in those territories since. In Malaya, the first country to be occupied in strength, the effect of a three-week anarchy was least unfortunate, but even so it was then estimated that, in order to bring the country back to its former tranquillity, a considerable occupation force would be needed for some years. In Java and Indo-China the delay considerably prejudiced the return of the Colonial Powers, for these countries had been partially controlled by nationalist governments for some weeks before the occupation forces arrived. The effect on the I.N.A. was the disappearance of nearly all the locally enlisted soldiers. When the British arrived in Malaya and Siam, few but the ex-prisoner-of-war members of the I.N.A. remained in their camps. Their examination and repatriation were nevertheless to take many months.

This was in a sense the second half of a problem. It will already have been clear that the disposal of members of the I.N.A. captured in battle must have been full of difficulties for the Indian government. The matter was not simply one of discipline and justice. These men had valuable military information about the Japanese and experience of Japanese methods which in some ways enhanced their value as soldiers. The information could be written down and handed on, but it was dangerous to allow a soldier, full of the propaganda of Subhash Chandra Bose, to return to the Indian Army which had been so carefully protected against subversive nationalism, even to improve its knowledge of enemy methods.

Besides interrogating the returned soldiers for enemy information, therefore, it was necessary to assess how safe it was to return a man to his battalion or regiment. Many were found fit to go back. The great majority, whose spirit was thought not to have been completely broken, were sent to rehabilitation centres before being returned to the Army. Those who had been so influenced that they were in effect virulent Axis propaganda agents were retained in custody. The Service organisations responsible for this assessment, and for the long succession or arduous interrogations which often preceded it, was housed, with its prisoners, in the Red Fort, that great walled palace of Delhi which had been the focal point of much of the drama of the Indian Mutiny of 1857, the goal of Bose's hopes and the battle-cry of his soldiers. Thousands of them reached it as prisoners.

In a very few cases, and it must be remembered that every one of the 1,500 members of the I.N.A. taken in the Imphal Campaign had committed the gravest possible military offence, the disciplinary aspect predominated. A few Viceroy's Commissioned Officers, N.C.O.'s and senior sepoys caught in battle distributing or shouting propaganda, firing on British-Indian soldiers or betraying them to the Japanese, were tried by court martial and imprisoned or executed. A like fate overtook some of the submarine and parachute agents who tried to carry out their espionage missions in India. These cases numbered less than thirty, and the executions only nine. No other disciplinary action was taken at all.

The mass surrenders at Zeyawaddy, in Rangoon, and in Singapore and Bangkok when the war ended, presented the second half of the problem. There was still information to be gleaned for security or historical purposes, but, partly because of the animosity displayed by the returned prisoners of war against the I.N.A., discipline became the main consideration. The marks of the earlier security classification – 'Black,' 'Grey', and 'White' – were retained but the question was now the degree of man's guilt and whether or not, with or without his arrears of pay, he should be discharged from the Indian Army. Over ten thousand I.N.A. soldiers were repatriated from Rangoon between May and October 1945. In September a further seven thousand surrendered in Malaya and Bangkok. The evacuation of many thousands of Allied prisoners from their fearful camps was the first call on shipping and it was not until March 1946 that the last of the I.N.A. left South-East Asia for home. This had certain consequences. In the eleven months which had then elapsed since the first contact of the Indian Army, Navy and Air Force with the mass of the I.N.A. in Rangoon, there had been widespread fraternisation. This could not be avoided – all were Indians serving in a foreign country, and contact with the I.N.A. often meant the reunion of close relatives separated since 1941. Its result was a political consciousness which the Indian Serviceman had never before possessed. He received a picture of the I.N.A. uncorrected by the observations of prisoners of war or by any official statement. He saw it as a band of oppressed heroes and listened eagerly to the hospitable and now fully politically conscious Indian civilians of South–east Asia, who had their own tale to tell about an independent Indian Government and the departed glories of Bose's Cabinet.

Indian soldiers who had seen the truth about the I.N.A. at Imphal were fast leaving the Army and there was often no voice to contradict the stories of universal I.N.A. heroism in battle. Thus gradually the Indian Services came to have a certain sympathy with the popular clamour about the I.N.A. which was being raised in India, and there can be little doubt that the serious naval mutinies and the unrest in the other two Services early in 1946, owed something to its influence. The British Prime Minister himself was compelled to recognise the new feeling: 'Today,' said Mr. Attlee on March 15th 1946, 'the national idea has spread... not least perhaps among some of those soldiers who have done such wonderful service in the war.'

Popular reaction in India had been slow at first. In July 1945 the battle between the Indian National Congress and the Muslim League on the one hand, and between the Congress and the British on the other, had been resumed. It seemed in Delhi that the apparent impossibility of a communal settlement might delay India's independence for a further decade. The mass of the Indian people was contented and peaceful, and while the Congress might abuse the British, there was no theme to arouse popular indignation, no General Dyer, no massacre of Jallianwala Bagh.

Then the war ended, and the story of the I.N.A., hitherto regarded as a military secret, was released in an official announcement. Mr. Nehru referred to the matter on August 20th:

> Now a very large number of officers and soldiers of the I.N.A.... are prisoners and some of them at least have been executed... At any time it would have been wrong to treat them too harshly, but at this time – when it is said big changes are impending in India, it would be a very grave mistake leading to far-reaching consequences if they were treated just as ordinary rebels. The punishment given them would in effect be a punishment on all India and all Indians, and a deep wound would be reacted in millions of hearts.

At the same time bodies of Legionaries from Germany, unrepentant, truculent, and some still in German uniform, were seen in trains and on stations as they were taken to their camps and regimental centres. Bose's death caused further publicity. A film was smuggled out of Singapore and shown privately in Delhi. By the end of September as much as could be obtained from unofficial sources, supplemented by the stories of returning prisoners of war and Indian civilians form Rangoon and Malaya, had been widely circulated.

The Government of India had announced that the rank and file of the I.N.A. 'who yielded to pressure and were so misguided as to join forces raised by the enemy' would be leniently and generously treated. Only the leaders were to be court-martialled and those charged with atrocities. The first Congress reaction was favorable, but in mid-September the All-India Congress Committee resolved that 'it would be a tragedy if these officers, men and women, were punished for the offence of having laboured, however mistakenly, for the freedom of India.... The A.I.C.C. therefore earnestly trusts that (they) .... will be released'. Two days later the Congress set up a Defence Committee, to handle the cases of I.N.A. soldiers and civilian members of the Indian Independence League brought to trial.

It soon became known that three of the commanders in the I.N.A. campaign near Mount Popa in 1945 were to be tried by court martial in November. There was immediate and widespread public interest. The trial was attacked by the Congress as an act of savage oppression, and the handling of the whole matter by the British was condemned. The I.N.A. was eulogised and glorified in the most fulsome terms of its own propaganda: its object was the same as that of the Congress itself, and its sufferings were in the same cause. Nehru 'had no doubt... that the men and women who had enrolled in this Army... had done so because of their passionate desire to serve the cause of India's freedom; also that if, owing to some technical interpretation of military law, large numbers of them received severe sentence, it would be a tragedy for India'.[1] This was clearly to be a test case. The Defence Committee went immediately into action, with the most illustrious members of the Indian Bar prepared to do battle. Mr. Bhulabhai Desai was chosen to conduct the defence.

---

[1] Foreword by J.L Nehru to *My Memories of the I.N.A. and Its Netaji,* by Shah Nawaz.

The accused were Shah Nawaz, Sahgal and Dhillon, all regular officers of the Indian Army, whose actions in the Mount Popa operations are described in Chapter VII. There were seventeen defence counsels, among them Mr. Nehru himself, when the trial opened in the Red Fort on November 5th. The charges were of some complexity, involving not only the general conduct of the officers in 'waging war against the King', but death sentences they were alleged to have had carried out on soldiers of the I.N.A. The trial lasted until December 31st. Every word of it was reported throughout India, with long commentaries day by day. The defence was a bold challenge to the legality of the trial. It was argued that the I.N.A. was the military force of a properly constituted and widely recognised government, which the accused had joined as true patriots. There were long and intricate appeals to historical precedent and international law. As for the death sentences, the defence challenged the evidence that any executions had taken place at all, forcing one prosecution witness to admit in court that he had been tutored. There were thirty witnesses for the prosecution and twelve for the defence, some of them men who had themselves been prominent under Bose. One hundred and twenty-five exhibits were produced, and the published report runs to three hundred and eighty-seven closely printed pages.

From the first day the attention of India was focussed on the courtroom and the Red Fort, whose place in nationalist history greatly heightened the drama. Long before the end the country was in an emotional uproar, 'The honour and the law of the Indian National Army are on trial before this court,' said Mr. Desai, 'and the right to wage war with immunity on the part of a subject race for their liberation.' The trial of Bahadur Shah, last of the Moghuls, was recalled, as so often by Bose himself. Mr. Nehru has said of the country's feeling:

> Behind the law there was something deeper and more vital, something that stirred the subconscious depths of the Indian mind. Those three officers and the I.N.A. became symbols of India fighting for her independence. All minor issues faded away... The trial dramatised... the old contest: England versus India. It became in reality not merely a question of law or of forensic eloquence... but rather a trial of strength between the will of the Indian people and the will of those who hold power in India.[2]

Within the courtroom, the law was still the law. The charges of waging war were found proven and likewise one of the charges arising out of the death sentences. All three officers were sentenced to cashiering and transportation for life.

It was clear that the matter could not rest there. Apart from other considerations; there was by this time strong if uninformed feeling on the subject in England. The Commander-in-Chief, Field-Marshall Sir Claude

---

[2] Foreword by J.L. Nehru to the published proceedings of the I.N.A. Court Martial.

Auchinleck, remitted the sentences of transportation, but confirmed the other penalties, 'since it is in all circumstances a most serious crime for an officer or soldier to throw off his allegiance and wage war against the State.' The principle had to be upheld for the sake of the stability of all lawful governments.

The wisdom and severity of this sober judgement were lost upon India. The Commander-in-Chief's action amounted, in the popular mind, to an acquittal, and the announcement a few days earlier than there would be no more I.N.A. trials except for atrocities was seen as an admission that there had been no case to bring. The Congress was triumphant: it had rallied the people of India and revived the old militant anti-British feeling of the civil disobedience days. It at once began to agitate for the speedy release of the men whose cases had not yet been examined, and harried the Government to complete the repatriation of those still held abroad. Mr. Gandhi visited the Red Fort frequently and conferred with the detained. The prisoners themselves made life increasingly uncomfortable for those responsible for the disciplinary assessment. This remaining task was hurried through and the returned I.N.A. soldiers sent back to their villages with all speed.

There were a few more court martials – of those concerned with atrocities, at the Bidadari Concentration Camp – but in May 1946, just as the trials of the officers who had tortured Captain Durrani were about to commence, all remaining charges were withdrawn.

When he visited Singapore in March 1946, Mr. Nehru was given an unofficial military reception by thousands of local civilian ex-members of the I.N.A. who, no longer afraid to admit their membership, had put on their old uniforms and lined the streets down which he would drive with Lord Mountbatten. He was not much impressed, soundly rebuking a uniformed group which made a disturbance outside his hotel. Like other Congress leaders he was anxious about the effect of such jubilant young men upon the discipline of the Indian Army, for which he would some day be responsible. But as a political weapon the I.N.A. had been the greatest use to the Congress in India. It had restored to it the ability to cause widespread civil commotion, and that in circumstances where the Government might hesitate to use the Indian Army. The essential soundness of the Indian Army was in fact to carry it through worse matters than the I.N.A. agitation. But in 1946, with the Bombay and Karachi naval mutinies fresh in the public mind, few outside the Army itself could be confident of that.

There can thus be little doubt that the Indian National Army, not in its unhappy career on the battlefield, but in its thunderous disintegration, hastened the end of British rule in India. The agitation which surrounded the trials turned the issue of independence for India into an instant burning question once more. 'Subhash's suddenly amplified figure,' says Dilip Kumar Roy, 'added to the romance of an Indian Army marching singing to Delhi, galvanised a frustrated nation out of its torpor, and substantially damaged the insulation of the Indian Army from the magnetic currents of popular enthusiasm for immediate independence'.

It would be too much to suggest that Bose had seen with any clarity what might occur after Japanese defeat although he certainly counted on the disbanded I.N.A. to influence the Indian Army in Burma after he left it. But he knew that the Indian struggle would soon be renewed, and he had urged his followers to remain steadfast in the faith he had given them, believing that, somehow or other, they would have their part to play. That the greatest influence he ever exerted lay in the accidental effect of the trials, whose setting in the Red Fort, nationalist goal, symbol of alien Imperial power, and centre of the Indian world, turned so much to the advantage of the Congress, does not diminish the authenticity of his vision.

The loss of that vision was, to India on the threshold of independence, a portent only less significant than the murder of Mr. Gandhi in 1948. For when he died S.C. Bose was only forty-eight, eight years younger than Mr. Nehru, still comparatively a young man for all his twenty-four years of politics, still somewhat the voice of Youth, still with an irresistible appeal to the young and with unquestionably a distinguished contribution to make. His own countrymen must assess both what his contribution was and what it might have been: they must judge of the validity of his non-communalism, of the soundness and expediency of his domestic policies. Here let us attempt to answer only the question he would himself have posed: 'Will he live in History?'

There were undeniable faults. His undergraduate self-assurance grew with the years into a prodigious arrogance. In 1928, as a young man with little more than his years in prison to serve for political experience, he had no hesitation in asserting not only that the British were wrong, but that Gandhi was wrong, that the Indian Struggle had no place for mystics and vague philosophers. In the following ten years he grew only more certain that Gandhi was wrong, and that he alone was right: Gandhi was 'an old, useless piece of furniture'. Bose's Congress Presidential year in 1938, by which perhaps Gandhi hoped to bring the angry young man into the main stream of Congress development, led in 1939 to open defiance; and in his short-lived triumph Bose talked to Gandhi as to an opponent he had beaten at the hustings. Even the crushing defeat which removed him from office, the failure of the popular support of which he had been so sure and the reluctant Congress disciplinary action against him held no message for his impenetrable self-esteem. He was still right, so right that he must escape from poor, enslaved, misguided India, in order to save her not only from the British, but from herself.

Under Axis patronage he behaved more and more like a dictator. The arch-rebel tolerated no rebellion against himself, no criticism, no failure to cooperate in the way he had chosen; the man who had been so sensitive to the sufferings of others could now condone brutality towards his opponents. At the end, when he was too remote from the political scene for sound judgement, when his own intolerance had cut him off from any corrective friendship, the Congress, Jinnah, Lord Wavell were still wrong: Mr. Gandhi could not be trusted to do the best for India; Russia, of all people, could be relied upon to help.

Some other things we seek in vain. There was laughter, but no humour, his wit was bitter, leaden-footed. The distinction between friend and flatterer was not always clear to him. His rhetoric, stirring perhaps in Bengali or Urdu, held in English only the stereotyped phrase, the toneless repetition. There was no lack of physical courage, he could stand as straight as any under aerial bombs or bullets. The escape from India, the journey to the Far East needed great spirit. He maintained a brave independence from the Japanese. But there were moments of unsteadiness – the flight from Meiktila, the hysterical outburst against the staff officers' desertions and the orders against treachery. The final plan to put himself at the mercy of the advancing Russian armies in Manchuria was bold enough, but many vacillations preceded it, at Siagon, Singapore, Rangoon – even at Pyinmana where he first said that he would fight to the last. The revolt against the Congress in 1939 was bold; indecision preceded that too. There were the illusions about the outcome of the war, about communalism, about Russia, about Indian Army and I.N.A. morale, the readiness to believe what suited him, the utter failure to grasp the social and political changes which war had brought about in India; the incredible *naivete* in matters military, Fujihara said of him:

> As leader of the Army Bose became the foundation of spiritual strength and was the pivot of the I.N.A. organisation. However, the standard of his operational tactics was, it must be said with regret, low. He was inclined to be idealistic and not realistic. For instance, without being familiar with the fighting power of the I.N.A., he was always demanding that the I.N.A. be employed in a separate and decisive role... and when the tide turned and the Japanese Army had retreated... he urged that the I.N.A. should continue to confront the Allies until their aim was achieved.

Yet it is something to be sure of oneself, to stake all on one's own judgement. Many of Bose's weaknesses were the weaknesses of his single-minded strength. For most, the personality of the man was overwhelming: there was a genius of enthusiasm, of inspiration. Men found that when they were with him only the cause mattered, they saw only through his eyes, thought the thoughts he gave them, could deny him nothing. For the I.N.A. as for Bengal, there was no resisting his compulsion. Rabindranath Tagore had once hailed him as the long-sought Deliverer of the Bengali nation, the one who would unite and reawaken. Shah Nawaz echoed the feelings of many other officers when he said of him:

> From the moment I came into personal contact with him he exercised a strange influence over me. Even now, I do not know in what proportion the man, the soldier and the statesman in him were blended. At home the man in him seemed to dominate; at the front and in the midst of his troops, the soldier in him shone in splendid glory and in the councils and conferences and at his desk... his brilliant statesmanship made a profound impression on one and all of us.

The fact that he was neither a good soldier, nor the infallible political genius his disciples believed, makes only more remarkable his power of fascination. He gave to the Indian communities of South-East Asia, for the first time, a common idea, and inspired in many of the soldiers a loyalty which for the time obliterated their sentiment for the remote King-Emperor.

In this alone there was an element of greatness, the greatness of this single-minded dedicated leader, if only of a forlorn hope. Was he then more than this? The answer must be found in the nature of his dream for India. To what end did he wish to lead? In considering this there is to be remembered his predominant feeling for the unity of India, and his sense of the ingrained, vested evils which possessed her. Poverty, ignorance, the caste system and the other social anachronisms of Hinduism would not disappear of themselves. This ills could be removed, the many social and religious components held together and India turned into a modern industrial democracy only by a very strong authority acting on a well-made, long-prepared plan. Bose's belief in an authoritarian government for India had grown up in the West, but his model was the Turkish regime of Mustapha Kemal who seemed to have faced the same problems of social adaptation that confronted India, and not the Nazi or Fascist caricatures. Bose saw a strong Congress Government settling down to the accomplishment of a great social and industrial revolution in India and then handing over, after perhaps twenty years, to the processes of democracy.

Mr. Gandhi, on the other hand, was not only unwilling to make any plan beyond independence, he seemed to lack the determination to wield power at all. Here lay the heart of Bose's quarrel with him: beneath it was the turbulent Bengali inheritance. Bose believed that a constitutional transfer of power would leave India divided and the new governing party without the authority and prestige it needed to carry out the reforms. Fighting the British was an essential source of unity for India and of political prestige for her future governors. The more bitter the struggle, the greater the glory. Hence came his insistence that the struggle must continue to the last, his advocacy of revolution in 1939, his horror of a negotiated settlement at any time and his leaning even towards terrorism as the ultimate means of preventing it.

Bose had always seen that British defeat in war might create the opportunity for the essential seizure of power. When, after his failure to lead the Congress to rebellion in 1939, impatience overmastered him, his first idea was for Russia to champion Indian independence before the Germans won the war, his next that he should influence German treatment of India himself. His move to the Far East reflected the early Japanese victories. He obtained from Tojo what Hitler had withheld and planned to save India from Japanese military government, heading the Congress dictatorship if necessary himself. Even after he realised the certainty of Japanese defeat, he hoped for a foothold in India from which, with an expanded I.N.A. he could keep the Indian crisis in being.

The loss of Burma and the hard, sorrowful march to Bangkok did not destroy that vision. Bose still thought his objective attainable in India, whatever happened in South-East Asia. He now saw the I.N.A. carrying the infection of his influence into the Indian Army, to loosen still further the British grasp and to deepen nationalist confidence. Still he must battle against any political compromise in India, still outside help must be secured for the struggle – whether from America, whose continued sympathy he sensed, or from Russia, whose post-war opposition to the West he clearly foresaw. Never would he give up: somehow, he was sure, the dream would be fulfilled. After its fulfillment must come reform. He believed with every fibre of his being that until the ills of illiteracy, caste, public corruption and the near slavery of women had been eliminated India would not be ripe for democracy. Until these things had been set right, until the people had some idea of why they were voting, until some degree of responsibility had been induced in the press, no administration could hope to govern save as the British had done, by benevolent autocracy. Nor could anything but autocracy accomplish those reforms: the ills were too deep, rooted in too many vested interests.

By the magnitude of this conception, by the example of his magnetic, burning zeal, his tenacity and personal force, by the tradition he left of sacrificial patriotism, must be measured the stature of Subhash Chandra Bose. His place in Indian history cannot be denied. Idol of the masses in Bengal, his youthful daring, his *panache*, his reckless courage caught the imagination of India. He gave much to his country. Even after the ruin of all he built, something of substance remained. Had he lived to see the Republic of India, he would assuredly have given much more.

There is something yet to be said before we leave the tragedy of Bose. Bose played his part – some would say an heroic part – in the history of his country. Had his early life not been scarred with racial hatred and had Indian politics taken a different course in the years 1919 to 1921, his part might have been incomparably greater. Bose can be read as a symbol of all that went wrong between Britain and the people of India, whom he had tried so long and earnestly to rule. This study cannot end without some attempt to define what that was. What if any was the justification for the revolt of the popular leaders of India? What justification was there for the Indian National Army? What in fact is there to regret in Britain's record?

The story has often been told. There was, over more than a century, a consistent progress in the British conduct of Indian affairs. Warren Hastings in 1818, Sir Thomas Munro in 1824, Sir Henry Lawrence in 1844 looked forward to a time when British rule would cease. And these men did not live in an age when for a nation to hold an empire was to court obloquy and slander from half the world, but the height of Western Civilisation's self-confidence, when it was assumed that Western contacts must necessarily benefit the backward Orient. For India was backward, decimated often by plague and famine, her people in thrall to arbitrary and indifferent rulers, her economy and administration in chaos. To see a day when she could be 'a noble ally, enlightened and brought into the scale of nations', was vision indeed. Yet this ideal was pursued. Successive British Governments showed themselves sensitive to the development of nationalism and granted stage after stage of ordered constitutional advance. Finally two enlightened and independent nations emerged. Britain need look no further for justification of her rule.

To the unclouded brain that could see the century of progress in India as a whole, there could be no rational doubt, even in 1939, of the British determination eventually to grant independence to India. The decision to do so was in effect taken in 1917; once made it was irrevocable. But by 1939 few Indians brains were unclouded by the massive hatred of British rule which had grown up in the past thirty-five years.

In accounting for this Mr. Guy Wint[3] takes a longer and more coherent view than has been possible in these pages. He shows how the modernising influence of the British administration had produced an educated class, which in accepting the modern Western outlook, surrendered the normal direction of the Hindu Universe: 'there was no longer any religious or moral sanction,' he says, behind men's lives'. There resulted materialism and self-interest which led to social desperation and at last nihilism. Hence both the Hindu revival of the 1890's and the bomb-worshipping revolutionaries of Bengal and the Punjab in the next decade.

There was also the element of political frustration which I have examined in Chapter II.[4] The Indian right to eventual self-government was admitted, and the British intention to grant it was at first clearly stated. Then, in all the afterthoughts of the Indian Mutiny and the immense pomp of Imperial Victorian India, this purpose grew dim. Constitutional progress continued but with no clear end in view, until, during the First World War, it was realised that a crisis was near. Liberal statesmen saw that the Viceregal

---

[3] *The British in Asia.*

[4] See p. 23 ff.

Court must be brought into touch with the needs and mood of the country, that radical constitutional reforms must bring independence rapidly into view and that the European community must change its attitude towards the Indians. This latter – the social factor – was considered of paramount importance if the British partnership in India was to survive. England had given her laws, her civilisation and her culture, but had withheld her society. The social life of the European community must now be integrated with that of the many educated and cultured Indians if there was to be any harmony in political development.

A similar problem was faced with frankness and great courage in Malaya during 1952. But behind the partial solution achieved then lay thirty long years of the British social revolution. In the India of 1918 social contact with Indians on terms of equality was for the European not merely distasteful, it was unthinkable: the colour bar was discreet, but quite rigid. For this there were many reasons. There was difference of temperament; there were the European clubs, to which the community had an undoubted right, but whose exclusiveness came to symbolise the strict racial barrier. There were also social reasons – the caste system and the customary seclusion of Indian women made a mixed society unnaturally difficult, while the bourgeois background of some of the Europeans was itself a further obstacle. But the main reason was in its various forms, fear: fear for life, with old roots in sudden savagery of the Indian Mutiny, and new ones in the recent terrorism: fear of genetic mixture,[5] fear of competition for the privileged positions which Europeans held. Unconscious fear it may have been; fear often is. It manifested itself in irrational feelings of racial superiority and of loathing for a coloured skin, in talk of white prestige or in the assumed conviction that the Indian would never display the high courageous leadership necessary for political independence.

It was too much to hope that all this could be broken down overnight. Perhaps a gradual change would have been tolerable. Indian opinion, which probably understood the situation at least as well as the British did, was not pressing, though it would have needed objectivity indeed not to resent the indignities which were sometimes heaped even on Indians of culture and high social standing. But the Montagu-Chelmsford proposals of 1918, with their exhortation to social change, were bitterly resented by the European community. The Rowlatt Report, revealing for the first time the extent of terrorist activity in India during recent years, had just appeared. The old feeling of insecurity was returning – this was no moment for fraternisation, let public security be firmly established before any new risks were taken. Airy idealism was all very well for visitors for England, whose lives and families were not in constant danger: such persons could not understand and must not be allowed to dictate. In such a climate of opinion the Indian Government brought forward with speed the Rowlatt Bill, to preserve some of the powers it

[5] Philip Mason, *An Essay on Racial Tension*, p. 80 ff.

had used in wartime to deal with civil emergency.

From this grew the crisis of racial hysteria and nationalism of which, in a sense, the Amritsar tragedy was the natural outcome. As Indian opposition to the Bill grew, so the Europeans in India became more and more nervous about their personal safety. To the Indian the measure spelt the betrayal of the new liberal reforms: to the European it became the indispensable guarantee of security, the only condition on which the reforms would be tolerable at all. In this atmosphere, with political unrest rising in the Punjab, the advocates of the firm hand and the 'teaching of lessons' could secure a ready hearing – and it was one of these, buoyed up by the knowledge that the great majority of his countrymen in India supported him, who was unhappily in charge at Amritsar. He summed up in himself the loss of nerve, panic, of his whole community.

For the massacre he perpetrated no amends could be made: after it no reconciliation was possible. Racial relations had been critical, they could never be normal again. The Congress revolt, the long political struggle in which Bose and his Indian national Army were mere incidents, and the present aloofness of India from the West, followed naturally and inevitably from this one hysterical outburst.

In the immediate situation, the wise instinct of the British Parliament soon prevailed. General Dyer was necessarily condemned: 'Frightfulness' was 'absolutely foreign to the British way of doing things'.[6] Earlier direction from home had been less distinct. Montagu and Chelmsford had advocated social equality and the elimination of racial prejudice, but there had been no interference with the Rowlatt Bill – the man on the spot had been allowed to legislate for his own security in his own way.

History may question whether this was wise. The man on the spot has a strong claim to be heard in such a matter but, however, impartial, he is inevitably involved in the interests and fears of his own racial group, matters on which it is much easier to have feelings than objective views. He is concerned with immediate interests, not with long-term national responsibilities. He will always consider that affairs are best handled in his fortnight way, and will oppose interference from home. But it is at home, where the long-term responsibility lies, that the most serious consequences of his actions will often be felt. The consequences in India were twenty-seven years of racial conflict, borne not by the men of 1919 in India, but by the British people who eventually, in disgust, ended it.

This may then be the lesson of Amritsar, the lesson of Subhash Chandra Bose, the lesson of India. Racial prejudice breeds racial hatred; racial hatred breeds hysteria and racial conflict. Social equality as between governor and governed – the equality of the railway train, the hotel, the school, the restaurant – may be more important than the

[6] Sir W. Churchill, in the decisive speech in the Commons debate on the subject.

transfer of political power. If racial prejudice can be eliminated – and constant pressure from home may be needed to secure this – tolerance and goodwill may work to produce the steady, unhindered political progress that is in the real interest of all. The lesson is inescapable; it has not yet been learned.

Appendix I

THE DOCUMENTS OF 1942

1. *Letter from Indian prisoners of war to Major Fujihara.*
2. *The Bangkok Resolutions.*

THE PRISONER'S LETTER

TAIPING, 1st January 1942.

Reference your notes and memorandum handed over to us on 30th and 31st December, 1941, *we have thoroughly studied all points and in principle we agree with them. Certain minor modifications and suggestions are placed before you for your consideration.

1. OUR MODIFIED VIEWS AS REGARDS COOPERATION WITH INDIAN NATIONAL CONGRESS

We consider it a point of great honour for us to accept kind, valuable and reverent leadership of Mr. S.C. Bose and his party in Berlin. We all know that he is an extremist who believes in revolutions and radical changes. People in India are most anxiously waiting for any movement started by Mr. Bose and they are ready to support him. He is extremely popular amongst all

* They have not survived.

freedom loving Indians, even his political enemies have great respect and regard for him. His photos can be seen in practically every house in India. In most cases people worship him like a god. He is a leader whose very name will stir up a great revolution amongst the Indian masses, which will cause a split in the Indian Army. It will cause a split in the Indian National Congress circle and the majority of the Congress will join Mr. Bose. We the members of the Indian National Army, are prepared to shed every drop of our blood for S.C. Bose. His very name puts new life into us.

We sincerely appreciate the Japanese government's efforts to cooperate with Mr. S.C. Bose. We further request that the Japanese Government may kindly use all its political influence to get Mr. S.C. Bose's support and leadership for such a great movement. If the Japanese Government is successful in it, then in our opinion half the battle in India is won. The day Mr. S.C. Bose's name comes before us we promise that if it suits our purpose we will openly condemn the Indian National Congress.

We appreciate very valuable work done by Mr. Pritam Singh in Malaya. We have great respect and regard for him and will do our best to enhance his influence and prestige. We are willing to cooperate with him with great pleasure.

2. We request that as far as Co-Prosperity Sphere is concerned the Japanese Government may very kindly

discuss it directly with Mr. S.C. Bose. We will be most willing to agree to any decision mutually agreed upon by the Japanese government and Mr. S.C. Bose. We only want to see for our information details and description of Co-Prosperity.

3. PARTICIPATION OF INDIAN NATIONAL ARMY IN MALAYA AND BURMA

It is true that the Army which is not prepared to fight in the front line is not worth its name. We do not want to be disinterested and passive observers of the Japanese operation. We also realise that we will not be able to show our face to the world if Indians do not play any active part in freeing their motherland. On the other hand it will be an honour to the Indian National Army to fight side by side with the glorious and world-famed Japanese Army. We request that before sending the Indian National Army to the front line the following points should be considered:

(a) The present Indian National Army consists of men belonging to about twenty different regiments coming from different parts of India. It is in fact a very strange mixture. In several cases they speak different languages. To train them under new leaders and under new ideas to fight against the army from which they have come requires some time.

(b) It is also essential that when the Indian National

Army is used for the first time it should set a very good example of its bravery and fighting spirit. It should enter the battlefield most modernly armed and equipped. As it is going to fight side by side with the Japanese Army, it is requested that it should be armed and equipped and trained in the same manner. It is just a foundation today, we hope in the near future it is going to be a very big Army. Putting it in the front line with inferior equipment is sending it to be butchered as was done by the English. This will set a bad example and morale will be lost.

(c) If the Indian National Army is used in Malaya we must not forget that in several cases our men will be fighting against their own units. In certain cases they have got their real brothers and other near relations serving in their own and other units in Malaya. To prepare our men to fight against all this again requires time.

(d) We should also remember that the Indian National Army consists of soldiers who have once thrown their arms away on the battlefield. The soldier who lays down his arms in battle may be:

(i) Timid and thus frightened to fight.

(ii) Discontented and thus not willing to fight.

(iii) Exhausted by continuous troubles and hardships which he has undergone since he has come to this country. He might have made up his mind to do no more fighting.

(iv) In certain cases he is just separated from his unit by force of circumstances, otherwise he would be fighting for his regiment.

To build up the morale and fighting spirit of such soldiers requires selected leaders and stern discipline.

(e) The present strength of the Indian National Army is very small. For its reinforcement and further expansion it is entirely dependent on the Indian Army and the Indians in India. Therefore it is essential that the chief theatre where this army should be used should be India where it will attract several Indians to join and enlarge it.

Considering all these points we request that the first time the Indian National Army is used in the front line should not be in Malaya but Burma or better still in India. This will give us some time to prepare. We do not want to set any bad example.

4. As far as the leadership of the Indian National Army is concerned all the officers attending the conference held at Alor Star on the morning of 31st December raised a strong unanimous objection to the words 'in Malaya', and they requested that 'in Malaya' may very kindly be deleted from that sentence.*

---

*Referring to limit placed on Mohan Singh's jurisdiction.

THE BANGKOK RESOLUTIONS

1. WHEREAS it is the objective of the war of Greater East Asia to destroy British Imperialism in Asia; and

   WHEREAS it gives an opportunity for India to realise the goal of complete independence; and

   WHEREAS it is the belief of this Conference that a new and regenerated Asia of Free Nations is certain to arise as a result of this said war:

   This Conference expresses its sincere gratification at the war policy of Japan and conveys to the Imperial Government its best wishes for the continued success of the Imperial Japanese Armed Forces.

2. This Conference conveys to all the powers fighting against British Imperialism its sincere congratulations and prays that their efforts may meet with complete success.

3. This Conference places on record its sense of deep admiration for the most determined manner in which the Nationalist Leaders at home have been trying to

refuse to be drawn into this war on the side of the British and their Allies, and for the frank and definite demand for the withdrawal of the British from India. In the opinion of this Conference, unless the British withdraw from India and the Allied forces cease to make use of India as a base for war operations and war preparations unimaginable and innumerable sufferings will be the lot of the people of India.

4. Resolved that a Movement for achieving complete and immediate independence of India be sponsored by this Conference.

OBJECT

5. This conference endorses the view of the Tokyo Conference held in March 1942 that the complete Independence of India free from any foreign control, domination or interference of whatever nature shall be the object of this Movement, and is emphatically of opinion that the time has arrived to take necessary steps for the attainment of that object.

GUIDING PRINCIPLES

6. Resolved that the Indian Independence Movement sponsored by this conference shall be guided by the principles indicated below:

(a) That UNITY, FAITH, SACRIFICE, shall be the motto of the Indian Independence Movement.

(b) That India be considered as ONE, and indivisible.

(c) That all activities of this Movement be on a national basis, and not on a sectional, communal or religious basis.

(d) That in view of the fact that the Indian National Congress is the only political organisation which could claim to represent the real interests of the people of India, and as such to be acknowledged the only body representing India, this Conference is of the opinion that the programme and plan of action of this Movement must be so guided, controlled and directed as to bring them in line with the aims and intentions of the Indian National Congress.

(e) That the framing of the future constitution of India be only by the representatives of the people of India.

(f) That a joint Axis policy favourably towards India will be advantageous to India.

(g) That the sympathy, co-operation and support of Japan is invaluable in securing the object of this Movement, namely the Independence of India.

7. Resolved that an organisation be started for carrying on the Indian Independence Movement and that it shall be known as the Indian Independence League.

8. Resolved that the Indian Independence League shall immediately proceed to raise an Army called the Indian National Army from among the Indian soldiers (combatants and non-combatants) and such civilians as may hereafter be recruited for military service in the cause of Indian Independence.

CONSTITUTION

9. This Conference adopts the following Constitution for the Indian Independence League organisation.

   (i) The Indian Independence League shall consist of:

      (a) A Council of Action.

      (b) A Committee of Representatives.

      (c) Territorial Branches, and

      (d) Local Branches.

   (ii) (a) Local branches of the Indian Independence League may be formed only at a public meeting of Indians in any locality who shall elect a Committee and a President.

      (b) Vacancy of such Committee or in the Office of the President may be filled up by the Committee.

      (c) All Indians above the age of eighteen shall

be entitled to be members of such Branch on compliance with the rules of the Branch.

(d) No such Branch shall be recognised as a Branch unless the Territorial Committee as constituted hereinafter accords and continues to accord to such Branch due recognition, provided however that all Branches of the Indian Independence League now in existence and recognised in the various territories mentioned in article (vi) hereof shall until otherwise decided upon be recognised by this Movement.

(iii) Representatives elected by the Committee of Local Branches in each territory shall form a Territorial Committee, and the Territorial Committee shall make such rules as it may consider necessary for the effective working of the Movement within the territory.

(iv) The Territorial Committee in each territory shall guide, supervise and control the work of the Movement within its territory and shall also elect representatives as constituted hereinafter.

(v) Territorial Committees and Committees of Local Branches under them shall have power to make rules not inconsistent with the rules by the Committee of Representatives or in case of

Local Branches by the Territorial Committees.

(vi) (a) A Committee of Representatives shall be constituted by civilian representatives selected by the Territorial Committees in the territories herein below set out and by representatives selected by the Indian National Army.

Japan and Machukuo	4
Philippines	2
Thailand	6
Malaya	14
Burma	21
Borneo and Celebes	1
Hongkong, Canton and Macao	2
Other parts of China, including Shanghai	2
Indo-China	1
Java	2
Sumatra	1
Andamans	1
	57
Indian National Army	33
	90

(b) The Council of Action shall be at liberty to include in the above list of territories any other territory and fix the number of representatives from such territory to the Committee of Representatives, providing in that event for increase in the representatives from the Indian National Army, equal to two-thirds of the number fixed for such territory.

(vii) Every member of the Committee of Representatives shall sign the Oath of Secrecy in the prescribed form before he takes his seat on the Committee.

(viii) The Committee of Representatives shall be responsible for the general policy and programme of the Indian Independence Movement and its decision shall in every case be final and binding on each and every member of this Movement.

(xi) The Committee of Representatives shall have power to alter, amend or rescind any previous decisions made by it, including any decision arrived at in this Conference.

(x) No meeting of the Committee of Representatives shall be valid unless two-thirds in number of the Members of the Committee are present (either in person or by proxy).

(xi) A Council of Action consisting of a President and four (4) members, of whom at least one half shall be from the Indian National Army in East Asia, shall be appointed by the delegates to this Conference. The first President shall be Sjt. Rash Behari Bose and the four members shall be:

1. Sri N. Raghavan.
2. Captain Mohan Singh.
3. Sri. K.P.K. Menon.
4. Colonel G.Q. Gilani.

(xii) Any vacancy in the Council of Action caused by death, resignation or otherwise of Members not exceeding two in number at a time, may be filled up by the other Members of the Council, and in the event of more than two such vacancies the Council of Action shall call a meeting of the Representatives to fill such vacancies.

(xiii) The Council of Action shall be Responsible for the carrying out of the policy and progrmame of work laid down by this Conference and as may hereafter be laid down by the Committee of Representatives and shall deal with all new matters that may arise from time to time and which may not be provided for by the Committee itself.

(xiv) For the proper and efficient carrying out of the work the Council of Action shall have power to create as many departments as are necessary and to appoint and dismiss administrative officers and staff whenever necessary.

(xv) The Council of Action shall have no power to alter or amend the Policy laid down by this Conference without the sanction of the Committee of Representatives.

(xvi) The Council of Action may at any time summon a meeting of the Committee of Representatives to be held at such places as the Council may decide provided that necessary facilities for travel to Representatives and at least 14 days' notice of such meeting have been given to the Secretaries of the Territorial Committees and to the Headquarters of the Indian National Army. On a requisition by twenty members (Representatives) hailing from more than one territory such a meeting shall be called by the Council of Action and the necessary notices and facilities for travel shall be given.

(xvii) The Council of Action shall have general superintendence and control over all Branches of the Indian Independence League in all territories mentioned in article (vi) and over the Indian National Army.

(xviii) The Council of Action shall cause to be kept a register of all the territorial and local organisations and may remove therefrom the names of any such organisations and withhold or withdraw recognition of any such organisation.

(xix) The Council of Action shall have collective responsibility.

(xx) The allotment of Portfolios shall be amongst the Members of the Council of Action and at the discretion of the President.

(xxi) The Headquarters of the Movement shall be at Bangkok or such other place as may hereafter be decided upon by the Committee of Representatives or the Council of Action.

(xxii) The deliberations of the Committee of Representatives and the Council of Action shall be privileged and no action of a disciplinary character can be taken against any member in consequence thereof by any Branch or Territorial Committee of the Indian National Army.

(xxiii) Changes in the Constitution of the Indian Independence League may be made only by vote to that effect by three-fourths of the Members of the Committee of Representatives.

10. Resolved that a request be made to the Nippon Government that it may be pleased to place immediately all Indian soldiers in territories in East

Asia under their control at the disposal of this Movement.

11. Resolved that the formation, command, control and organisation of the Indian National Army be in the hands of Indians themselves.

12. Resolved that it is the earnest desire of this Conference that the Indian National Army from its inception be accorded the powers and status of a free National Army of an Independent India, on a footing of equality with the armies of Japan and other friendly powers.

13. Resolved that the Indian National Army shall be made use of only:
    (a) For operations against the British or other foreign powers in India.
    (b) For the purpose of securing and safeguarding Indian National Independence, and
    (c) For such other purpose as may assist the achievement of the object, viz: the Independence of India.

14. Resolved that all officers and men of the proposed Indian National Army shall be members of the Indian Independence League and shall owe allegiance to the League.

15. Resolved that the Indian National Army shall be

under the direct control of the Council of Action and that the said Army shall be organised and commanded by the General Officer commanding, Indian National Army, in accordance with the directions of the Council of Action.

16. Resolved that in the event of military action being taken against the British or other foreign powers in India, and for the said purpose the Council of Action may be at liberty to place the military resources available to it, under the unified command of Indian and Japanese Military Officers under the direction of the said Council of Action.

17. Resolved that before taking any military action against the British or any other foreign power in India, the Council of Action will assure itself that such action is in conformity with the express or implied wishes of the Indian National Congress.

18. Resolved that the Council of Action shall make all efforts to create an atmosphere in India which would lead to a revolution in the Indian Army there, and among the Indian people, and that before taking military action the Council of Action shall assure itself that such an atmosphere exists in India.

19. In view of the great urgency and imperative necessity of informing and convincing our countrymen in India and abroad, and friends of India all over the world of the meaning and purpose of this movement, and in

view of the fact that propaganda in and outside India is one of the most effective means of waging the war for Indian independence, this Conference resolves to take immediate steps to carry on active and vigorous propaganda by Broadcasts, Leaflets, Lectures and by such other means as may be found possible and practicable from time to time.

20. That all foreign assistance of whatever nature shall be only to the extent and of the type asked for by the Council of Action.

21. Resolved that for the purpose of financing the Independence Movement the Council of Action be authorised to raise funds from Indians in East Asia.

22. The Conference places on record its grateful appreciation of the support and encouragement given to this Movement by the Imperial Government of Japan, and resolves that the Council of Action be authorised to approach if and when necessary the said Government with a request to render such monetary help as may be required from time to time for the successful carrying out of the object of this Movement, on the distinct understanding that such monetary help is to be treated as a loan repayable to the Imperial Government of Japan by the National Government of India.

23. Resolved that the Imperial Government of Japan be

requested to be good enough to provide all facilities for Propaganda, Travel, Transport and Communication within the area under the control of the Imperial Government of Japan, in the manner and to the extent requested by the Council of Action, and also all facilities to come into contact with the National leaders, workers and organisations in India.

24. Resolved that the Imperial Government of Japan be requested to be good enough to arrange with the local authorities concerned that in matters of administration affecting the Indian community, the Indian Independence League in the respective places, and in places where there are no branches of the League, recognised leaders of the community approved by the League Branch nearest to such places, be consulted.

25. Resolved that the Government of Thailand be requested to be good enough to consult the Indian Independence League (formerly known as the Indian National Council and the Independence League of India) in matters of administration affecting the Indian Community in Thailand.

26. The Conference, while recording its grateful appreciation of the various pronouncements made by General Tojo the Premier of Japan, expressing the preparedness of the Nipponse Government to give its unstinted support to the cause of Indian

Independence, reiterates the Resolution of the Tokyo Conference that in further clarification of the attitude of Japan towards India, the Imperial Government be good enough to make a formal declaration to the effect:

(a) That immediately on the severance of India from the British Empire, the Imperial Government of Japan shall respect the territorial integrity and recognise the full sovereignty of India free from any foreign influence, control or interference of a political, military or economic nature.

(b) That the Imperial Government of Japan will exercise its influence with other powers and induce them to recognise the National independence and absolute soveriengty of India.

(c) That the framing of the future Constitution of India will be left entirely to the representatives of the people of India without interference from any foreign authority.

27. Resolved that this Conference is committed to a definite policy of close cooperation with Japan, and it shall, on eliciting an official definition satisfactory to this Movement of the term 'Greater East Asia Co-Prosperity Sphere' and its implications, endeavour to persuade Independent India:-

(a) To be a member of such Sphere or a member of

any other international combine of which Japan is a member, on a footing of equality with Japan; and

(b) To confer on Japan the most favoured nation treatment on a reciprocal basis.

28. WHEREAS it has come to the knowledge of this Conference that Indians in the territories which are now freed from the domination of the Anglo-Saxons and their Allies by the Imperial Forces of Japan own considerable movable and immovable properties in these territories; and

WHEREAS owing to the exigencies of war a number of Indians had to leave these territories, leaving behind their properties without making arrangements for their care and management; and

WHEREAS the Imperial Government of Japan has promised its unstinted support to the cause of Indian Independence; and

WHEREAS an enormous amount of money is required to carry on and complete the object of the said movement in East Asia; and

WHEREAS an appreciably steady income is likely to be derived from the said properties in the said territories; and WHEREAS in the opinion of the Conference, the handing over of such properties to the Indian Independence League by the authorities concerned, on the distinct understanding that the said properties are to be returned to their rightful owners when claimed, will be welcomed as a sign of goodwill and encouragement towards this Movement.

NOW THIS CONFERENCE RESOLVES:

That the Imperial Government of Japan may be pleased to arrange with the authorities in the territories now freed from the domination of the Anglo-Saxons and their Allies by the Imperial Forces of Japan, to hand over the properties owned by the Indians (including those owned by Indian Companies, firms and partnerships) and left by them owing to the existences of war, to the Council of Action in this Movement in trust for their rightful owners, to manage and control the said properties, and advance the income thereof for the use of this Movement, to be repaid as and when claimed by the said owners.

29. This Conference having learned with regret that Indians residing in certain countries under the occupation of the Imperial Forces of Japan are being treated as enemy aliens, and suffer hardships and loss in consequence; resolves that the Imperial Government of Japan may be pleased to make a declaration to the effect:

(a) That Indians residing in the territories occupied by the Imperial Forces of Japan shall not be considered enemy nationals so long as they do not indulge in any action injurious to this movement or hostile to the interest of Japan, and

(b) That the properties both movable and immovable of those Indians who are now residing in India or elsewhere (including the properties of Indian companies, firms and partnerships) be not treated by Japan as enemy properties so long as the management or control of such properties is vested in any person or persons residing in Japan or in any of the countries occupied by or under the influence or control of the Imperial Japanese Forces, and to instruct the authorities concerned in the respective territories to give effect to this policy as early as possible.

30. That this Movement adopts the present National Flag of India and requests the Imperial Government of Japan and the Royal Government of Thailand and the Governments of all other friendly powers to recognise the said flag in all territories under their jurisdiction.

31. This Conference requests Sjt. Subhash Chandra Bose to be kind enough to come to East Asia, and appeals to the Imperial Government of Japan to use its good offices to obtain the necessary permission and conveniences from the government of Germany to enable Sjt. Subhash Chandra Bose to reach East Asia safe.

32. That no unauthorised publicity be given to any of the Resolutions adopted at this Conference, but a manifesto be issued by this Conference setting out the purpose and policy of this Movement, and incorporating such decisions and details as may be found proper and beneficial to be made public.

33. This Conference places on record its deepest appreciation of and grateful thanks for the cooperation, assistance and support extended to this movement and its objective by the Imperial Government of Japan.

34. This Conference gratefully acknowledges the sincere and friendly attitude the Governments and the peoples of Germany and Italy have adopted towards our struggle for freedom, and places on record its deep appreciation and thanks for the offer of assistance and cooperation extended by them to this Movement.

35. This Conference places on record its grateful thanks to the Government and people of Thailand for the opportunity given to hold this Conference at Bangkok, for their kind hospitality, and for their sympathy and co-operation in India's struggle for freedom.

RASH BEHARI BOSE

President

Indian Independence League, 30th June, 1942.

Appendix II

PROCLAMATIONS, SPECIAL MESSAGES AND ORDERS OF THE DAY

1. Special Order on assuming Direct Command of the I.N.A. – *25th August, 1943.*
2. Proclamation of the Provisional Government – *21st October, 1943*
3. Special Order on the I.N.A.'s Departure for the Front – *9th February, 1944*
4. I.N.A. proclamation on entering India – date blank.
5. Provisional Government Proclamation No.2 – *4th April, 1944.*
6. Special Order on the Imphal Defeat – *14th August, 1944*
7. Special Order on New Year's Day *1945*
8. Special Order (on Desertions) – *13th March, 1945.*
9. Special Order (on the Traitors) – *13th March, 1945.*
10. Special Order on leaving Burma – *24th April, 1945.*
11. Message to the League in Burma – *24th April, 1945.*
12. Statement on the Treatment of I.N.A. Prisoners by the British – *30th May, 1945.*
13. Special Order on Surrender Rumours – *14th August, 1945.*
14. Special Order on the Japanese Surrender – *15th August 1945.*
15. Special Message to the Indians of East Asia – *15th August, 1945.*

I

SPECIAL ORDER OF THE DAY ON THE OCCASION OF TAKING OVER DIRECT COMMAND OF THE ARMY

In the interests of the Indian Independence Movement and of the Azad Hind *Fauj* I have taken over the direct command of our army from this day.

This is for me a matter of joy and pride – because for an Indian, there can be no greater honour than to be a Commander of India's Army of Liberation. But I am conscious of the magnitude of the task that I have undertaken and I feel weighed down with a sense of responsibility. I pray that God may give me the necessary strength to fulfil my duty to India under all circumstances, however difficult or trying they may be.

I regard myself as the servant of thirty-eight crores of my countrymen who profess different religious faiths. I am determined to discharge my duties in such a manner that the interests of these thirty-eight crores may be safe in my hands, and that every single Indian will have reason to put complete trust in me. It is only on the basis of undiluted nationalism and of perfect justice and impartiality that India's Army of Liberation can be built up.

In the coming struggle for the emancipation of our Motherland, for the establishment of a government of Free India, based on the goodwill of thirty-eight crores of Indians and for the creation of a permanent army which will guarantee Indian independence for all time, the Azad Hind *Fauj* has a vital role to play. To fulfil this role, we must weld ourselves into an army that will have only one goal – namely, the freedom of India – and only one will – namely to do or die in the cause of India's freedom. When we stand, the Azad Hind *Fauj* has to be like a wall of granite: when we march, the Azad Hind *Fauj* has to be like a steam-roller.

Our task is not an easy one: the war will be long and hard, but I have complete faith in the justice and the invincibility of our cause. Thirty-eight crores of human beings, who form about one-fifth of the human race, have a right to be free and they are now prepared to pay the price of freedom. There is consequently no power on earth that can deprive us of our birthright of liberty any longer.

Comrades, Officers and men! With your unstinted support and unflinching loyalty, the Azad Hind *Fauj* will become the instrument of India's liberation. Ultimate victory will certainly be ours, I assure you.

Our work has already begun. With the slogan 'Onward to Delhi' on our lips, let us continue to labour and fight till our National Flag flies over the Viceroy's House in New Delhi, and the Azad Hind *Fauj* holds its victory parade inside the ancient Red Fortress of India's metropolis.

SUBHASH CHANDRA BOSE

Supreme Commander, 25th August, 1943.

2

PROCLAMATION OF THE PROVISIONAL GOVERNMENT OF AZAD HIND

After their first defeat at the hands of the British in 1757 in Bengal, the Indian people fought an uninterrupted series of hard and bitter battles over a stretch of one hundred years. The history of this period teems with examples of unparalleled heroism and self-sacrifice. And, in the pages of that history, the names of Sirajuddoula and Mohanlal of Bengal, Haider Ali, Tippu Sultan and Velu Tampi of South India, Appa Sahib Bhonsle and Peshwa Baji Rao of Maharashtra, the Begums of Oudh, Sardar Shyam Singh Atariwala of Punjab and last, but not least, Rani Laxmibai of Jhansi, Tantia Topi, Maharaja Kunwar Singh of Dumraon and Nana Sahib – among others – the names of all these warriors are for ever engraved in letters of gold. Unfortunately for us, our forefathers did not at first realise that the British constituted a grave threat to the whole of India, and they did not therefore put up a united front against the enemy. Ultimately, when the Indian people were roused to the reality of the situation, they made a concerted move – and under the flag of Bahadur Shah in 1857, they fought their last war as free men. In spite of a series of brilliant victories in the early stage of this war, ill-luck and faulty leadership gradually brought about their final collapse and subjugation. Nevertheless, such heroes as the Rani of Jhansi, Tantia Topi, Kunwar Singh and Nana Sahib live like eternal stars in the nation's memory to inspire us to greater deeds of sacrifice and valour.

Forcibly disarmed by the British after 1857 and subjected to terror and brutality, the Indian people lay prostrate for a while – but with the birth of the Indian National Congress in 1885, there came a new awakening. From 1885 until the end of the last World War, the Indian people, in their endeavour to recover their lost liberty, tried all possible methods – namely agitation and propaganda, boycott of British goods, terrorism and sabotage – and finally armed revolution. But all these efforts failed for a time. Ultimately in 1920, when the Indian people, haunted by a sense of failure, were groping for a new method, Mahatma Gandhi came forward with the new weapon of non co-operation and civil disobedience.

For two decades thereafter, the Indian people went through a phase of intense patriotic activity. The message of freedom was carried to every Indian home. Through personal example, people were taught to suffer, to sacrifice and to die in the cause of freedom. From the centre to the remotest villages, the people were knit together into one political organisation. Thus, the Indian people not only recovered their political consciousness but became a political entity once again. They could now speak with one voice and strive with one will for one common goal. From 1937 to 1939, through the work of the Congress Ministries in eight provinces, they gave proof of their readiness and their capacity to administer their own affairs.

Thus, on the eve of the present World War, the stage was set for the final struggle for India's liberation. During the course of this war, Germany, with the help of her allies has dealt shattering blows to our enemy in Europe – while Nippon, with the help of her allies, has inflicted a knockout blow to our enemy in East Asia. Favoured by a most happy combination of circumstances, the Indian people today have a wonderful opportunity for achieving their national emancipation.

For the first time in recent history, Indians abroad have also been politically roused and united in one organisation. They are not only thinking and feeling in tune with their countrymen at home, but are also marching in step with them, along the path to freedom. In East Asia, in particular, over two million Indians are now organised as one solid phalanx, inspired by the slogan of 'Total Mobilisation'. And in front of them stand the serried ranks of India's Army of Liberation, with the slogan 'Onward to Delhi', on their lips.

Having goaded Indians to desperation by its hypocrisy and having driven them to starvation and death by plunder and loot, British rule in India has forfeited the goodwill of the Indian people altogether and is now living a precarious existence. It needs but a flame to destroy the last vestige of that unhappy rule. To light that flame is the task of India's Army of Liberation. Assured of the enthusiastic support of the civil population at home and also of a large section of Britain's Indian Army, and backed by gallant and invincible allies abroad – but relying in the first instance on its own strength, India's Army of Liberation is confident of fulfilling its historic role.

Now that the dawn of freedom is at hand, it is the duty of the Indian people to set up a Provisional Government of their own, and launch the last struggle under the banner of that Government. But with all the Indian leaders in prison and the people at home totally disarmed – it is not possible to set up a Provisional Government within India or to launch an armed struggle under the aegis of that government. It is, therefore, the duty of the Indian Independence League in East Asia, supported by all patriotic Indians at home and abroad, to undertake this task – the task of setting up a Provisional Government of Azad Hind (Free India) and of conducting the last fight for freedom, with the help of the Army of Liberation, (that is, the Azad Hind *Fauj* or the Indian National Army) organised by the League.

Having been constituted as the Provisional Government of

Azad Hind by the Indian Independence League in East Asia, we enter upon our duties with a full sense of the responsibility that has devolved on us. We pray that Providence may bless our work and our struggle for the emancipation of our Motherland. And we hereby pledge our lives and the lives of our comrades in arms to the cause of her freedom, of her welfare, and her exaltation among the nations of the world.

It will be the task of the Provisional Government to launch and to conduct the struggle that will bring about the expulsion of the British and their allies from the soil of India. It will then be the task of the Provisional Government to bring about the establishment of a permanent National Government of Azad Hind constituted in accordance with the will of the Indian people and enjoying their confidence. After the British and their allies are overthrown and until a permanent National Government of Azad Hind is set up on Indian soil, the Provisional Government will administer the affairs of the country in trust for the Indian people.

The Provisional Government is entitled to, and hereby claims, the allegiance of every Indian. It guarantees religious liberty, as well as equal rights and equal opportunities to all its citizens. It declares its firm resolve to pursue the happiness and prosperity of the whole nation and of all its parts, cherishing all the children of the nation equally and transcending all the differences cunningly fostered by an alien government in the past.

In the name of God, in the name of bygone generations who have welded the Indian people into one nation, and in the name of the dead heroes who have bequeathed to us a tradition of heroism and self-sacrifice – we call upon the Indian people to rally round our banner and strike for India's freedom. We call upon them to launch the final struggle against the British and all their allies in India and to prosecute that struggle with valour and perseverance and full faith in final victory – until the enemy is expelled from Indian soil and the Indian people are once again a Free Nation.

SIGNED ON BEHALF OF THE PROVISIONAL GOVERNMENT OF AZAD HIND.

Subhash Chandra Bose : (Head of the State, Prime Minister and Minister for War and Foreign Affairs)

Captain Mrs. Lakshmi : (Women's Organisation)

S.A. Ayer : (Publicity and Propaganda)

Lt. Col. A.C. Chatterjee : (Finance)

Lt. Col. Aziz Ahmed, Lt. Col. N.S. Bhagat,
Lt. Col. J.K. Bhonsle,
Lt. Col. Gulzara Singh,
Lt. Col. M.Z. Kiani,
Lt. Col. A.D. Loganadhan,
Lt. Col. Ehsan Qadir,
Lt. Col. Shah Nawaz
(Representatives of the Armed Forces)

A.M. Sahay,	: Secretary (with Ministerial rank)
Rash Behari Bose	: (Supreme Advisor)
Karin Ghano, Debnath Dass, D.M. Khan, A. Yellappa, J. Thivy, Sardar Ishar Singh	(Advisers)
A.N. Sarkar	: (Legal Adviser).

Syonan, 21st October 1943.

3

SPECIAL ORDER OF THE DAY

—9th February, 1944

The eyes of the whole world are focussed on the Arakan Front, where events of far-reaching consequence are taking place today. The glorious and brilliant actions of the brave units of Azad Hind *Fauj* working in close concert with the forces of the Imperial Nippon Army, have helped to foil all attempts by the Anglo-American forces to start a counter-offensive in this sector.

I am sure that the brave deeds of our comrades on the Arakan Front will be a great inspiration to all officers and men of the Azad Hind *Fauj* wherever they may be stationed at the present moment. Our long awaited march to Delhi has begun, and with grim determination, we shall continue that march until the tricolour National Flag that is flying over the Arakan mountains is hoisted over the Viceregal Lodge, and until we hold our victory parade at the ancient Red Fortress of Delhi.

Comrades, officers and men of India's Army of Liberation.

Let there be one solemn resolve in your hearts – 'Either Liberty or Death.' And let there be but one slogan on your lips – 'Onward to Delhi.' The road to Delhi is the road to freedom. That is the road along which we must march. Victory will certainly be ours.

Inquilab Zindabad: Azad Hind Zindabad
Subhash Chandra Bose

4

I.N.A. PROCLAMATION OF ENTERING INDIA

I. The Indian National Army, under the leadership of the Provisional Government of Azad Hind, has now massed in force and advanced into a territory of Eastern India as the spearhead for the creation of a Free India.

The Indian National Army with the help and cooperation of the Imperial Nipponese Army, has pushed into Eastern India with the object of crushing the Anglo-American forces the common enemy of East Asia: of making India really an India for Indians by liberating her from the shackles of the despotic rule under which she has been groaning for ages; of bringing complete freedom and peace and order to three hundred and eighty million of our brothers and sisters in India; and also of driving away the Anglo-American menace from the borders of our neighbours – the Independent Burmese.

BROTHERS AND SISTERS IN INDIA!

Be engaged in your daily work without fear; gather wholeheartedly under your Tricolour Flag of Independence hoisted by the Provisional Government of Azad Hind; brace yourself up for winning Complete Independence by retaking our Motherland from the hands of our enemies, the Anglo-Americans.

The East Indian Territory into which the Indian National Army has advanced with the powerful aid of the Imperial Nipponese Army, as well as the people thereof, have now been liberated from the bondage of the Anglo-Americans. The territory has become the first free Indian territory on the Mainland of India under the Provisional Government and will serve as the base for liberating our Motherland. The Imperial Nipponese Army will not establish a military administration but will cooperate with and wholeheartedly help the Provisional Government of Azad Hind in maintaining perfect peace and order.

II. If any person fails to understand the intentions of the Provisional Government of Azad Hind and the Indian National Army, or of our Ally, the Nippon Army, and dares to commit such acts as are itemised hereunder which would hamper the sacred task of emancipating India, he shall be executed or severely punished in accordance with the Criminal Law of the Provisional government of Azad Hind and the Indian National

Army or with the Martial Law of the Nippon Army, the application of which has been agreed upon between the two allied Armies, namely, the Indian National Army and its Ally, the Imperial Nipponese Army.

PUNISHABLE ACTS

(1) Rebellious acts against the Provisional Government of Azad Hind or the Indian National Army, or our Ally, the Nipponese Army.

(2) Acts of spying.

(3) Acts of stealing and taking by force, damaging and destroying war materials which are in the possession of the Provisional Government or belong to our Ally, the Nippon Army.

(4) Acts of damaging or destroying of valuable material resources controlled or utilised by the Provisional Government of Azad Hind or by the Nippon Army under previous agreement with the Provisional Government.

(5) Acts of destroying various installations or equipments for traffic, communication, transportation, broadcasting etc. which are controlled or utilised by the Provisional Government of Azad Hind and the Indian National Army, or by the Nippon Army under previous agreement with

the Provisional Government; or acts of interference with the employment and utilisation thereof.

(6) Violent acts against, intimidation of, killing or wounding of, or doing other harmful acts to those who belong to the Provisional Government of Azad Hind and the Indian National Army or our Ally, the Nippon Army.

(7) Acts of spreading enemy propaganda or wild and false rumours, and other acts of disturbing and misleading the minds of the inhabitants.

(8) Acts of disturbing the money circulation and economic organisation or of obstructing the production and free interchange of commodities.

(9) Any act other than those contained in the above items, that benefits the enemy or is harmful to peace and order, and the well-being of the provisional Government of Azad Hind and the Indian National Army or our Ally, the Nippon Army.

(10) Acts of attempting, instigating and abetting those acts contained in the above items.

The trial and punishment of such criminals will entirely be at the discretion of the Provisional Government of Azad Hind except when crimes committed are of such a nature of necessity, owing to war-time emergency, must be dealt with by the

Nippon Army as agreed upon between the two Allied Armies.

III. The Nippon Army will maintain strict discipline and protect in the area into which they have advanced the lives and properties of the Indian masses who do not commit any hostile act; and due respect will be paid to the religions, customs and manners of the Indian people.

It is guaranteed that any Nippon soldier that may violate these strict injunctions shall be severely punished in accordance with the Martial Law of the imperial Nipponese Army.

The Indian National Army will maintain strict discipline and protect, in the area into which it has advanced, the lives and properties of the Indian Masses who do not commit any hostile act; and due respect will be paid to the religions, customs and manners of our countrymen.

It is guaranteed that any Indian soldier that may violate these strict injunctions shall be severely punished in accordance with the Martial Law of the Indian National Army.

THE ABOVE IS SOLEMNLY PROCLAIMED IN THE MONTH OF... IN THE YEAR 1944 BY THE SUPREME COMMANDER OF THE INDIAN NATIONAL ARMY.

5

SECOND PROCLAMATION

4th April, 1944

Under the leadership of the Provisional Government of Azad Hind which was formed on the 21st October 1943, at Syonan (formerly Singapore) by the unanimous will of the three million Indians in East Asia, the Indian National Army has crossed the frontier and has penetrated deep into Indian territory.

The Provisional Government of Azad Hind, your own Government has only one mission to fulfil. That mission is to expel the Anglo-American armies from the sacred soil of India by armed force and then to bring about the establishment of a permanent National Government of Azad Hind, in accordance with the will of the Indian people.

The Provisional Government of Azad Hind will continue the armed struggle until the Anglo-American forces are annihilated or expelled from India.

While prosecuting the armed struggle for the complete liberation of India, the Provisional Government of Free India will push on with the work of reconstruction of the liberated areas.

The Provisional Government of Azad Hind is the only lawful Government of the Indian people. The Provisional Government calls upon the Indian people in the liberated areas to render all assistance and cooperation to the Indian National Army and to the civilian officials appointed by the Provisional Government.

The Provisional Government guarantees the safety of life and property of the Indian population in the liberated areas, but will inflict severe punishment on those who carry on any activities, overt or covert, which might be of help to our Anglo American enemies or their allies, or might disturb the work of reconstruction to be started by the Provisional Government.

The Provisional Government calls upon the Indian people to co-operate whole heartedly with our Ally, the Nippon Army, who are giving unstinted and unconditional assistance in defeating our enemies. In the last two years, the British have been strongly reinforcing themselves with troops from America, Australia, Chungking-China and East and West Africa. The Provisional Government has, therefore, felt compelled to avail itself of the generous offer of all-out aid made by Nippon, whose armed forces have scored unparalleled victories over the Anglo-

Americans, since the beginning of the war in East Asia. The Provisional Government of Azad Hind is supremely confident that the Indian National Army, with the aid of the invincible forces of our Ally, the Nippon Army, will crush the Anglo-Americans and bring about the complete liberation of India.

The Provisional Government is fully convinced of Nippon's sincerity towards India. The Provisional Government is convinced that Nippon has no territorial, political, economic or military ambitions in India. The provisional Government is convinced that Nippon is interested only in destroying the Anglo-American forces in India which are the enemies not only of India, but of Asia as well. The destruction of Anglo-American Imperialism alone will terminate this war and bring peace to the world.

In accordance with its status as an independent Government, the Provisional Government of Azad Hind is arranging to issue its own currency in Rupee-Notes of different denominations. But owing to the rapid development of the war situation, culminating in our quick advance into India, it has not been possible to bring into India, in time, the currency of the Provisional Government. The circumstances have therefore, rendered it necessary for the Provisional Government to borrow from the Nipponese Government the currency (viz. military rupee notes) already in its possession and to use that currency as a temporary measure. As soon as the Provisional Government's own currency is available, the currency borrowed from the Nipponese Government will be gradually withdrawn from circulation.

Brothers and sisters! Now that our enemies are being driven out of Indian soil, you are becoming once again what you were before – namely, free men and women. Rally round your own Government – the Provisional Government of Azad Hind – and thereby help in preserving and safeguarding your newly-won liberty.

SUBHASH CHANDRA BOSE

Head of the State etc. 4th April, 1944

6

SPECIAL ORDER OF THE DAY ON THE WITHDRAWAL FROM IMPHAL

COMRADES OF THE AZAD HIND *FAUJ*,

In the middle of March this year, advanced units of the Azad Hind *Fauj*, fighting shoulder to shoulder with their valiant allies, the Imperial Nippon Forces, crossed the Indo-Burma border and the fight for India's liberation thereupon commenced on Indian soil.

The British authorities, by ruthlessly exploiting India for over a century and bringing foreign soldiers to fight their battles for them, had managed to put up a mighty force against us. After crossing the Indo-Burma border, inspired by the righteousness of our cause, we encountered these numerically superior and better equipped, but heterogeneous and disunited forces of the enemy and defeated them in every battle. Our units, with their better training and discipline, and unshakeable determination to do or die on the path of India's freedom, soon established their superiority over the enemy, whose morale deteriorated with each defeat. Fighting under the most trying conditions, our officers and men displayed such courage and heroism that they have earned the praise of everybody. With their blood and sacrifice, these heroes have established traditions which the future soldiers of free India will have to uphold. All preparations had been completed and the stage had been set for the final assault on Imphal when torrential rains overtook us, and to carry Imphal by assault was rendered a tactical impossibility. Handicapped by the elements, we were forced to postpone our offensive. After the postponement of the offensive it was found disadvantageous for our troops to continue to hold the line that we then had. For securing a more favourable defensive position, it was considered advisable to withdraw our troops. In accordance with this decision, our troops have withdrawn to a more favourable defensive position. We shall now utilise the period of lull in completing our preparations, so that with the advent of better weather, we may be in a position to resume our offensive. Having beaten the enemy once in several sectors of the front, our faith in our final victory and in the destruction of the Anglo-American forces of aggression has increased tenfold. As soon as all our preparations are complete, we shall launch a mighty offensive against our enemies once again. With the superior fighting qualities, dauntless courage and unshakeable devotion to duty of our officers and men, victory shall surely be ours.

May the souls of those heroes who have fallen in this campaign inspire us to still nobler deeds of heroism and bravery in the next phase of India's war of Liberation. Jai Hind.

SUBHASH CHANDRA BOSE
Supreme Commander, Azad Hind Fauj
Burma, *14th August, 1944.*

7

SPECIAL ORDER OF THE DAY – NEW YEAR'S DAY 1945

COMRADES OF THE AZAD HIND *FAUJ*,

On this auspicious New Year's Day, I want you, first of all, to look back on your achievement and on your progress since the formation of the Azad Hind *Fauj*. There can be no doubt whatsoever that in spite of many difficulties and drawbacks, your achievement and progress may have been truly remarkable. This has been possible because of the passionate desire for freedom which inspires the Indian people today, the many-sided assistance rendered by our countrymen in East Asia, the valuable aid offered by our Allies, and – above all – the hard work and sacrifice that you yourselves have put in.

Before the end of 1943, units of the Azad Hind *Fauj* began moving in the direction of the Indo-Burma frontier. On the 4th February, 1944, India's War of Independence was launched in the Arakan region of Burma. On 21st March 1944, we were able to proclaim to the whole world that the Azad Hind *Fauj* had crossed the eastern frontier of India and was fighting on the sacred soil of India. Since then, the fight has been going on and in the course of that campaign, many of our comrades, while fighting heroically, have laid down their lives on the field of battle.

The heroism and self-sacrifice of the officers and men of the Azad Hind *Fauj* in India's War of Independence have already become a priceless heritage for the India of tomorrow – while for the Azad Hind *Fauj* itself, they have become a glorious and undying tradition which will serve as an inspiration for all time.

Comrades! On this auspicious day, I want you all to pay a silent homage to our immortal heroes and to renew your solemn pledge to continue to fight until complete victory is achieved. India is calling you. The souls of your comrades are urging you on to still braver deeds. Therefore, gird up your loins for the hard battle that lies ahead. There can be no rest and no pause for us, until our tricolor national flag is hosted over India's metropolis.

Comrades! Our immortal heroes have paid for India's liberty with their own blood. We are proud of them. But we too must be ready for that supreme sacrifice. The Azad Hind *Fauj* can justify its name and fulfil its task – only if it is ready to fight and die to the last man. We have to give our blood and take the blood of our enemies. Therefore, let your slogan – your battle-cry – for the year 1945 be... 'Blood, blood and blood.'

SUBHASH CHANDRA BOSE

1st January 1944

8

SPECIAL ORDER OF THE DAY (ON THE DESERTIONS) — 13TH MARCH, 1945

TO ALL OFFICERS AND MEN OF THE AZAD HIND ARMY

COMRADES!

As you all know, the positive achievements of the Officers and men of the Azad Hind *Fauj* last year on the field of battle, and the victories that they scored over the enemy through their patriotism, bravery and self-sacrifice were marred to some extent by the cowardice and treachery of a few officers and men. We were hoping that with the advent of the New Year all traces of cowardice and treachery would be wiped out; and that in this year's operations the Azad Hind *Fauj* would be able to put up an unsullied record of heroism and self sacrifice. But that was not to be. The recent treachery of five officers of the H.Q. of the 2nd Division has come as an eye-opener to us that all is not well within our ranks, and that the seeds of cowardice and treachery have yet to be wiped out. If we now succeed in exterminating cowardice and treachery once for all, this shameful and despicable incident may, through God's grace, ultimately prove to be a blessing in disguise. I am, therefore, determined to take all possible measures necessary for the purification of our Army. I am confident that in this I shall have your full and unstinted support. In order to destroy completely the germs of cowardice and treachery, the following measures will have to be adopted:

1. Every member of the Azad Hind *Fauj*, Officer, N.C.O. or Sepoy will, in future, be entitled to arrest any other member of the Azad Hind *Fauj*, no matter what his rank may be, if he behaves in a cowardly manner or to shoot him if he acts in a treacherous manner.

2. I am giving an opportunity to all members of the Azad Hind *Fauj* who may not feel inclined to work dutifully or fight courageously in future to leave the ranks of the Azad Hind *Fauj*. This offer will be open for one week from the time of its communication.

3. In addition to giving an opportunity to unwilling elements to leave voluntarily the ranks of the Azad Hind *Fauj*, I want to carry out a thorough purge of our Army. During the course of this purge, all those will be removed against whom there is suspicion that they may fail us, or betray us, at the critical moment. In order to carry out this purge successfully I want your fullest cooperation and I want you, therefore, to give me and

my trusted officers all available information about any cowardly or treacherous elements that may still exist in our Army.

4. It will not be enough to carry out a thorough purge now. In future, also, vigilance will have to continue. It will, therefore, be the duty of every member of the Azad Hind *Fauj*, in future, to keep his eyes and ears open in order to detect in good time any tendency towards cowardice or treachery. In future, if any member of the Azad Hind *Fauj* detects any tendency towards cowardice or treachery, he should report at once, either orally or in writing, either to me or to the officers who may be within reach. In other words, from now onwards and for all time, every member of the Azad Hind *Fauj* should regard himself as the custodian of the honour and reputation of the Azad Hind *Fauj* and of the Indian Nation.

5. After the purge has been carried out and unwilling elements have been given an opportunity of leaving our Army, if there is any case of cowardice or treachery, the punishment will be death.

6. In order to create within our Army a moral bulwark against cowardice and treachery, we have to create an intense hatred against cowardice and treachery in any form. A strong feeling has to be created in the mind of every member of this Army that for a member of a revolutionary army, there is no crime more heinous and despicable than to be a coward or a traitor. Instructions

are being issued separately as to how we can create such an intense hatred against cowardice and treachery so that there will be no more cowards or traitors within our ranks.

7. After the purge has been carried out, every member of the Azad Hind *Fauj* will be required to renew his oath to fight on bravely and courageously until the emancipation of our dear Motherland is achieved. Instructions regarding the form and manner of this oath will be issued separately.

8. Special rewards will be given to those who give information regarding cowardly and treacherous elements or who arrest or shoot at the front cowardly and treacherous elements.

SUBHASH CHANDRA BOSE

Supreme Commander, Azad Hind Fauj

Burma, *13th March, 1945.*

9

SPECIAL ORDER OF THE DAY (ON THE TRAITORS) — 13TH MARCH, 1945

COMRADES,

In order to express our indignation, disgust and hatred, against cowardice and treachery, a special observance will be held in every camp of the Azad Hind *Fauj* on a day to be previously fixed for the purpose. All officers and other ranks must take part in the observance. With regard to the details of the observance, each camp will be free to draw up its own programme with a view to making the observance a complete success. Directions in broad outlines are, however, being given herewith:

(a) Poems or articles may be written and read, expressing hatred and disgust against cowardice and treachery.

(b) Dramas may be improvised and acted for expressing abhorrence against cowardice and treachery.

(c) Effigies of the traitors (Riaz, Madan, Sarwar, Dey,

Mohammad Baksh and others) in cardboard or straw or clay or any other suitable material, either in human or in animal form, should be prepared and every member of the camp should give full vent to his disgust and hatred against the traitors.

(d) Lectures should be delivered praising Indian heroes of the past and lauding the brave deeds of the members of the Azad Hind *Fauj* in the course of the present War of Liberation.

(e) The day's observance should end with the singing of the National Anthem and collective shouting of slogans.

Special reward will be given to the camp that can put up the best show.

SUBHASH CHANDRA BOSE

Supreme Commander, Azad Hind Fauj

Burma, *13th March, 1945.*

10

SPECIAL ORDER OF THE DAY ON LEAVING BURMA — 24th APRIL, 1945

BRAVE OFFICERS AND MEN OF THE AZAD HIND *FAUJ*:

It is with a very heavy heart that I am leaving Burma – the scene of the many heroic battles that you have fought since February 1944 and are still fighting. In Imphal and Burma, we have suffered a reverse in the first round in our Fight for Independence. But it is only the first round. We have many more rounds to fight. I am a born optimist and I shall not admit defeat under any circumstances. Your brave deeds in the battle against the enemy on the plains of Imphal, the hills and jungles of Arakan and the oil field area and other localities in Burma will live in the history of our struggle for Independence for all time.

Comrades: At this critical hour, I have only one word of command to give you, and that is that if you have to go down temporarily, then go down fighting with the

National Tricolour held aloft; go down as heroes; go down upholding the highest code of honour and discipline. The future generations of Indians who will be born, not as slaves but as free men, because of your colossal sacrifice, will bless your names and proudly proclaim to the world that you, their forbears, fought and suffered reverses in the battle in Manipur, Assam and Burma, but through temporary failure you paved the way to ultimate success and glory.

My unshakeable faith in India's liberation remains unaltered. I am leaving in your safe hands our National Tricolour, our national honour, and the best traditions of Indian Warriors. I have no doubt whatsoever that you, the vanguard of India's Army of Liberation, will sacrifice everything, even life itself, to uphold India's National Honour, so that your comrades who will continue the fight elsewhere may have before them your shining example to inspire them at all times.

If I had my own way, I would have preferred to stay with you in adversity and share with you the sorrow of temporary defeat. But on the advice of my Ministers and high ranking officers, I have to leave Burma in order to continue the struggle for emancipation. Knowing my countrymen in East Asia and inside India, I can assure you that they will continue the fight under all circumstances and that all your suffering and sacrifices will not be in vain. So far as I am concerned, I shall steadfastly adhere to the pledge that I took on the 21st October 1943, to do all in my power to serve the interests of thirty-eight crores of my countrymen and fight for their liberation. I appeal to you, in conclusion, to cherish the same optimism as myself and to believe like myself, that the darkest hour always precedes the dawn. India shall be free – and before long

May God Bless you!

I*nquilab Zindabad, Azad Hind Zindabad*

JAI HIND.

SUBHASH CHANDRA BOSE
Supreme Commander, Azad Hind Fauj
Dated: *24th April, 1945.*

11

SPECIAL MESSAGE ON LEAVING BURMA – 24TH MARCH, 1945

TO MY INDIAN AND BURMESE FRIENDS IN BURMA

Brothers and Sisters! I am leaving Burma with a very heavy heart. We have lost the first round of our fight for Independence. But we have lost only the first round. There are many more rounds to fight. In spite of our losing the first round, I see no reason for losing heart.

You, my countrymen in Burma, have done your duty to your Motherland in a way that evoked the admiration of the world. You have given liberally of your men, money and materials. You set the first example of Total Mobilisation. But the odds against us were overwhelming, and we have temporarily lost the battle in Burma.

The spirit of selfless sacrifice that you have shown, particularly since I shifted my headquarters to Burma, is something that I shall never forget as long as I live.

I have the fullest confidence that spirit can never be crushed. For the sake of India's Freedom, I beseech you to keep up that spirit, I beseech you to hold your heads erect, and wait for that Blessed Day when once again you will have an opportunity of waging the War for India's Independence.

When the History of India's Last War of Independence comes to be written, Indians in Burma will have an honoured place in that History.

I do not leave Burma of my own freewill. I would have preferred to stay on here and share with you the sorrow of temporary defeat. But on the pressing advice of my Ministers and high-ranking Officers, I have to leave Burma in order to continue the struggle for India's liberation. Being a born optimist, my unshakeable faith in India's early emancipation remains unimpaired and I appeal to you to cherish the same optimism.

I have always said that the darkest hour precedes the dawn. We are now passing through the darkest hour: therefore, the dawn is not far off.

INDIA SHALL BE FREE

I cannot conclude this message without publicly acknowledging once again my heartfelt gratitude to the Government and people of Burma for all the help that I have received at their hands in carrying on this struggle.

The day will come when Free India will repay that debt of gratitude in a generous manner.

INQUILAB ZINDABAD
AZAD HIND ZINDABAD
JAI HIND

SUBHASH CHANDRA BOSE

12

STATEMENT ON THE TREATMENT OF I.N.A. PRISONERS — 30th MAY, 1945.

Information that has reached us from reliable sources in Burma go to show that vindictive and brutal treatment is being meted out to officers and men of the Azad Hind *Fauj* (Indian National Army) who have been captured by the Anglo-Americans in Burma. As the whole world knows, the Anglo-Americans - and in particular the British – have always been in the habit of condemning Germany and Japan for their supposed ill-treatment of Anglo-American prisoners of war. But I would now like to ask what the Anglo-Americans are themselves doing with the members of the Azad Hind *Fauj* who happened to fall into their hands in Burma. Though the Allied Forces in Burma belong to several nationalities, the responsibility as regards the ill-treatment of the officers and men of the Azad Hind *Fauj* devolves solely on the British Authorities. The British Authorities cannot even invent the excuse that we ill-treated their troops who fell into our hands. The only

Allied Troops who fell into our hands were those who voluntarily came and joined the Azad Hind *Fauj*. And even Delhi Radio admitted some days ago that all those who joined the Azad Hind *Fauj* received good treatment.

It may be that the British Authorities think that we are not in a position to retaliate, and that they can, therefore do what they like with our officers and men. But I would like to warn the British Authorities that this is not the case. If we are forced to do so we can find ways and means for adopting retaliatory measures in case they continue to ill-treat and persecute the officers and men of the Azad Hind *Fauj*. But before we are forced to think of retaliatory measures, there is one remedy open to us, which is not only efficacious but also easy. If our countrymen at home take up this matter and carry on a raging and tearing campaign inside India, I am absolutely sure that the British Authorities will be brought to their senses and will see the error of their ways. Public opinion in India may not be strong enough to force the British to concede independence to India, but it is certainly strong enough to stop the ill-treatment and persecution of members of the Azad Hind *Fauj* who have become prisoners of war at the hands of the British. Members of the Azad Hind *Fauj* are honest patriots and revolutionaries fighting for the freedom of their Motherland. They, no doubt, fought bravely and stubbornly against the British, but they fought with clean hands and with a clear conscience. They are, therefore, entitled to decent treatment during captivity, in accordance with international usage and convention. Consequently, I appeal to my countrymen at home to take up the cause of their own prisoners of war, who fought for India's liberation and who are now receiving brutal and vindictive treatment at the hands of the British. I appeal to them also to compel the British Authorities to divulge correct information about the fate of these prisoners of war, so that the world may judge how far the British themselves observe the rules and canons of international warfare, to which they pay so much lip-homage.

SUBHASH CHANDRA BOSE

Bangkok, *30th May, 1945*.

13

SPECIAL ORDER OF THE DAY ON THE RUMOUR OF SURRENDER — 14th AUGUST, 1945

COMRADES,

All sorts of wild rumours are now afloat in Syonan and other places, one of them being that hostilities have ceased. Most of these rumour are either false or highly exaggerated. Till this moment fighting is going on on all fronts, and I say this, not only on the basis of reports from friendly sources, but also of reports given out by the enemy radio. If there is any change in the war situation, I shall be the first to inform you. Therefore I want all of you to remain perfectly calm and unperturbed and carry on your duties in a normal way. Above all, do not allow yourselves to be influenced in any manner by wild bazaar rumours. We have to face any situation that may arise, like brave soldiers fighting for the freedom of their Motherland.

Jai Hind

SUBHASH CHANDRA BOSE

Supreme Commander, Azad Hind Fauj

Syonan, *14th August 1945. 1500 hours*

14

SPECIAL ORDER ON THE JAPANESE SURRENDER — 15th AUGUST, 1945

COMRADES,

In our struggle for the independence of our Motherland, we have now been overwhelmed by an undreamt-of crisis. You may perhaps feel that you have failed in your mission to liberate India. But let me tell you that this failure is only of a temporary nature. No set-back and no defeat can undo your positive achievements of the past. Many of you have participated in the fight along the Indo-Burma frontier and also inside India and have gone through hardship and suffering of every sort. Many of your comrades have laid down their lives on the battle-field and have become the immortal heroes of Azad Hind. This glorious sacrifice can never go in vain.

Comrades, in this dark hour I call upon you to conduct yourselves with the discipline, dignity and strength befitting a truly Revolutionary Army. You have already given proofs of your valour and self-sacrifice on the field of battle. It is now your duty to demonstrate your undying optimism and unshakeable will-power in the hour of temporary defeat. Knowing you as I do, I have not the slightest doubt that even in this dire adversity you will hold your heads erect and face the future with unending hope and confidence.

Comrades, I feel that in this critical hour thirty-eight crores of our countrymen at home are looking at us, the Members of India's Army of Liberation. Therefore, remain true to India and do not for a moment waver in your faith in India's destiny. The roads to Delhi are many and Delhi still remains our goal. The sacrifices of your immortal comrades and of yourselves will certainly achieve their fulfillment. There is no power on earth that can keep India enslaved. India shall be free and before long.

Jai Hind.

SUBHASH CHANDRA BOSE

15

SPECIAL MESSAGE TO INDIANS IN EAST ASIA — 15th AUGUST, 1945

SISTERS AND BROTHERS,

A glorious chapter in the History of India's struggle for Freedom has just come to a close and, in that chapter, the sons and daughters of India in East Asia will have an undying place.

You set a shining example of patriotism and self-sacrifice by pouring out men, money and materials into the struggle for India's independence. I shall never forget the spontaneity and enthusiasm with which you responded to my call for 'Total Mobilisation'. You sent an unending stream of your sons and daughters to the camps to be trained as soldiers of the Azad Hind *Fauj* and of the Rani of Jhansi Regiment. Money and materials, you poured lavishly into the War Chest of the Provisional Government of Azad Hind. In short, you did your duty as true sons and daughters of India. I regret more than you do, that your sufferings and sacrifices have not borne immediate fruit. But they have not gone in vain, because they have ensured the emancipation of our Motherland and will serve as an undying inspiration to Indians all over the world. Posterity will bless your name, and will talk with pride about your offerings at the altar of India's Freedom and about your positive achievement as well.

In this unprecedented crisis in our history, I have only one word to say. Do not be depressed at our temporary failure. Be of good cheer and keep up your spirits. Above all, never for a moment falter in your faith in India's destiny. There is no power on earth that can keep India enslaved. India shall be free and before long.

Jai Hind

SUBHASH CHANDRA BOSE

Appendix III

YAMAMOTO FORCE AND THE 1ST I.N.A. DIVISION

Imphal was to have fallen, according to the Japanese plan, by April 10, 1944. On that assumption it was already too late, when the 2nd and 3rd Guerrilla Regiments of I.N.A. reached Rangoon in March, for them to have any part in the battle. But Bose had persuaded General Kawabe to let them at least enter Imphal on the heels of the Japanese and the 2nd Guerrilla Regiment, together with the headquarters of the 1st I.N.A. Division, began their move to Kalemyo on March 25th. Three days later the Divisional Commander, Colonel Mohammad Zaman Kiani, reached Maymyo, where Mutaguchi at the peak of his optimism told him to join Yamamoto Force (part of the Japanese 33rd Division) at Tamu immediately if he wished to be present at the fall of Imphal. Eagerly Kiani hastened a battalion of his 2nd Regiment forward from Mandalay and himself followed with the Regimental Commander, his kinsman Lieutenant-Colonel Inayat Jan Kiani, close behind.

The Kianis met General Yamamoto in the mountain village of Chamol on April 17th. All confirmed that Imphal would certainly fall any day, but Yamamoto could still use the I.N.A. force now allotted to him and directed the 2nd Guerrilla Regiment to cover the left flank of his advance to Palel, blocking the Mombi track along the great ridge of mountains running S.S.W. from Chamol. So great was the haste and so urgent the anticipation of victory, that the regiment left all its heavy baggage, its mortals and heavy machine-guns at Kalewa and travelled with only a blanket, a rifle and fifty rounds of ammunition per man. Regimental Headquarters was established on April 28th at the village of Khanjol, on a high spur to the south of the vast hump of jungle over which the Japanese were fighting their way onwards from Chamol. Almost immediately there came orders for the regiment to take part in an attack on the Palel airfield. The Japanese planned a thrust from the east on 1st May. The I.N.A. was to attack from the south at the same time with one battalion.

This was no easy task: all battalions contained a high proportion of civilian recruits and there were already many sick. In spite of Japanese confidence, the I.N.A. Commander realised that the British, who had already been dependent on air supply since 18th April, would fight for the airfield. For such a battle the best he could do was to form a task force of three hundred odd soldiers from the whole regiment and place it under the command of Major Pritam Singh, a divisional staff officer who had volunteered to lead it. There was now no time to send back for equipment: although rations were not yet arriving regularly and the men had not been properly fed for three days. Pritam singh led his force down the precipitous jungle track from Khanjol on the night of April 30th, into the deep, dense valley which led westwards and then northwards to Palel. On the map the distance does not appear more than about twelve miles, but it took two exhausting night marches to bring the soldiers to Purum Chumpang, the village which had been selected at the base. By now the day of the Japanese attack was past, but Pritam Singh prepared his own, nevertheless, for the night of May 2nd.

The rank and file were still full of confidence, obsessed with the strong assurances they had heard that when at last they came face to face with British-Indian troops, neither British nor Indians would fire on them. At about half past ten that night, the leading company, proceeding up a ridge in extended order, ran into a Gurkha platoon position about five miles from their objective. The Gurkhas, No. 11 Platoon of "B" Company of the 4/10 Gurkhas, saw them in the moonlight and heard them as they came on, talking, with cigarettes lit and with no noticeable discipline. They waited for them to reach a suitable position and then opened fire.

The I.N.A. panicked and scattered, but after a time Pritam Singh rallied some of his men and approached once again with more caution. There ensued a parley in which the I.N.A. leader tried to induce the Gurkhas not to fire.

This failing, the post was charged in style with shouts of 'Chalo Delhi'. Pritam Singh and another officer who had shown great bravery were expelled from the post after wounding the Gurkha Bren-gunner. There followed seven attacks, each of which was broken up, before the I.N.A. finally retired. Two I.N.A. officers and many soldiers were killed; about thirty-five more surrendered or were captured. The Gurkhas lost two killed.

Pritam Singh withdrew to Purum Chumpang and sent out a Bahadur Group patrol to reconnoiter for a new attack, at the same time calling on his regimental commander, who was leading a follow-up force, for prompt assistance. But the message had hardly reached Kiani in his position a few miles to the rear when he himself was attacked by a company of the Frontier Force Rifles. This infantry attack was not pressed, but it was followed by an air strike, in which the I.N.A. lost fifty killed and about the same number wounded, and an artillery concentration which severely shook the morale of the rest. Kiani ordered a general withdrawal to Khanjol and the two forces reached their base, greatly depleted, on 4th May. Pritam Singh's Bahadur Group patrol had surrendered.

The failure at Palel and the subsequent casualties to Kiani's force were perhaps the most significant events in I.N.A. history since the arrival of S.C. Bose in the Far East. Bose had hoped, and his hope had become an axiom of I.N.A. propaganda, that when a formed body of the I.N.A. confronted British-Indian troops in the field, propaganda and not fire-power would decide the day. This belief had been confirmed by Misra's easy subversion of an outlying picquet in the Arkan battle, and Misra himself had told the newly arrived regiments at Rangoon in March that the Indian Army was demoralised and would not stand up to I.N.A. determination. Now this cherished illusion was shattered; that they were regarded by their former comrades of the Indian Army as traitors was suddenly plain to all. Commanders and soldiers were alike confused, resentful, disheartened. Apart from a few enthusiasts it had not been easy for them to march against their late comrades – often also their kinsmen – and it had only been possible at all because so many believed that the battle would be no more than a token. The walls of Jericho were to have fallen to a shout: they proved well armed, relentlessly defended, and the wishful conquerors, marching carelessly round them, had paid the penalty.

Lieutenant-Colonel I.J. Kiani, though deeply cast down by this, attributed the defeat chiefly to the Japanese failure to supply and support him, although it can hardly have been a matter of surprise that on May 2nd his men had seen nothing of a Japanese attack scheduled for 1st May. In fact the Japanese, who had relied on capturing British-Indian supply dumps by mid-April, were themselves now very short of ammunition and supplies, and the Hikari Kikan Liaison officers responsible for supplying the I.N.A. could not obtain what was required, even if they were prepared to see the I.N.A. supplied at the expense of the Japanese themselves. The I.N.A. Divisional Commander at Chamol had little influence in the matter, nor were local supplies available in any quantity. The I.N.A. continued, therefore, to suffer, and only Chatterji, with his swift realisation of disaster impending from this cause and his energetic use of Bose's funds, enabled it to remain in the field after the beginning of June.

When the attempt on the Palel airfield was made, the offensive of Yamamoto Force was already past its peak. The British-Indian 23rd Division was already beginning to re-establish itself in the mountains S.E. of Palel, and on about May 7th it forced the I.N.A. to withdraw from Khanjol. The village was reoccupied next day, and the 2nd I.N.A. Regiment held firm there and at Mittong Khunue on the next spur of mountain towards Chamol, throughout May, in spite of frequent attacks and temporary withdrawals from the two villages. Sickness and battle casualties were meanwhile wearing the regiment down and morale began to drop. When Kiani visited Chamol on May 26th to argue once more about supplies, he had to report that twenty-five of his men had self-inflicted wounds. The greater part of the regiment had now to be employed on the transporting of rations; only three companies could be left to hold the mountain ridge and the Mombi track.

Throughout June the rains restricted the activity of both sides of patrolling and the 2nd Guerrilla Regiment had no more pitched battles. But the effects of climate and hunger, and of malaria, against which the I.N.A. had none of the protection which so signally benefited the Indian Army in 1944, reduced the Regiment by June 15th to less than a thousand men. The force on the Mombi track was reduced to two companies and then to one. By early July desertions were also taking their toll. The Second-in-Command of the Regiment, who had been in hospital at Chamol, deserted almost immediately on his return to the front. Before long 'Safe-Conduct Passes' and leaflets signed by him, urging members of the I.N.A. to return without fear to the Indian Army as he had done, were scattered by aircraft over I.N.A. areas. Another officer who deserted said of I.N.A. morale at this time:

> The feeling that they will be shot if caught is so strong that it produces a state of hopelessness, i.e. a loathing for the Japanese, a desire to return home, and a fear of being shot if they do. (Because of stool pigeons) discussion of escape plans is out of the question.

The leaflets and passes had an excellent effect on this state of mind. The Punjabi Muslims, of whom there was a proportion in each battalion, began to desert in such numbers that eighty of them had to be disarmed and sent to the rear. Colonel Mohammed Zaman Kiani wrote despairingly to Bose, but at first concealed the desertions from the Japanese by reports of men 'missing'. When the Japanese found out they insisted that all communications from Kiani to Bose should go through their hands. They even blamed the I.N.A. in part for their own failure.

At the beginning of July the 2nd I.N.A. Regiment was only seven hundred and fifty strong; these men were formed into four new companies which were again disposed to cover Khanjol, Mittong Khunue and the Mombi track. On July 3rd and 4th an Indian battalion of the Fourteenth Army (the 4th Battalion, the Mahratta Light Infantry) attacked and cleared Khanjol, which was held by fewer than fifty men, and occupied Mittong Khunue and a strong hill position to the east of it. But the Battalion went no further and the I.N.A. Regiment retained its precarious hold on the end of the Mombi track until it finally withdrew.

There is less to be told about the 3rd Guerrilla Regiment, although some who fought against it have said that in its few weeks at the front it showed more zeal and will to fight than either of the other two I.N.A. regiments. The 3rd Regiment reached Tamu under its commander Lieutenant-Colonel Gulzara Singh, on May 26th after the monsoon had broken. Yamamoto ordered it to a defensive position around Narum, to cover the tracks runnings eastwards down the slopes of Sita Hill, whose summit was once more in the hands of the Indian Army. From here it would, he hoped, also be able to raid the British supply route to Sita Hill from Wangjing, on the fringe of the Imphal Plain. Gulzara Singh established his headquarters at Narum early in June, using his 1st Battalion on transport duties and the other two to occupy the villages of Lamyang, Keipham and Khosat.

Even on its first arrival in the battle area the regiment was sorely depleted by sickness. A company of the 2nd Battalion, for instance, which was detached at Tamu to patrol the area of Leibi village with a view to attacking the main Sita Hill positions, could only raise seventy out of its original one hundred and fifty men. As the rain poured down the casualties from sickness increased. On June 18th a second company, and at the end of June a third, had to be sent from the battalion to sustain the position to Leibi. By then the battalion's strength had fallen from some six hundred men to 332; 247 men being sick, twelve having deserted, three having been killed in battle and three having killed themselves. Patrol activity at Leibi was considerable in spite of the monsoon which turned the dry-weather mountain tracks into streams of mud.

The 3rd Battalion was similarly heavily engaged at the end of June and in early July around the village of Bongli. Two companies from this battalion had been despatched to Tamu as reinforcements for the weakening 2nd Guerrilla Regiment on June 6th, but they returned after a fortnight to accompany their battalion headquarters to Bongli, which they held against pressure down this more northerly spur of mountain, until ordered to withdraw.

Both regiments and the remnants of the 2nd and 3rd Battalions of the Subhash Regiment began to withdraw on July 18th, 1944.

BIBLIOGRAPHY

An Indian Diary Edwin S.Montagu

Biography of an Unknown Indian Nirad C. Chaudhuri

An Autobiography J.L. Nehru

The Discovery of India J.L. Nehru

Young India Lajpat Rai

Report of the Sedition Committee, India, 1918 (The Rowlatt Report)

India as I knew It Sir Michael O'Dwyer

My Indian Years Lord Hardinge of Penshurst

Indian Problems Lord Halifax

Pundits and Elephants Lord Lytton

Memoirs Franz von Papen

The British in India Sir Percival Griffiths

The British in Asia Guy Wint

While Memory Serves Lieutenant-General Sir Francis Tuker

Nationalism and Reform in India Hugh Byas

The Indonesian Story Wolf

The Eclipse of the Rising Sun Toshikazu Kase

Sunk Mochitsura Hashimoto

Beyond the Chindwin Brigadier Bernard Fergusson

This Europe Girija Mukherjee

Dictatorship and Political Police E.K. Bramstedt

The Subhash I knew Dilip Kumar Roy

Subhash Chandra Hemendranath Das Gupta

India Today R Palme Dutt

My Adventures with the I.N.A. K.R. Palta

My Memories of the I.N.A. and its Netaji Shah Nawaz Khan

Unto Him a Witness S.A. Ayer

Report of the Indian Statutory Commission, 1930 (The Simon Report)

An Indian Pilgrim S.C. Bose (autobiography)

Said Subhash Bose Amar Lahiri

Ciano's Diary Ed. Malcolm Muggeridge

Ciano's Diplomatic Papers Ed. Malcolm Muggeridge

The Goebbels Diary Ed. Louis P. Lochner

Two Historic Trials (The I.N.A. Court Martial of 1943, and the Trial of Bahadur Shah: pub. Moti Ram, January 1946).

The Transfer of Power in India V.P. Menon

S.C. Bose, his Personality and Political Ideas H.L. Seth.

On To Delhi Blood Bath *On With the Fight*	Collection of wartime Speeches by S.C. Bose, published by the Indian Independence League.

JAICO PUBLISHING HOUSE

Elevate Your Life. Transform Your World.

ESTABLISHED IN 1946, Jaico Publishing House is home to world-transforming authors such as Robin Sharma, Sadhguru, Osho, the Dalai Lama, Deepak Chopra, Eknath Easwaran, Paramhansa Yogananda, Devdutt Pattanaik, Radhakrishnan Pillai, Morgan Housel, Napoleon Hill, John Maxwell, Brian Tracy, and Stephen Hawking.

Our late founder Mr. Jaman Shah first established Jaico as a book distribution company. Sensing that independence was around the corner, he aptly named his company Jaico ('Jai' means victory in Hindi). In order to service the significant demand for affordable books in a developing nation, Mr. Shah initiated Jaico's own publications. Jaico was India's first publisher of paperback books in the English language.

While self-help; religion and philosophy; mind, body and spirit; and business titles form the cornerstone of our non-fiction list, we publish an exciting range of current affairs, history, biography, art and architecture, travel, and popular science books as well. Our renewed focus on popular fiction is evident in our new titles by a host of fresh young talent from India and abroad.

Jaico's translations division publishes select bestselling titles in over 10 regional languages including Gujarati, Hindi, Kannada, Malayalam, Marathi, Tamil, and Telugu. These include titles from renowned national and international authors like Sudha Murthy, Gaur Gopal Das, Swami Mukundananda, Jay Shetty. Simon Sinek, Ankur Warikoo and Jeff Keller.

Visit our Website

Boasting one of India's largest book distribution networks, Jaico has its headquarters in Mumbai, with branches in Ahmedabad, Bangalore, Chennai, Delhi, Hyderabad, and Kolkata. This network ensures that our books reach all parts of the country, both urban and rural.